Writing the Economy

To my parents, Bert and Ethel Smart

Writing the Economy

Activity, Genre, and Technology in the World of Banking

Graham Smart

LONDON   OAKVILLE

Published by
Equinox Publishing Ltd.
UK: Unit 6, The Village, 101 Amies Street, London, SW11 2JW
USA: DBBC, 28 Main Street, Oakville, CT 06779
www.equinoxpub.com

First published 2006
© 2006, Graham Smart.

British Library Cataloguing-in-Publication Data
A catalogue record for this book is available from the British Library.

ISBN 1-84553-066-7 (Hardback)
ISBN 1-84553-067-5 (Paperback.)

Library of Congress Cataloging-in-Publication Data
    Library of Congress Cataloging-in-Publication Data

Smart, Graham.
  Writing the economy : activity, genre and technology in the world of banking / Graham Smart.
      p. cm. -- (Studies in language and communication)
   Includes bibliographical references and index.
   ISBN 1-84553-066-7 -- ISBN 1-84553-067-5 (pbk.)
   1. Communication in organizations. 2. Communication in management. 3. Discourse analysis. 4. Bank of Canada. 5. Monetary policy--Canada. I. Title. II. Studies in language and communication (London, England)
   HD30.3.S565 2006
   332.4'971--dc22
                          2005021565

Typeset by Catchline, Milton Keynes (www.catchline.com)

Contents

Chapter Three
Genres of knowledge-building and policy-making

Chapter Six
Conclusion: addressing the 'So what?' question

Appendices

Acknowledgements

Over the years I have spent working on the study presented in this book, I have been fortunate to have the friendship and support of many people. To begin, I want to thank a number of current and former colleagues at Carleton University. First and foremost is Aviva Freedman, whose continuing scholarly inspiration has meant a great deal to me. I am grateful as well to Ian Pringle, whose intellectual encouragement aided me at different points along the way. An ongoing conversation with Pete Medway about things 'virtual,' particularly virtual buildings and economies, helped give shape to some key ideas that emerged in my research. My friendship and shared interests with Devon Woods go back to our high school days. And I would also like to thank Natasha Artemeva, Claire Harrison, and Christine Adam for their interest in my research.

At the University of Wisconsin-Milwaukee and Purdue University, I benefited greatly from the support of congenial colleagues: Jerry Alred, Bill Van Pelt, Rachel Spilka, Dave Clark, Janice Lauer, Bud Weiser, Jim Porter, Johndan Johnson-Eilola, Sandy Goodhart, Janet Alsup, Samantha Blackmon, Margie Berns, Tony Silva, Bob Lamb, and Nicole Brown. I would also like to thank two people at McGill University: Patrick Dias, my dissertation adviser, who helped me navigate the currents and shoals of doctoral work; and Anthony Paré, with whom I have enjoyed a fine blend of friendship and scholarly exchange for many years.

As well, I owe a great debt (no pun intended) to my former colleagues at the Bank of Canada in Ottawa, particularly the economists and other staff members who participated in my research during my time at the Bank and in the years after I left the organization. Without their generosity and trust, I could never have carried out my study. Similarly, I am extremely grateful to the ten economists outside the Bank who agreed to be interviewed for my research.

I would also like to thank a number of friends who have been unwavering in their encouragement over the years: Beth McFarlane, Virginia Balson and Allan Andren, Ray and Elaine Gagné, Tom and Marilyn Henighan, Paul Strople, Ian McCrorie, Paul Savoie, Dan Woolford, Ed and Joy Trott, David Woods, and the late Susan Lafleur.

Finally, and most importantly, I am grateful to my parents, Bert and Ethel Smart, for their unfailing faith in me.

Persuasive economies

Graham Smart's ethnographic account of the genres and activities by which monetary policy is produced, promulgated, and promoted at the Bank of Canada is in itself an exemplary study of how knowledge work is accomplished in complex professional organizations, through the production and circulation of written documents. Further his account gives a unique view of how complex computer models are structurally integrated into that literate work. Smart's study is additionally fascinating because it is about money and the economy, or more precisely monetary and economic policy – subjects that have loomed increasingly large in the life of people, nations, and the world. Smart's study reveals that the institutions that shape those policies, despite the perceptions of hard-edged economic mathematicians, are built on the soft world of words. But even more fundamentally, Smart's account reveals that the Bank of Canada, in producing and disseminating policy, is engaged in a the rhetorical activity of keeping the economy persuasive – that is in maintaining people's trust, interest, and activity in the economy, thereby keeping that economy going. The work of the Bank of Canada is to persuade all with a stake in the economy of Canada that that economy is sound.

In the latter half of the eighteenth century, Adam Smith advanced the ideas that the wealth and prosperity and happiness of a nation is to be found in a vital market economy and that the aim of government should be to advance economic activity. Since then the economy has become an ever more central concern of nations and now international bodies. Now the economy is a major political force, not only as an expression of the interests of key economic actors like corporations and market traders, but as a proper end of governance itself. The economy contests other forms of value, such as equity, compassion, communal responsibility, religion, peace. Consequently the state of the economy is central to political debates in most nations and economic rights are viewed as central to the operation of modern liberal democracies, at least from the U. S. perspective. Interestingly, the U.S. Bill of Rights, dating from shortly after Smith, defines only one economic right – the fifth amendment guarantee not to be deprived of property without due process in criminal matters or without just compensation when it is appropriated for government use. Equally interestingly, economic rights are now argued most vigorously on behalf of corporations treated legally as artificial persons. Nonetheless, a thriving free market economy is viewed as the sine qua non of modernity, particularly since the collapse of the socialist states toward the end of last century.

But the market as Smith recognized is itself a world of meanings based on persuasion and the creation of value.

> The real foundation of [the disposition to barter] is that principle to perswade which so much prevails in human nature. When any arguments are offered to perswade, it is always expected that they should have their proper effect. If a person asserts anything about the moon, tho' it should not be true, he will feel a kind of uneasiness in being contradicted, and would be very glad that the person he is endeavouring to perswade should be of the same way of thinking of himself. We ought then mainly to cultivate the power of perswasion, and indeed we do so without intending it. Since a whole life is spent in the exercise of it, a ready method of bargaining with each other must undoubtedly be attained. (Smith, 1978, 493)

As trade moved from the occasional barter at the oasis, persuasion became not of the particular value of some beads but of commitment to the market and institutions around it, and ultimately to the abstraction of the economy (see Bazerman, 1991). Faith and trust had to be created in ever more abstracted means of exchange: precious metals, coinage, paper financial instruments and government issued paper currency, and finally the electronic records of accounts, the institutions which circulate and guarantee these abstractions of monetary value, the markets on which they are traded, and the mechanisms of audit and accounting that provide information upon which exchange can be made – both of the specific commodity and service, but also of the amount, flow, and location of abstracted monetary value, which provides the market context of every specific exchange. With abstracted means of exchange, economic actors had to come to rely on the trustworthiness, stability, reliability of the entire system of exchange – a new abstraction of the economy. Despite the fiction of the invisible hand which would regulate price, the vitality of the economy depended not only on the persuasiveness of all actors to assert the value of the products and services they had to offer – the institutions that stood behind the markets and the currency had to persuade users of the very coin of the realm so to speak – but also on the perceived fairness of the marketplace and the assured value of the currency. Thus government regulation of markets became important as markets grew in complexity and abstraction so that each actor no longer could inspect each bushel of wheat to assure its value. But also the government regulation of the currency became important to persuade users that they should convert their valuable wheat or gold into currency and play the market game (see Bazerman, 2000)

Governments became guarantors of the currency, responsible for its soundness upon which the health of the economy depended. Today that function no longer is primarily carried out by the assay and weighing of gold, the minting of true weight coins, or designing devices to fool counterfeiters and shavers. Rather the health is measured in inflation rates and measures of the circulation of money. These are abstractions built on collected and calculated data, sampling and other economic mathematical techniques, with the result that the periodic release of economic indicators (GNP, GDP, inflation rates, M1 monetary flow, etc) is major news affecting the aggregate wealth represented in markets. Governments as well as the economic players have theoretical notions about acceptable ranges of inflation and growth, usually having some basis in the academic field of economics. These data and precepts are used by all economic participants to evaluate the state of the abstract economy, so as to guide their decisions and actions. Government institutions have grown to make a particular class of decisions aimed at keeping these measures within acceptable ranges, so that people would maintain faith in the currency and economy, would continue to spend, and would continue to support the government as a producer of a strong economy.

Further, with the globalization of currencies, governments have had a stake in maintaining their own currencies as strong and stable in comparison to currencies of other governments, so capital would remain or even flow to its economies, rather than fleeing. Some governments which have not been successful in maintaining their local currencies have had them replaced (often in practice, but sometimes even in law) by the dollar, pound, or euro. In losing control of its own currency, a government loses control of a key mechanism to make choices regulating its economy and becomes beholden to the choice makers of the stronger currencies.

Central banks, with their responsibility for conducting national monetary policy, work to retain people's faith in their countries' currencies by influencing the flow of money in order to keep its growth within acceptable parameters, particularly in relation to growth of productivity. In the not too distant past governments may have been able to control the money in circulation simply by adjusting the print runs of paper currency. But now only small parts of modern complex economies are transacted through physical currency. One of the few ways to influence and shape the profligate creation of value through loans, credit, and other virtual money transactions is to prompt interest rates to dampen or encourage the rapidity of flow of money. Thus monetary policy became expressed through the nation's central bank lending rates that affect interbank transfers and through their symbolic force influence loan rates offered by all lending institutions. So, somewhat bizarrely, this technical matter of interbank transfers buried within the banking system has become of great interest to people, and has become major economic news. The adjustments of central bank lending rates give an institutional assessment of the health of the economy, influencing people's judgments about their participation in the economy. Further adjustments affect the faith people have in this currency and in the nation's markets. Countries viewed as having weak currencies have a hard time borrowing money and must pay high rates of interest in the anticipation of instability and inflation. Countries with strong countries are able to attract foreign capital into their markets and are able to maintain large government debts at favourable interest rates.

Faith in the economy is based on a belief that governmental choices influencing monetary flow are well-informed and wise, with a history of prudent choices that seem to anticipate economic trends and adjust for them. To achieve these public goals, central banks must determine criteria for gathering data on the economy, aggregate that data, develop models for analyzing what the data indicate about the current dynamic activity of the market and its trends, and then use this analysis to inform specific decisions about economic policy. These epistemic procedures must lead to wise conclusions that anticipate economic trends reasonably well. Spokespeople for the central banks must then persuasively present their actions so they are perceived as wise and keeping the economy on course.

How these data, models, analysis and conclusions are produced in one such institution, the Bank of Canada, is the subject of much of Graham Smart's book. How these policies are then sold to the public to elicit further confidence is the subject of the latter part. This complex inward- and outward-facing activity is one of symbolic exchange, discourse – people talking, writing, producing reports and documents and speeches. These communications integrate professional knowledge of economics, computing, statistics, data management, law, government policy, and public psychology. These knowledges and practices are finely honed and delicately articulated in massive collaborations of institutionally-embedded participants, with visible spokespeople then communicating with all the economic actors engaged with Canadian currency and markets.

The Canadian economy monitored by the central bankers that Smart studies is constituted through disciplinary knowledge, inscription and institutions so as transform individual exchange – of trading beads for clams – into complex abstract entities of the economy, viewed through statistically gathered indicators. The participation of many individuals making local decisions based on their economic interest makes it appear that the economic system is all about individual choice and free markets, free from the heavy hand of regulation and direction. The success of the markets, however, in maintaining the faith and confidence of these participants requires the deft and knowledgeable hand of those who inscribe that economy and regulate it through inscription so as to keep it all going. A failure in persuading people of the viability of a currency in the markets can have a devastating effect on the lives of people in those countries, as hinted at by the Asian currency crises in the later 1990s. Graham Smart's volume in mapping the rhetorical terrain of one nation's central bank helps us understand where and how the arguments that affect the future of nations are carried out. This is a necessary step to open up issues of political economy to public debate.

Such incidents as the Asian monetary crisis, however, remind us that we have become dependent not only on our own currency, but on the economies of other nations. Canadian currency knows it sits in the shadow of both sterling and the dollar. The dollar has accrued great strength, but that is no guarantee it will remain the persuasive currency for the future. Increasingly the key arguments about the political economy of the world are moving to international economic bodies like the International Monetary Fund, the World Bank, and UN economic agencies that integrate and discipline the economies of the world's nations. How those emerging economic bodies of increasingly great influence produce policy, how internal arguments contribute to shaping international economic policy, how those policies are sold to the governments and citizens of the various nations affected, and how those arguments and policies can be opened up for public deliberation is an important next stage in the extremely valuable inquiry Graham Smart has set in motion.

Charles Bazerman

Chapter One

Introduction

In recent years, the economic policies of major financial institutions such as the European Union Central Bank, the U.S. Federal Reserve and central banks of other countries, the International Monetary Fund, and the World Bank have received growing attention in the news media, reflecting increased public awareness of the impact of these financial institutions on the global economy and, more concretely, on the material conditions of our every-day lives. As a consequence, public interest in the goals, economic analyses, and decision-making processes that guide these institutions' policy actions has greatly intensified. This book takes readers inside one such site, the Bank of Canada, that country's central bank, to look at its knowledge-building, policy-making, and external communications, revealing significant socio-rhetorical, ideological, and technological dimensions of this work.

The study

An overview

The ethnographic study presented in this book examines the intellectual collaboration of economists at the Bank of Canada, focusing on the discourse practices they employ as they build knowledge about the Canadian economy, apply this knowledge in making decisions about the direction of national monetary policy, and communicate with external audiences regarding the policy – a broad writing-intensive activity known within the Bank as the 'monetary-policy process.'[1] Drawing on qualitative data gathered during my 13 years' tenure as an in-house writing consultant and trainer in the Bank and in the nine years since I left the organization (I continued to gather data at the Bank until May 2005), the book explores two key dimensions of the economists' discourse. First, it describes how the economists use a group of written and oral genres, employed jointly with the technology of computer-run economic models, to collaborate in creating specialized written knowledge[2] about current and future developments in the Canadian economy and in applying this knowledge in formulating and implementing the country's monetary policy. Here the relationship between writing, spoken language, and the technology of economic modelling is closely observed, with a focus on the social and epistemic, or knowledge-generating, functions of the computer-run Quarterly Projection Model (QPM), a mathematical representation of the Canadian economy that is the organization's primary analytic tool. And second, the book examines the economists' use of another group of technology-supported discourse genres to orchestrate the Bank's external communications with government, the media, the business sector, financial markets, labour, and academia – communications that for a central bank are a vital part of maintaining public legitimacy. At the same time, the book explores the ways in which the economists' discourse practices engender intersubjectivity and enable individual and organizational learning.

The research site

The site of the study is the head office of the Bank of Canada in Ottawa (see Photograph 1).

Photograph 1: Bank of Canada building, Ottawa (Photo: William P. McElligott / Bank of Canada)

Founded in 1935, the Bank of Canada is responsible for directing the country's monetary policy, a role that involves managing the national money supply by influencing interest rates, with the larger goal of improving the performance of the Canadian economy over time.[3] Ongoing decisions on monetary policy are made by an executive group known as the Governing Council that includes the Governor of the Bank and five deputy governors. Providing this group of decision-makers with economic analysis are some 175 staff economists situated in four departments – Research, Monetary and Financial Analysis, International, and Financial Markets (known collectively as the 'economics departments') – with each department headed by a chief. In addition, five other departments house employees with expertise in areas such as corporate communications, information technology, personnel management, and editorial services (see for the organizational structure of the Bank).

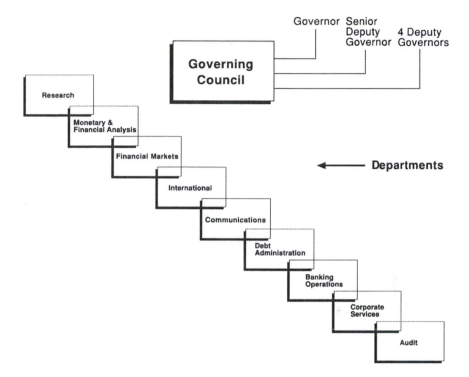

Diagram 1: The Bank of Canada organization chart

In addition to staff in the Ottawa head office, the Bank has regional representatives in five cities – Halifax, Montreal, Toronto, Calgary, and Vancouver – who provide economic information and analysis from their respective regions of the country, as well as a senior person in Toronto and another in Montreal whose role is to maintain ongoing communication with key players in the financial markets.

The methodology: interpretive ethnography

The methodology I have employed in the study is interpretive ethnography, a qualitative approach that enables a researcher to explore a professional organization's repertoire of shared symbolic resources, or discourse, in order to learn something of how its members view and function within their particular, self-constructed corner of the world. As we will see in Chapter Five, interpretive ethnography also allows a researcher to investigate how members of an organization differentiate among, characterize, and communicate with outside audiences.

Interpretive ethnography, in striving to explore and represent the web of shared meanings that constitutes reality within a particular social group, relies heavily on the practice of eliciting and presenting 'displays of members' thoughts, theories, and world views' (Van Maanen, 1988). Thus the accounts produced by researchers typically have a multi-vocal, polyphonic quality, with informants' voices and perspectives given pride of place – all with the aim of achieving a 'thick description' (Geertz, 1973) of the group's 'structures of meaning... and systems of symbols' (p. 182). Accordingly, the account presented in this book is grounded in commentary from the Bank's economists themselves and includes quotes from 34 individuals (30 economists and four other Bank employees). As well, to gain a critical perspective on the Bank's economic ideology, a perspective free of the 'naturalization of ideology' (Fairclough, 1995, cited in Dias, Freedman, Medway, & Paré, 1999), the account also draws on interviews with ten economists from outside the Bank. (See Appendix A for an inventory of the data used in the study.) With its focus on a group's discourse and meaning-making – its 'symbolic action' (Geertz, 1973) – interpretive ethnography has provided me with a way of examining the intellectual collaboration of the Bank's economists as they go about their work of theoretical research, monitoring and analysis of economic developments in Canada and abroad, policy-making, and external communications.

The theoretical orientation

This study of the discourse practices enacted by the Canadian central bank's economists as they collaborate in the work of knowledge-building, policy-making, and external communications draws on a number of theoretical perspectives. Most broadly, current views on the indivisible, mutually constitutive relationship between discourse – broadly understood to encompass not only language, but also a way of thinking, believing, and acting – and disciplinary knowledge have been central to the study (Barron, Bruce, & Nunan, 2002; Gee, 1999; van Dijk, 2003). In particular, I have employed the concepts of intertexuality (Bauman, 2004; Bazerman, 2003; Fairclough, 1992), the presence within a text of extracts of prior texts; interdiscursivity (Fairclough, 1992; Chouliaraki & Fairclough, 1999; Candlin & Maley, 1999), the occurrence within a text of language and conventions reflecting other genres, discourses, and styles; and multimodality (Kress, 2003; Kress & van Leeuwen, 2001; New London Group, 1996), the semiotic interplay of language, image, and sound that characterizes meaning-making in much contemporary technology-mediated discourse.

I have also been guided, in a more specific way, by the socio-rhetorical notion that it is through their discourse practices that members of professional organizations collaborate in creating and applying the specialized knowledges they need for accomplishing their work (Bazerman, 2003; Doheny-Farina, 1992; Gunnersson, 1997, 1998; Harper, 1998; Heath & Luff, 2000; Iedema, 2003; McCarthy, 1991; Myers, 1990; Suchman, 2000; Van Nostrand, 1997; Winsor, 2003; Yates, 1989). In this regard, scholarship revealing the degree to which epistemic discourse in professional organizations is frequently poly-symbolic, with alpha-numeric writing used jointly with other symbolic forms such as mathematics, statistics, and diagrams, has also informed my work (Ackerman & Oates, 1996; Bazerman, 1999; Journet, 1990; Latour, 1990; Medway, 1996; Sauer, 2003; Winsor, 1992). I have been influenced as well by research pointing to the centrality of acts of persuasion in professional discourse and knowledge-building (Bazerman, 1999; Sarangi, 2000; Sauer, 2003), with recent work in pragmatics on the relationship between persuasion and genre also proving extremely useful (Halmari & Virtanen, 2005).

Dorothy Smith's critical sociological work (1974, 1990, 1999, 2005) has also offered important insights into the knowledge-constituting textual practices of professional organizations. Similarly, in research that is perhaps even more relevant to a study of knowledge-building, policy-making, and external communications in a central bank, work in the 'anthropology of policy,' as exemplified by the collection edited by Cris Shore and Susan Wright (1997), has suggested useful ways of thinking about the socio-cultural dimensions of public-policy discourse.

In addition, I have drawn extensively on theories of genre and activity. Contemporary genre studies, following in the wake of Carolyn Miller's (1984) groundbreaking scholarship, characterizes written genres as recurrent, textually-mediated social actions. Working with the frame of genre analysis, researchers have shown how professional organizations employ genres of written discourse to produce the particular types of knowledge they need for their work (Bargiela-Chiappini & Nickerson, 1999; Bazerman, 1988; Bhatia, 2004, 1993; Devitt, 1991; Myers, 1990; Paré, 2000; Schryer, 1993; Smart, 1998, 1999; Swales, 1990, 1998; Winsor, 2003). Anthony Paré and I offer a view of genre that underscores this knowledge-building function (1994):

> [W]hen an organization has a stable mandate and a well-defined structure, recurrent problems or exigencies arise, each of which calls for a different type of discourse and knowledge. [A] written genre can be seen as a broad rhetorical strategy enacted within an [organization] in order to regularize

> writer/reader transactions in ways that allow for the creation of particular knowledge. (p. 146)

More specifically, Paré and I argue for a conception of genre that includes regularities in texts as well as repeated patterns in the production and interpretation of these texts and in 'an organization's drama of interaction, the interpersonal dynamics that surround and support certain texts' (p. 148).

Researchers have recognized that certain genres are frequently linked to one another in their occurrence and functions. Norman Fairclough (2000, 2003), John Swales (2004), and John Flowerdew (2004), for example, have written of 'genre chains' – sequences of genres that exhibit what Fairclough refers to as 'systematic transformations from genre to genre' (2003, p. 31). Fairclough provides the following example: official documents ➤ related press releases or press conferences ➤ TV or newspaper reports (2003, p. 216). On another level of connection, researchers have described the various genres employed by the members of a professional organization as a 'genre set' that functions as a provisionally stable discursive system for creating, negotiating, circulating, and applying specialized knowledge (Bazerman, 1994b; Bhatia, 2004; Devitt, 2004; Paré, 2000; Yates & Orlikowski, 2002). Moving beyond the scope of a single professional organization, researchers have also identified the 'genre system' – an inter-organizational realm of discourse comprising genres used by two or more organizations to interact communicatively and develop knowledge mutually relevant to them (Bazerman, 1994a; Bhatia, 2004; Paré, 2000; Yates & Orlikowski, 2002b). (Related concepts in the literature of genre studies include the 'genre ecology' [Spinuzzi, 2003; Spinuzzi & Zachry, 2000] and the 'genre repertoire' [Devitt, 2004]). In the study presented in this book, I have broadened the concept of the genre set and the genre system, as defined by the scholars cited above, to include not only written but also oral genres, since written and spoken discourse are so closely linked within the activity of the Bank's monetary-policy process.

The concept of a genre system encompassing a variety of genres produced by several organizations suggests a further aspect of genre theory relevant to this study: Anne Freadman's (1994) notion of 'uptake,' a tennis metaphor, where a text in one genre – a shot served over the net, as it were – will frequently elicit, in the natural course of social events, a response in the form of another text. In the context of a genre system, we might think of a pair of genres, each originating in a different social group, that exist 'in some sort of dialogical relation' (Freadman, p. 48) – so that the appearance of a text in one genre invites a responding text in the second genre, an occurrence that we will see exemplified in Chapter Five.

A number of genre theorists have appropriated Anthony Giddens's (1979, 1984) concept of 'structuration' to explain how written genres in professional environments function to balance social convention and stability with individual agency and social change. Giddens describes social structure as both the 'medium and the outcome' (1979, p. 5) of social practices: on the one hand, social conventions strongly influence the behaviours of people comprising a collective, but on the other, these conventions exist only as long as they are maintained in memory and enacted by individuals – a 'duality of structure' (1984, p. 25) that results in recurrence and continuity, but also allows for individual judgment, personal creativity, and change. Genre theorists have used the notion of structuration to explain how genres both influence and are shaped by their social contexts (Bargiela-Chiappini & Nickerson, 1999; Berkenkotter & Huckin, 1995; Bazerman, 1994a; Giltrow & Valiquette, 1994; Miller, 1994; Schryer, 2002). Viewed from this perspective, genres are created through, but also serve to enable and coordinate, the discursive actions of the members of an organization as they collaborate in creating the particular kinds of knowledge needed to accomplish their work. In Chapter Three I take up this idea when I describe several writers' individual innovations in genres associated with the Bank of Canada's monetary-policy process. JoAnne Yates and Wanda Orlikowski (1992), in their discussion of written communication in professional organizations, demonstrate how structuration theory can also be used to account for the way that social and technological changes within an organization are accompanied by new and evolving genres. This point that will be illustrated with several examples from the Bank of Canada in later chapters. Here we will also see evidence of a related tension between, on the one hand, an organization's tendency to impose a narrow, constraining conformity on its members' language, thinking, and knowledge-building – to 'normalize' the discourse (Foucault, 1972) – and on the other hand, the countervailing presence of individual agency and creativity, intellectual self-reflexivity, and lively debate.

A final aspect of genre theory pertinent to my study at the Bank of Canada is the concept of 'genre knowledge' – that is, a rhetorical awareness on the part of writers and readers of the ways in which a particular genre or genre set functions (Beaufort, 1999; Berkenkotter & Huckin, 1995; Devitt, 2004; Giltrow, 2002; Giltrow & Valiquette, 1994; Orlikowsky & Yates, 1994; Paré, 2000; Tardy, 2003). In the present study, the genre knowledge of members of the Bank staff who participate in the discourse associated with the monetary-policy process will be displayed prominently in Chapters Three, Four, and Five.

To complement genre theory, I have drawn on North American, British, and Scandinavian extensions of the Soviet historical-cultural approach known as activity theory (Leont'ev, 1978; Luria, 1976; Vygotsky, 1978). From this theoretical vantage point, a set of organizational genres can be viewed as one element in an 'activity system' (Cole & Engestrom, 1993): an historically- and culturally-situated sphere of goal-oriented collaborative endeavor, in which cognition – thinking, knowing, and learning – is diffused, or distributed, across a number of individuals and their work practices and, at the same time, mediated by culturally-constructed tools. An organizational activity system, while having a strong cultural-historical dimension, is constituted through the moment-to-moment agency and social negotiations of the people who participate in it. Thus the system changes constantly, continuously recreated in response to internal tensions or initiatives, to the possibilities afforded by newly available tools, or to external pressures and influences. Chapters Three, Four, and Five provide clear examples of this particular characteristic of organizational activity systems.

The various cultural tools – physical, social, and symbolic – used within an organizational activity system, with their respective affordances, or functional capacities, both extend and exert a mediating influence on participants' cognition, discourse, and work practices, and are frequently, if not always, infused with particular values and interests. Such tools can include, for example, digital technologies, built environments, analytic methods, systems of classification, conventionalized roles and social interactions, and genres employing texts in different symbol systems. (This description of activity theory is derived from the work of scholars such as Yrjö Engeström, 1987, 1992; David Russell, 1997; Charles Bazerman, 1994b; Bazerman and Russell, 2003; Dorothy Winsor, 1999; Aviva Freedman and myself, 1997; Edwin Hutchins, 1995; Lucy Suchman, 1998; James Wertsch, 1991, 1997; Charles Goodwin, 1997; and Jeoffrey Bowker and Susan Leigh Star, 1999.)

The concept of distributed cognition, a strand of activity theory, requires particular mention here. Viewed from this theoretical perspective, intelligence, reasoning, and knowledge arise as people collaborate, using shared cultural tools, in performing their work. As Roy Pea (1993) points out, 'the environments in which humans live are thick with invented artifacts that ... both organize and constrain activity [and] include not only designed objects such as tools, control instruments, and symbolic representations like graphs, diagrams, text, plans, and pictures, but people in social relations' (p. 48). In recent years computer technology, one such cultural tool, has come to play a particularly significant role in facilitating collaborative activity within organizations. An important implication of this development is the degree to which computer technology influences the thinking and actions of the people who employ it. As Pea (1993) observes: 'computer tools serve not [only] as they are often construed – as amplifiers of cognition – but [rather also] as reorganizers of mental functioning. [W]hat humans actually do in their activities changes when the functional organization of that activity is transformed by technologies' (p. 57).

This observation regarding the mediating effects of computer technology on cognition and action will become salient in later chapters, particularly Chapters Four and Five, as I examine the role of computer-run economic models in the intellectual collaboration of the Bank of Canada's economists.

Knowledge produced in professional organizations through distributed cognition in collaborative intellectual activity is instantiated in symbol-based representations of many types, such as alpha-numeric texts, diagrams, graphs, photographs, computer programs, and mathematical equations. These representations – used to generate, embody, and communicate information, ideas, and knowledge claims – are embedded in the social environment through links to other types of representations as well as to an organization's repertoire of shared analytic practices (Lynch & Woolgar, 1990). As Charles Bazerman (1994a) observes, such symbolic representations serve to 'mediate between private spaces of cognition and public spaces in which intersubjectivity is negotiated [and] can provide shared information, perception, [and] orientation of large numbers of people engaged in coordinated activities' (pp. 146–147). As we shall see, this concept of intersubjectivity – a domain of shared focus, perception, and understanding that connects individuals intellectually within an organization – features prominently in my Bank of Canada study. And while I would certainly acknowledge that in the Bank as elsewhere such intersubjectivity always co-exists with the 'private spaces' of individual cognition – and we will see clear evidence for this in Chapter Three – nevertheless the accomplishment of intersubjectivity is crucial for collaborative knowledge-building.

This last point prompts me to mention that the present study employs what Gavriel Salomon (1993, p. xiv) refers to as the 'weak' version of distributed cognition theory, where although the communal thinking-in-activity of a social group may be privileged by a researcher, individual cognition is also recognized as significant and seen to interact with collective cognition. This is distinct from the 'strong' version of the theory in which the existence of 'solo' cognition is denied or ignored.

In another line of theorizing often associated with activity theory, Jean Lave and Etienne Wenger (Lave & Wenger, 1991) describe the 'situated learning' that occurs within any organization. They consider such learning, 'the development of knowledgeably skilled identities' (p. 55), to be an inherent and continuous aspect of involvement in a community-of-practice[4] – for all members, veterans as well as newcomers. Looking beyond the individual, Wanda Orlikowski (2001) points to the collective learning that occurs on an organizational level. Chapters Four and Six reveal ways in which the discourse practices of the Bank's economists' enable both individual and organizational learning.

Taken together, theories of genre and activity have provided me with a broad conceptual framework for exploring and developing an account of the

ways in which the Bank of Canada's economists employ a discourse mediated by a variety of cultural tools to enable and coordinate their intellectual
collaboration. In addition to these two bodies of theory, Chapters Two, Three,
and Four also draw on theories of inscription, narrative, and modelling, while
Chapter Five draws on theories regarding organizational change, the social
aspects of information production and use, and the fusing of texts and digital
technologies. Relevant aspects of these theories will be presented later in the
book as needed.

To borrow from Stephen Fishman and Lucille McCarthy (2001), I have
used the theories mentioned above to 'help name, explore, and explain what
[I was] seeing' in the data I gathered at the Bank of Canada during the time I
worked there and in the years since I left the organization. Collectively, these
theories have helped me recognize and describe how the Bank's economists
use a set of discourse genres, in combination with technology, to engender and
coordinate a complex configuration of collaborative intellectual activity.

The organization of the book

Chapter Two begins with a discussion of knowledge-building in economics,
suggesting that the 'economy' itself is a symbol-based representation constructed and constantly revised through the discursive and analytic practices
of economists, with professionals in any given organization producing their
own particular version of the economy for specific occupational purposes.
Next I turn to the Bank of Canada and its specific linguistic and mathematical
representation of the Canadian economy. I show that this representation is
constructed through, and also permeates, the thinking, speaking, and writing
of the organization's economists, and that it is instantiated in the mathematical
equations of the computer-run Quarterly Projection Model.

The chapter then provides an overview of the Bank's 'monetary-policy
process' – a broad writing-intensive activity of knowledge-building, policy-
making, and external communications. I explain that the monetary-policy
process, as viewed by the Bank's economists, comprises three facets: building
specialized knowledge about the state of the Canadian economy; applying
this knowledge in making decisions about the country's monetary policy; and
communicating with external audiences regarding the policy.

Chapter Three, the longest in the book, describes the activity of the monetary-policy process in greater detail, showing how tightly enmeshed written
and spoken discourse genres are with the technology of computer-assisted
economic modelling. The account is organized around four cultural tools
that mediate the collaborative work of the Bank's economists: the Quarterly
Projection Model, the Projection Exercise, the *White Book*, and a narrative

known as the 'monetary-policy story.' The chapter provides a close-up view of the process through which the results of economic monitoring and analysis by junior staff economists are developed by more senior staff economists into a broad, forward-looking view of the Canadian economy and a set of policy recommendations for the Governor and his senior colleagues, who in turn draw on this view of the economy and these policy recommendations in directing Canada's monetary policy and in communicating with external audiences regarding policy.

The chapter begins with a description of the Quarterly Projection Model, a complex computer-run mathematical representation of the Canadian economy that functions as the Bank's primary analytic tool. Next, I discuss the Projection Exercise, a quarterly month-long operation in which the organization's staff economists use QPM to analyze statistical data and produce a key policy document known as the *White Book*. After providing an overview of the Projection Exercise, I describe in some detail the sequence of formal meetings around which the operation is organized, making reference to related work documents, and also explain the contribution of the meetings and documents to the economists' knowledge-building and policy-making.

The chapter then turns to the *White Book* as another important symbol-based, knowledge-bearing representation. I begin by describing the *White Book's* discourse structure and the document's dual function as an end-of-quarter input into the processes of decision-making that underlie the Bank's monetary-policy actions and as a benchmark for 'current analysis,' the ongoing monitoring and interpretation of recent economic developments. I then describe the part that the *White Book* plays in another sequence of regular meetings during the quarter in which the chiefs of the four economics departments (Research; Monetary and Financial Analysis; Financial Markets; International) brief the Governor of the Bank and his colleagues on the Governing Council on the policy implications of the staff economists' ongoing current analysis work.

Next I discuss a narrative representation known in the Bank as the 'monetary-policy story.' After looking at the generic use of the term 'story' within the organization to refer to a particular form of economic analysis and representation of economic reality, I turn to the 'monetary-policy story' itself. First I describe how this narrative is produced, then how it functions as an essential social organizing device for coordinating the staff economists' work of collaborative knowledge-building, and finally how the narrative is used by the Governing Council as a shared cognitive and rhetorical resource for making decisions about monetary policy and for explaining these decisions to the Canadian public. In this close examination of the monetary-policy process, the chapter also explores the tension within the economists' intellectual collaboration between, on the one hand, the 'normalizing' influence of the Bank as an organization, and on the other, the clear presence of individual agency, contested interpretations, and rigorous negotiation of ideas.

Chapter Four describes the symbol-based structure of the Quarterly Projection Model, outlines its functions, recounts the history and politics of QPM's in-house construction and implementation, and looks at the model's role as a cultural tool mediating the intellectual activity of knowledge-building. At the same time, I continue to examine the interplay between, on the one hand, written and spoken discourse and, on the other, the technology of computer-assisted economic modelling. One aspect of this interplay is seen in the role of writing in the development, 'selling,' and enhancement of QPM, while another aspect appears in the various ways that the model, as a 'tool of reasoning,' influences the discourse of the Bank's economists. Here as well, I discuss the role of written genres and QPM as joint contributors to the intersubjectivity that underlies and enables the economists' knowledge-building and policy-making.

Chapter Five examines how the Bank's economists employ technology-mediated genres of discourse to orchestrate the organization's communications with government, the media, the business sector, financial markets, labour, academic economists, and the general public – an activity known in the Bank as the 'Communications Strategy.' After identifying the technology-supported group of written and oral genres associated with the Communications Strategy, I describe two key features of these genres: the rhetorical and other knowledge associated with them and their relationship to processes of organizational change. Next I discuss the part the genres play in the activity of the Communications Strategy, focusing on three primary functions: coordinating the intellectual work of numerous individuals performing a variety of professional roles; generating, shaping, and communicating the 'public information' that constitutes the Bank's official public position on its monetary policy; and acting as a site for individual and organizational learning. The chapter also considers the relationship between the internal and external dimensions of the economists' discourse.

The final chapter, Chapter Six, presents an overview of the study and explores its implications. The chapter begins with a summary of the account presented in the book, first providing a wide-angle description of the monetary-policy process and then focusing in on the discourse genres associated with this activity. Next the chapter traces the implications of the study for discourse theory, for research in professional organizations, and for the teaching of professional discourse.

Reflections on my experience using the methodology of interpretive ethnography in the study appear at the end of Chapters Two, Three, Four, and Five. In these reflections, I discuss methodological practices and issues I believe to be significant for other researchers who might wish to explore discourse and intellectual collaboration in professional organizations. In Chapter Two, I outline a number of key concepts from the work of Clifford Geertz, the originator of interpretive ethnography; in Chapter Three, I describe how I developed my research questions and also how I went about gathering and analyzing data; in Chapter Four, I discuss the tension inherent in the ethnographer's need to engage with the conceptual world of his or her informants while also maintaining a certain critical distance from that world; and in Chapter Five, I discuss the issues of validity, reliability, and generalizability.

As background for this study of the discourse practices of central bank economists, I felt that certain readers might it helpful if I were to situate the Bank of Canada's economic ideology within the larger disciplinary field of economics. Therefore a text presenting such a perspective is provided in Appendix B. I begin by describing the prevailing 'Neo-Classical' theory of how economies function, and then present the 'Neo-Keynesian' counter-view, outline certain criticisms mounted within the profession against both the Neo-Classical and Neo-Keynesian perspectives, and finally, consider where the Bank of Canada's conception of the Canadian economy fits into this disciplinary landscape.

Chapter Two

The monetary-policy process: the big picture

This chapter begins with a discussion of knowledge-building in the profession of economics, and then moves on to portray 'the economy' as a site-specific, symbol-based representation that is created, maintained, and revised through the discourse practices of economists collaborating for specific occupational ends. Looking at the particular representation of the Canadian economy created by economists at the Bank of Canada to accomplish their work of economic research, analysis, and policy-making, I suggest that this 'economy' permeates the economists' thinking, speaking, and writing, and is instantiated in the mathematical equations of the Quarterly Projection Model. With this background, and also drawing on inscription theory, the chapter then provides an overview of the Bank's 'monetary-policy process' – a broad writing-intensive activity that encompasses knowledge-building, policy-making, and policy-related communications with outside groups.

Knowledge-building, ideology, and rhetoric in economics

The study presented in this volume takes its place alongside previous scholarship that views economic knowledge as socially constructed in local sites – 'made, not found ... and made by groups of people, not by individuals,' to borrow a phrase from Debra Journet (1990, p. 162). According to Vivienne Brown (1993), 'Instead of seeing the development of economics as the steady march of progress towards a scientific understanding of the real economy, this approach is concerned with the ways in which economic knowledge is produced within specific discursive conditions, and how it comes to be culturally inscribed and socially constructed' (p. 64). In a similar vein, Robert Heilbroner (1990) points to the 'ideological nature of economic inquiry' (p. 104). Defining ideology as 'the frameworks of perception by which all social groups organize and interpret their experience' (p. 103), Heilbroner asserts that when 'economics [is] understood as a belief system,' it then follows that the economy itself, as an object of research and analysis, is seen as socially constructed and ideologically inflected.[1] For Heilbroner, a key implication here is that the knowledge claims of economists, while typically backed with 'empirical data or plausible generalizations,' are nevertheless part of 'the general field of rhetoric, taking that word to mean the art of persuasion' (p. 103).

This brings us to two economists who explore the rhetorical strategies associated with knowledge-building in their discipline. For Deidre McCloskey, economic knowledge depends on persuasion, the effective marshalling of arguments. As McCloskey (1990) puts it, economics 'is rhetoric, human argument, all the way down...' (p. 8). Consequently, despite the discipline's scientific posture and empirical methodologies, economists depend on rhetorical strategies such as narrative and metaphor to argue knowledge claims. According to Arjo Klamer (1990), this view would have us 'look beyond the propositions that economists produce and consider their discursive practice in its entirety, [remaining] alert to the various rhetorical devices that economists use to make their case' (p. 130). The study presented here proceeds from the theoretical stance described above: it assumes that economic knowledge is socially constructed, ideologically grounded, and rhetorically established. And in looking at how language and technology are used together in a central bank's knowledge-building, policy-making, and external communications, the study acts on Klamer's prompt to take a broad contextual view of economic discourse and rhetoric.

'The economy' as a cultural construct

As mentioned in the last chapter, theorists in discourse studies have pointed out that while written discourse plays a central role in knowledge-building within professional sites, it is often used in combination with other types of symbols. And of course this is very much the case in economics, where knowledge is created and conveyed through a discourse encompassing written and spoken language, mathematical equations, statistics, numerical tables, and visual forms such as graphs and charts – with computer technologies used heavily to support this poly-symbolic discourse.

With regard to knowledge-building in economics, it can be argued that 'the economy' itself – the profession's object of research and analysis – is a cultural construct, an intersubjective reality established through the discourse practices of collaborating economists. The economic historian Vivienne Brown (1993) articulates this view: '[T]he 'real economy' is not knowable as a direct or brute fact of existence independently of its discursive construction. The 'economy' is represented as an object of analysis by a set of discourses which constitute it as such; it is these discourses that provide the economic concepts, modes of analysis, statistical estimates, econometric methods and policy debates that constitute the different analytic understandings of the economy' (p. 70). Bruno

Latour (1990) offers a similar perspective on the 'the economy' as a cultural construct:

> It is of course impossible to talk about the economy of a nation by looking at 'it.' The 'it' is plainly invisible, as long as cohorts of enquirers and inspectors have not filled in long questionnaires, as long as the answers have not been punched onto cards, treated by computers, [and] analyzed… Only at the end can the economy be made visible inside piles of charts and lists. Even this is still too confusing, so that redrawing and extracting is necessary to provide a few neat diagrams that show the Gross National Product or the Balance of Payments (p. 38).

From the perspective of activity theory, a socially-constructed 'economy' is a cultural tool that mediates – that is, both enables and shapes – the thinking and actions of the particular group of economists who create and employ it.[2] And while, as Brown puts it, written texts 'are constitutive of ways of seeing the economy' (p. 70), as I will demonstrate in later chapters, within the Bank of Canada the technology of mathematically-based economic models is an essential complement to written and spoken discourse in the construction of the economy as an object of research and analysis.

As cultural tools, however, 'economies' are not all cut from the same discursive cloth; their specific character is determined by location and use. Professional economists are always situated somewhere, either in universities or in public-sector, private-sector, or non-governmental organizations. And in the case of non-university economists, the occupational setting – government department, labour union, business lobby group, economic forecasting firm, NGO, or central bank – shapes the particular version of the economy that is constructed, reflecting the organization's mandate, goals, history, bureaucratic and technological systems, theoretical assumptions, ideological orientation, and so on.

For economists in any given professional site, the discursive creation of a particular version of 'the economy' is a means to an end: the economists use its structure of conceptual categories – such as household consumption, commodity prices, exports, and government expenditures – and the inter-relationships among these categories to analyze empirical data and produce 'stories' that identify and explain recent developments and expected future trends, knowledge that is applied in accomplishing the organization's work. As employed by economists at the Bank of Canada, the term 'story' is similar in meaning to its use by Deidre McCloskey (1985, 1990, 1994) in that both refer to the interpretation of economic developments empirically observed in the 'real world' (to use McCloskey's phrase), as opposed to the revelations or prophecies of armchair speculation. However, as we will see, for Bank economists the word 'story' also has a more specific meaning related to – and no doubt shaped by – factors such as the Bank's mandate for conducting monetary policy and the way that work is organized within the organization.

Metaphorically speaking, a conceptual economy functions as a kind of 'interpretive engine'[3] for analyzing data and helping to transform them into institutionally-sanctioned knowledge about the state of the economic world, or more specifically, about the state of that particular territory of occupational interest to economists in any given professional site. With this as context, then, we will now turn to the Bank of Canada and the monetary-policy process with its three functions of knowledge-building, policy-making, and external communications.

Knowledge-building, policy-making, and external communications

In Bruno Latour and Steve Woolgar's *Laboratory Life*, a landmark ethnography of scientists and technicians in a biochemical laboratory, as well as in subsequent work by Latour (1990), the authors use the term 'inscription' to refer to the process of collaborative knowledge-building enacted in many research-oriented professional organizations. Within such an organization, inscription occurs as empirical data reflecting some aspect of the world are interpreted, in stages, with the aid of 'inscriptional devices' and through the prism of particular theories and methodological practices, in a sequence of texts – here taken to include both documents and artifacts such as graphs and numerical tables. Successive interpretations are negotiated among members of the organization, eventually leading to a knowledge claim argued in a written research report and, possibly, accepted in due course by the larger research community. Below, the theory of inscription is used to conceptualize the activity of knowledge-building and policy-making within the Bank.

Latour and Woolgar's account of knowledge inscription raises the question of what kind of texts a researcher's busy colleagues will select for reading. Speaking of scientists, Thomas Huckin (1987) suggests that to attract other researchers' attention, texts have to combine 'factuality' and 'surprise value':

> On the one hand scientists subscribe to what Kinneavy (1971) calls 'factuality,' that is, to the degree of certainty that results from the use of well-established rules of inference and evidence and well-established quantitative methods. But scientists are also aware that absolute certainty is a chimera, and that so-called hard facts are always subject to revision. Hence they subscribe as well to ... what Kinneavy would call 'surprise value.' (pp. 2–3)

To turn once again to the Bank of Canada, as a central bank the organization's primary role is to direct the country's monetary policy, that is, to manage the growth of the national money supply by influencing interest rates, with the larger aim of improving the performance of the Canadian economy over time. During the last 15 years or so the Bank has made the pursuit of price stability, or low inflation, its primary policy goal (as have central banks in other industrialized countries). Accordingly, the Bank has committed itself to guiding the Canadian economy towards a series of 'inflation-control targets' running out into future years, staged in five-year periods.[4]

As the Governor of the Bank explains:

> *To do our job of conducting monetary policy, we have to know what's happening in the Canadian economy. So the Bank follows economic developments more closely than anyone else in the country. We monitor daily what's going on in the real economy, what's going on in financial markets, and so on.*[5]

To a large extent, the monitoring that the Governor speaks of is performed through the collaborative interpretation – linguistic and mathematical – of statistical data. In a manner that recalls Latour and Woolgar's notion of knowledge inscription in science, a deputy governor describes the Bank of Canada as an '*information-processing factory*' in which statistical data are analyzed as they are communicated upward through different levels in the organizational hierarchy, gradually being transformed into the specialized economic knowledge needed by the Governor and his colleagues on the Bank's Governing Council to make decisions about the country's monetary policy:

> *What this place is when it comes to monetary policy is a big information-processing factory, structured like a pyramid. Enormous amounts of information come in at the bottom – all sorts of statistics covering a wide range of territory: financial markets, product markets, factor markets, and so on. And what we do is channel this information upwards through the different levels in the organization, distilling and synthesizing it. As the information moves upwards, through increasingly senior staff, it's analyzed in ways that are more and more pertinent to the decisions the Governing Council has to take, with people asking themselves: 'What are the implications of this information? What does it mean for the job that we do, for conducting monetary policy?'* (Executive 1)

Knowledge for decision-making

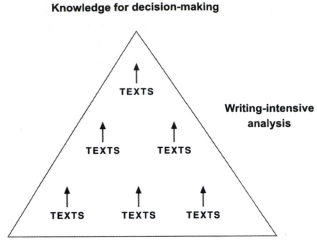

Writing-intensive analysis

Statistical data re. Canadian economy

Diagram 2: An economist's view of knowledge-building in the Bank of Canada

And as the deputy governor goes on to explain, written discourse plays a key role in this process of knowledge-building:

> *Given that the information and analysis has to get transported from level to level, the question is, 'Well, how's it going to get done?' And there's been a very great reliance put on the written page around this institution.*

But what is the nature of the ongoing discursive and analytic activity through which this community-of-practice transforms vast amounts of diverse statistical data into specialized knowledge about the Canadian economy to be used by the Bank's executives in making decisions about the country's monetary policy? Adapting Charles Bazerman's (1988, p. 62) question about knowledge-making in the natural sciences, how does the empirical world of economic developments get transformed into the virtual world of discourse?

I will begin to address this question by again turning to the idea of a site-specific 'economy' created through the discourse practices of a group of professional economists and used to create the knowledge needed to carry out the particular work of their organization. A department chief gives local expression to this idea:

> *The Bank of Canada's policy actions are based on a theoretical and empirical view of how the economy functions.* (Chief 1)

In words that echo Robert Heilbroner's previously cited reference to ideology as the shared 'frameworks of perception' that a social group uses to organize and make sense of its experience, the department chief goes on to describe the

central role that organizationally-created 'frameworks' play in the interpretation of incoming statistical data, a continuous operation known in the Bank
as 'current analysis':

> *Daily current analysis of incoming data employs frameworks. Data or*
> *events are not merely reported – they are analyzed in accordance with the*
> *various frameworks that have been built up over time at the Bank.*

Here we begin to get a sense of the historical legacy of cultural tools available
to the Bank's economists for accomplishing their work of knowledge-building
and policy-making.

Another department chief elaborates on this theme, referring to the 'various
frameworks built up over time' as the Bank's 'paradigm' of the economy, and
distinguishing between 'current analysis and the 'research' performed by the
institution's economists to develop this construct:

> *Current analysis involves using our paradigm of the economy – our view of*
> *how the economy works; that is, how it's structured and what the linkages*
> *are – to interpret the events of the day. Current analysis, in other words,*
> *is about developing stories, in the context of our state of knowledge. You*
> *start with the data and ask, 'What does our paradigm say about this?'*
> *Research, on the other hand, challenges the current paradigm; it questions*
> *our thinking on how the economy works. This involves taking new ideas*
> *out there in the profession and adapting them to Bank use, so that we're*
> *continually expanding our understanding.* (Chief 2)

Thus far in the book, I have been referring to the economists' shared 'conception' of the Canadian economy; from this point on, taking up the economists'
own term, I will use the word 'paradigm' to refer to the economists' conception
of the economy. (As it happens, this notion of what constitutes a paradigm fits
quite well with that espoused by Nigel Gilbert, 1976, who describes it as a
research organization's 'construct of the world and ... the methods [it] uses
to study it' p. 284.)

Broadly speaking, then, the work of the Bank's economists can be seen as
comprising three functions: building specialized knowledge about the state of
the Canadian economy; applying this knowledge in making decisions about
the country's monetary policy; and communicating with outside groups regarding monetary policy. As mentioned earlier, in the Bank vernacular this broad
three-part enterprise is known as the 'monetary-policy process.' We can also
view the economists' knowledge-building as having two primary sub-functions:
carrying out theoretical and empirical research that informs the institution's
evolving paradigm of the Canadian economy; and performing current analysis,
using this paradigm of the economy to interpret incoming statistical data and

other, more qualitative information and thereby produce 'stories' about recent economic developments and expected future trends.

In Chapter One, I described the concept of the 'activity system' – a local sphere of collaborative goal-oriented activity in which intellectual work is mediated by cultural tools such as built environments, analytic methods, technologies, conventionalized roles and social interactions, and texts constituted in various symbol systems. The Bank's monetary-policy process can be viewed as such an activity system – one in which the institution's economists collaborate, using cultural tools such as written genres, a regime of regularly-scheduled meetings with conventionalized roles and social interactions, and computer-run mathematical models, to accomplish the particular kind of intellectual work needed to produce and apply the specialized knowledge about the Canadian economy that the central bank needs in order to accomplish its mandate for directing the country's monetary policy.

To add resonance to the idea that looking at the Bank's monetary-policy process as an activity system casts light on important aspects of the organization's knowledge-building and policy-making, I want to quote from Edwin Hutchins (1993), who draws on the theory of distributed cognition to describe the knowledge, thinking, and actions involved in the navigation of a large ship. Specifically, Hutchins describes an activity system known as the 'fix cycle' in which several crew members, located in different parts of the ship and using a telescopic device called an alidade, simultaneously take the bearings of different landmarks; these bearings are reported by telephone to the pilot house, where another crew member first inscribes them on a navigation chart and then performs directional calculations to guide the ship's helmsman. Hutchins elaborates on the larger aim of the fix cycle:

> The central computations in navigation answer the questions, Where are we? and If we proceed in a certain way for a specified time, where will we be? Answering the first question is called 'fixing the position' or getting a fix. Answering the second is called 'dead reckoning.' It is necessary to answer the first in order to answer the second, and it is necessary to answer the second to keep the ship out of danger. This especially true for large ships that lack maneuverability. In order to make a turn in restricted waters in a big ship, it is not good enough to know when one has reached the point where the ship is to make the turn. Because of the lag in maneuvering response of such a massive object, when a ship reaches the turn point, if it has not already taken action to make the turn, it is too late to do so. (p. 39)

Economists at the Bank of Canada employ strikingly similar terms to describe the work of employing monetary policy to steer the country's economy in the currents of economic events.[6] Below are three quotations, the first and third

from staff economists and the second from a deputy governor, which illustrate
this analogy:

> *When you're conducting monetary policy, you have to think of three*
> *questions: First, where's the economy currently? Second, where do you want*
> *the economy to go? And third, how are you going to get there?*
> (Staff Economist 1)

> *Decisions on monetary policy are taken in a forward-looking way. The*
> *whole process is about how to get the economy from where we are now,*
> *with the current inflation rate, to where we want to be, the inflation-control*
> *targets. To do this, we have to make decisions about the appropriate path of*
> *interest rates. So all the economic analysis coming up to us from the staff is*
> *used to address one question: 'Are we on track?' As new information comes*
> *in, it changes one's views, and if evidence piles up that we're not on track,*
> *then at some point the [Governing Council] will have to make a decision*
> *about changing the policy.* (Executive 1)

> *Essentially, what the monetary-policy process does is this: You've got an*
> *objective; you say, for example, 'Here's where we want the economy to*
> *be in three years, at 2% inflation.' So each quarter there are some new*
> *events. And you say, 'OK, given these events, given what we think is going*
> *to happen over the near term, and given how we figure the economy works,*
> *what path for interest rates will get us to our target?' Now obviously there*
> *could be several paths. But we want a smooth landing when we get to the*
> *target point; we'd like the economy to come in at that point, not run past it.*
> (Staff Economist 2)

Just as the concept of the activity system helps Hutchins explain how knowledge needed to manoeuvre a large vessel is produced and applied through
interpersonal observations and reasoning mediated by various cultural tools,
so the concept offers a way of thinking about the Bank's knowledge-building
and policy-making. The monetary-policy process can be viewed as an activity system in which staff economists take repeated 'sightings' of statistical
landmarks in the Canadian economy and then interpret these data using a set of
written and oral genres in combination with computer-run analytic tools such
as mathematical models to create economic knowledge that is applied by the
Governor and his colleagues on the Governing Council in making monetary-
policy decisions intended to guide the future course of the Canadian economy.
As a further parallel, economists estimate that it takes from 18 months to two
years for the Bank's policy actions to have a significant impact on the economy,
a situation that parallels Hutchins's reference to the limited manoeuvrability of

large ships and the consequent lag in their response time, with the consequent need to take action well in advance of an intended effect.

At the ideological center of the monetary-policy process is the Bank's particular paradigm of the Canadian economy: its '*view of how the economy works; that is, how it's structured and what the linkages are*' (quoted earlier). As a key area of intersubjectivity – that is, a domain of shared focus, perception, and understanding – within the Bank, this paradigm of the economy permeates the thinking, speaking, and writing of the organization's economists. As well – and this is a key point for the present study – the economists' paradigm of the Canadian economy is formally instantiated in the mathematical equations of the Quarterly Projection Model, the Bank's primary analytic tool.

Activity systems in hierarchical organizations usually involve the 'division of cognitive labor' (Hutchins, 1995), where technical specialists perform analytic work, or 'surrogate thinking' (Smart, 1999), on behalf of more senior decision-makers. And indeed, we can see that this is the case at the Bank of Canada, where the structured social interaction associated with the monetary-policy process involves three primary roles: junior staff economists, who monitor and analyze developments in the Canadian economy; senior staff economists (including the department chiefs), who interpret the significance of the junior economists' output, '*continuously generating views, judgments, and ideas,*' as one department chief puts it (Chief 3); and the executives on the Governing Council, who apply this knowledge in making monetary-policy decisions and communicating with the public regarding policy.

The relationship between the staff economists and the Governing Council has a marked rhetorical dimension, in that the Bank's executives do not simply accept the 'views, judgments, and ideas' of the staff economists because they are available – rather, the executives need to be persuaded. A deputy governor describes the dynamic at play here as a 'dialectic':

> *As decision-makers, we have our own logic, which comes out of the ongoing discussions we have among ourselves. Our relationship with the staff involves a kind of dialectic, with them trying to convince us of their logic.* (Executive 2)

Another deputy governor describes the Bank as an '*extremely disputatious place,*' where the staff economists' intellectual input is always carefully scrutinized, and often challenged, before being accepted and applied:

> *If the staff want to influence our views, they've got to work to convince us of their ideas. The Bank is an extremely disputatious place; it's a very tough shop, intellectually. People like to probe and critique ideas before they accept them.* (Executive 1)[7]

He goes on to talk of the critical importance of being able to argue one's ideas in writing:

> *Most of this convincing will have to be done in writing. The Bank's culture is a written culture: if the staff want to make their contribution count, to have it absorbed and used, and if they want to have an impact on people, then they've got to write their ideas down in a clear and convincing way.*

These comments recall Dorothy Winsor's (1996) observation about knowledge-building in science and technology, an observation that holds equally well for the Bank:

> [K]nowledge is formed in interpersonal negotiation over interpretations of evidence rather than simply in the close individual observation of an unambiguous reality. ... People must convince one another of the factuality and truthfulness of their vision of the world as it exists before them. (pp. 5, 6)

Methodological reflections: foundations of interpretive ethnography

The methodology employed in my Bank of Canada study is interpretive ethnography, as originated by Clifford Geertz and further developed by other scholars (Adler & Adler, 1988; Agar, 1980, 1986; Atkinson, 1992; Denzin, 1997, 1999; Hammersley, 1992; Hammersley & Atkinson, 1995; Van Maanen, 1979, 1988, 1995). The philosophical perspective underlying this approach is conveyed by Clifford Geertz in these often-quoted lines from *The Interpretation of Cultures (IOC)*:

> Believing ... that man is an animal suspended in webs of significance he himself has spun, I take culture to be those webs, and the analysis of it to be therefore not an experimental science in search of law but an interpretive one in search of meaning.... The whole point of a semiotic approach to culture is ... to aid us in gaining access to the conceptual world in which our subjects live. (pp. 5, 24)

But just how does a researcher go about the task of 'gaining access to the conceptual world' inhabited by the members of a given social group? According to Geertz in *Local Knowledge (LK)*, achieving such access requires sustained engagement with informants in the group under study: 'The trick is to figure out what the devil they think they are up to. [And] no one knows this better than they do themselves; hence the passion to swim in the stream of their experience' (p. 58). On the other hand, however, Geertz denies the possibility of achieving a 'transcultural identification' or 'inner correspondence of spirit' with one's informants (*LK*, pp. 56, 58). Instead, the researcher needs to focus attention on what is accessible: the 'symbolic forms' of the informants' discourse (p. 58).

For Geertz, the larger goal of interpretive ethnography is to produce a 'thick description' (*IOC*, p. 6) of a social group's 'interworked systems of construable signs' (p. 14), its 'structures of meaning ... and systems of symbols' (p. 182). In order to develop such an account, a researcher must bring together two kinds of concepts, what Geertz calls 'experience-near' and 'experience-distant' concepts. He distinguishes between the two:

> An experience-near concept is, roughly, one which someone – a patient, a subject, in our case an informant – might himself naturally and effortlessly use to define what he or his fellows see, feel, think, imagine and so on, and which he would readily understand when similarly applied by others. An experience-distant concept is one which specialists of one sort or another – an analyst, an experimenter, an ethnographer – employ to forward their scientific, philosophical, or practical aims' (*LK*, p. 57).

According to Geertz, the researcher's job is to take the informants' own indigenous, locally-produced concepts and 'place them in illuminating connection' with the 'concepts theorists have fashioned to capture the general features of social life' in order to produce 'an interpretation of the way a people lives which is neither imprisoned within their mental horizons ... nor systematically deaf to the distinctive tonalities of their existence.' (*LK*, p. 57). The result is a 'thick description' of the community's meaning-making activity – its 'symbolic action' (*IOC*, p. 27) – that 'hovers over' informants' 'experience-near' constructs of reality (p. 25).

Interpretive ethnography, with its method of 'reading' a social group's discourse, or system of symbolic forms, offers a researcher a way to examine and represent the intellectual collaboration that enables a professional organization to produce and apply specialized knowledge. Indeed, in *Local Knowledge*, Geertz himself advocates the ethnographic study of knowledge-building in the local spheres of disciplinary and professional activity that comprise 'modern thought' (*LK*, p. 156). Such research, viewing cognition as largely social in nature, a 'matter of trafficking in the symbolic forms available within a particular community' (p. 153), would focus on 'systems of symbols' (p. 182) as 'modes of thought, idiom to be interpreted' (p. 120).

In *Local Knowledge*, Geertz outlines three methods a researcher might employ in developing an account of an organization's discourse and intellectual collaboration: the 'use of convergent data; the explication of linguistic classifications; and the examination of the life cycle' (*LK*, p. 156). Here is how Geertz defines 'convergent data':

> By convergent data I mean descriptions, measures, observations [which]
> turn out to shed light on one another for the simple reason that the
> individuals they are descriptions, measures, or observations of are directly
> involved in one another's lives.... [S]omething you find out about A tells you
> something about B as well, because having known each other too long and
> too well, they are characters in one another's biographies' (pp. 156, 157).

For Geertz, an important part of gathering 'convergent data' in an intellectual community involves locating and recording shared perspectives among its 'multiply connected individuals' (p. 157).

By the 'explication of linguistic classifications,' Geertz refers to the tactic of identifying frequently-used terms in an intellectual community's vernacular and probing these terms as indicators of significant shared meanings. Again, to quote Geertz, '[exploring linguistic categories involves] focus[ing] on key terms that seem, when their meaning is unpacked, to light up a whole way of going at the world. [T]he vocabularies in which the various disciplines talk about themselves to themselves [are] a way of gaining access to the sorts of mentalities at work in them' (p. 157). Finally, by the 'examination of the life cycle,' Geertz refers to the method of eliciting narratives from informants that recount lines of development in the community's history and examining these narratives as symbolic artifacts potentially rich in meaning. He elaborates:

> [The informants'] notions about maturation (and postmaturation) in the
> various fields, together with the anxieties and expectations those notions
> induce, shape much of what any given one is like, 'mentally,' from inside.
> They give a distinctive, life-cycle, age-structure tone to it, a structure of
> hope, fear, desire, and disappointment that permeates the whole structure of
> it. (*LK*, pp. 159–160)

Using Geertz's approach, a researcher exploring discourse and intellectual collaboration within a professional organization would draw on data yielded by these and similar methods to produce an account of the 'mutually reinforcing network of social understandings' (*LK*, p. 156) that constitute the particular shared vision/version of reality constructed by the members of the organization. Employing experience-distant theories from his or her discipline (and possibly from related disciplines) as lenses for 'reading' the experience-near concepts gathered from informants, the researcher would attempt to describe significant aspects of their work-world.

In my Bank of Canada study, drawing on a wide range of qualitative data, I have been able to map the symbolically-constituted shared reality of the organization's economists – the 'conceptual world' they create and inhabit as they collaborate in going about their work. Using, among other methods of inquiry, the three methods proposed by Clifford Geertz, and at the same time bringing into play experience-distant theories of, among others, genre, activity, and inscription, I have crafted an account of the Bank's knowledge-building, policy-making, and external communications. At the end of Chapter Four I describe how the research questions prompting this account emerged over time and how I went about the task of gathering and interpreting data.

Chapter Three

Genres of knowledge-building and policy-making

In this chapter I bring together, in Clifford Geertz's terms, 'experience-distant' concepts outlined earlier in the book – disciplinary theories of discourse, genre, activity, distributed cognition, and situated learning (here supplemented by modelling theory) – and 'experience-near' concepts embedded in commentary from the Bank's staff economists and senior executives to present a detailed account of knowledge-building and policy-making, a writing-intensive activity mediated by four cultural tools: the *Quarterly Projection Model*, the *Projection Exercise*, the *White Book*, and the *monetary-policy story*. In this account, we will see how the output from economic monitoring and analysis by junior economists is used by more senior economists to develop a broad, forward-looking view of the Canadian economy and a set of policy recommendations for the Governor and his colleagues on the Governing Council, who in turn draw on this view of the economy and these recommendations in making decisions about the direction of the country's monetary policy. A central aim in the chapter will be to examine closely the relationship between written and spoken discourse on the one hand and knowledge-building on the other (Barron, Bruce, & Nunan, 2002; van Dijk, 2003). At the same time, the chapter carefully traces out the ways in which written and spoken discourse genres are enmeshed with the technology of computer-assisted economic modelling.

In examining the discourse of the Bank's economists, we will observe a high degree of intertextuality (Bauman, 2004; Bazerman, 2003; Fairclough, 1992; Witte, 1992), with written and oral genres functioning interactively. More broadly, we will see a complex field of discourse in which written and oral genres are used jointly with various digital technologies and built environments in the accomplishment of collaborative intellectual work. We will also see how intellectual collaboration within the economists' community-of-practice (Lave & Wenger, 1991; Wenger, 1998; Wenger, McDermott, & Snyder, 2002) is characterized, on the one hand, by the 'normalizing' (Foucault, 1972) influence of the Bank as an organization, but also, on the other, by individual agency, contested interpretations, and the animated negotiation of ideas. At the same time, we will observe instances of individual and organizational learning.

Before moving to a discussion of mathematical models and then, more specifically, the Quarterly Project Model, we will first look at a list of ten oral genres (regularly scheduled meetings) and seven written genres that are associated with knowledge-building and policy-making within the activity of the Bank's monetary-policy process.[1]

Oral Genres (meetings)

- Friday Presentation *
- Tuesday Meeting *
- Governing Council Meeting *
- Issues Meeting **
- Starting Point Meeting **
- Project Round Meeting **
- Chiefs' Meeting **
- Presentation Meeting **
- Management Committee Meeting **
- Inter-Projection Monitoring Meeting
- *   These meetings occur weekly throughout the year
- **   These meetings occur as part of the Projection Exercise

Written Genres

- issue note *
- research memorandum *
- daily information package
- weekly information package
- output (from QPM) **
- Chiefs' Case **
- *White Book* **
- *   These genres are very widely used in the economists' work
- **   These genres are specific to the Projection Exercise

Mathematical models in disciplinary knowledge-building

Another body of theory used in the present study relates to mathematical modelling (Harre, 1970; Collins, 1976; Gilbert, 1976; Lynch & Woolgar, 1990; Schön, 1983). Mathematical models employed in the natural and social sciences function as representations of some entity in the physical or social world, such as an object, event, process, or system. Usually incorporating elements of disciplinary theory in their mathematical structure, these models are tools that allow researchers to analyze empirical data and explore conceptual relationships, thereby explaining and/or predicting problematic phenomena.

Since such models are typically designed for specific intellectual ends, their particular properties are determined by what they have been designed to do. Consequently, models reflect an organization's aims, theoretical assumptions, and methodological conventions, with all the heuristic, yet also potentially constraining, effects that this implies. Here we see obvious links to both inscription theory and activity theory: modelling can be viewed as a practice operating within the larger process of knowledge inscription, with models serving as 'inscriptional devices' (Latour & Woolgar, 1986) for interpreting data, while from the perspective of activity theory, models can be seen to act as cultural tools that mediate – that is, enable and influence – intellectual collaboration.

The Quarterly Projection Model

According to activity theorists, the cognition – that is, the thinking, knowing, and learning – associated with goal-oriented collaborative activity is distributed across a community-of-practice, its work procedures, and its cultural tools. As a consequence, if we wish to understand the nature of such cognition, we need to consider the various symbol-based representations mediating the activity with which it is associated (Wertsch, 1991). Within the activity of the Bank's monetary-policy process, mathematical models, a particular type of symbol-based representation, play a key role in analyzing economic data and generating specialized knowledge about the Canadian economy.

The Bank's economists use a variety of mathematically-based economic models in doing their work. According to one staff economist:

> Some models are local, ad hoc models that people have developed to do their jobs in a particular area – such as money-market demand models, trade models, and foreign exchange models. And then there are other models that are used widely by economists right across the Bank. (Staff Economist 3)

Sometimes a model may take the form of a simple equation or two quickly scribbled on a piece of paper or a whiteboard during a conversation; other, more formal and complex models are inscribed in software and run on computers.[2] Another staff economist explains:

> There's some paper-only analysis done, where you write down equations. But most of our stuff gets supported by computer code of some form. That's because wherever there's a link to data, either an historical one in an 'estimation,' or a hypothetical one in a 'simulation,' then you need to have a data-base and a computer system to use the model. (Staff Economist 4)

Of the various models used by economists across the Bank, the computer-driven Quarterly Projection Model is the most widely shared and most
important for the activity of the monetary-policy process. As a third staff
economist puts it:

> *We have different models for different purposes, but QPM is the central
> model, the core model, that we use all the time.* (Staff Economist 1)

As we shall see, the technology of QPM plays a pivotal role in the Bank's
knowledge-building, both as an analytic tool for interpreting statistical data and
as a vehicle of intersubjectivity that is essential to the intellectual collaboration
of the organization's economists.

The Quarterly Projection Model is an evolving mathematical representation
of the Bank's shifting paradigm of the Canadian economy – a representation
based on, and revised in response to, ongoing theoretical and empirical research
by the organization's economists. Originally developed by Bank staff over a
four-year period beginning in 1989, QPM was first used in September 1993,
replacing an earlier model known as RDXF, and continues in use today (May
2005).[3] Incorporating recent economic theory on issues such as the links among
interest rates, exchange rates, and inflation, and the significance of people's
expectations about future economic trends, the model is composed of some 30
interconnected equations that simulate the behaviour of households, business
firms, government, foreigners, and the central bank itself.[4] Run on a powerful
Sun-SPARK computer, which is linked to a network comprising other similar
computers, an extensive data-base, and an integrating device known as a server,
QPM represents 'sectors' of the economy such as consumption, government
expenditure, business investment, employment, importing and exporting, as
well as the influence of the Bank's monetary policy on interest rates and the
exchange rate. (Appendix C shows a sample of equations from QPM.) Viewed
within the Bank as, to quote a deputy governor, a '*state-of-the-art model with
a general equilibrium structure and steady-state, forward-looking, and stock-
flow properties*' (Executive 2), the Quarterly Projection Model, according to
a department chief, embodies '*our working understanding of the economy, as
derived from both theoretical and empirical studies*' (Chief 1).[5]

As a representation of the Canadian economy – or more accurately, of
the Bank's particular conception of the economy – the Quarterly Projection
Model is used both for economic research such as policy simulations and as
the primary analytic tool for the Projection Exercise, a quarterly month-long
operation in which a team of staff economists collaborates in producing a
pivotal document known in the Bank vernacular as the *White Book*, which is
used by the executives on the Governing Council in making key decisions about

monetary policy.[6] In a co-authored article, three of the Bank's staff economists describe these two functions in more detail:

> *The model has been designed to serve a dual purpose. First, as its name implies, the model is intended for use by the staff in preparing economic projections. Economic projection exercises are conducted quarterly at the Bank and form an important basis for discussions of monetary policy between the staff and [the Governing Council]. Second, the model is designed as a research tool, to be used when analyzing important changes to the economy or to macro-economic policies which require a deeper understanding of the longer-term equilibrating forces that influence economic behavior over time. That QPM succeeds in combining these two roles represents an important step forward in economic modelling.* (Poloz, Rose, & Tetlow, 1994, p. 22)

We can see, then, that the Quarterly Projection Model plays a central part in the creation of the economic knowledge needed by the Bank for making decisions about monetary policy. In the words of another department chief:

> *Using QPM as a model of the economy allows the Bank to formalize its decision-making process.* (Chief 3)[7]

From a vantage point informed by activity theory, we can see the Quarterly Projection Model as a prime example of a cultural tool used within a community-of-practice to accomplish complex collaborative intellectual work. And as a mathematical representation incorporating formal economic theory and accumulated organizational understandings, QPM exemplifies Roy Pea's (1993) observation that 'intelligence' is often embedded in a group's cultural tools, reflecting a decision at some point in the group's history that a particular form of knowledge should be stabilized and made available to the collective. This resonates with Latour and Woolgar's (1986) depiction of laboratory 'inscription devices' that embody the outcomes of previous debates within a research community regarding its theories and methodologies. I take up this point in more detail in Chapter Four when I describe the organizational politics surrounding the development and implementation of QPM as the Bank's paradigmatic model of the Canadian economy.

The Quarterly Projection Model, as a mathematical representation of the Bank's paradigm of the Canadian economy, plays a major role in the monetary-policy process. Donald Schön (1983) describes how people in different professions construct, and employ in their work, symbol-based models that represent particular disciplinary conceptions of reality. As 'virtual worlds,' such representations allow for experimentation that is not possible in the physical and social world. The Quarterly Projection Model is a good example of this. One of the ways that Bank economists use QPM is for policy simulations, experimenting with various scenarios to see, for example, what effects various monetary-policy actions would have on the Canadian economy. In this guise, QPM is a cultural tool that enables a particular kind of continuous organizational learning.

As mentioned earlier, however, the primary use of the Quarterly Projection Model is for the Projection Exercise. Here QPM, as an analytic tool incorporating formal disciplinary theory and accrued organizational understandings in a mathematical representation of the Canadian economy, is used to interpret the reams of diverse statistical data that come into the Bank. At the same time, QPM operates as a cornerstone of social organization, providing the Bank's economists with a common discursive and intellectual space for collaborative work. This intersubjective dimension of the model is most apparent in the Projection Exercise, where, according to a deputy governor, '*it plays a central part as an organizing framework*' (Executive 2).

The Projection Exercise

The Projection Exercise is the focal point of the Bank's knowledge-building and policy-making. It is a highly collaborative operation that occurs once a quarter, involves approximately two dozen staff economists, and usually lasts about a month.[8],[9] The primary textual product of the activity is the *White Book*, a document addressed to the Governing Council, in which the staff economists describe current developments in the Canadian economy, forecast future trends, and, accordingly, recommend a particular direction for monetary policy. From the perspective of both the staff economists and the executives on the Governing Council, the Projection Exercise plays an essential role in the Bank's work, a view reflected in the following quotation from deputy governor:

> *The Projection Exercise is a process that brings together all the understanding we've got on how the economy works and applies it to analyzing the data. It's central to the decision-making associated with conducting monetary policy. In fact, the contribution the Projection Exercise makes to decision-making has become even more important in the years since the introduction of the Bank's inflation-control targets.* (Executive 1)

The Projection Exercise offers an excellent opportunity for examining the 'inscription' of knowledge (Latour & Woolgar, 1986) that is achieved through the intellectual collaboration of professionals within a research-oriented organization and so is worth examining in some detail. In what follows we will be looking at stages in a process in which statistical data reflecting a wide range of economic variables are transformed into specialized knowledge needed by the Bank to carry out its mandate for directing monetary policy. To come back to an earlier point, we will see how the empirical world of economic events gets reduced to the virtual world of discourse.

At the same time, the Projection Exercise can be viewed as a classic example of distributed cognition. We will see how intelligence, thinking, and knowledge are diffused across the activity of people working together as a community-of-practice, using shared symbolic resources, to accomplish common goals. We will also see how the Projection Exercise is mediated by various cultural tools – physical technologies (computers and software programs), symbolic representations (alpha-numerical text and mathematical equations), collaborative arrangements (a regular series of formal meetings), and built environments (economists' workstations, meeting rooms).

In addition, we will see a tension between, on the one hand, an organization's tendency to enforce a narrow, constraining intellectual conformity, and on the other, the countervailing presence of individual agency and creativity, intellectual self-reflexiveness, and lively debate. This observation resonates with a tension that we can recognize in the work of two groups of scholars: on the one hand, Michel Foucault (1972), Pierre Bourdieu (1991), Dorothy Smith (1990), and Mary Douglas (1986) suggest that organizations tend to 'normalize' (Foucault, 1972) – that is, to limit and shape – the discourse, thinking, and knowledge-building of their members in ways that efface individual agency and lead to a narrow and static intellectual conformity; while other theorists such as Anthony Giddens (1979, 1984), with his theory of structuration, Mikhail Bakhtin (1986), Carolyn Miller (1994), and Charles Bazerman (1994a) argue that individuals, although influenced by social structures and conventions, nevertheless enjoy considerable freedom of thought, expression, and action, and with that, the possibility of effecting change.

During the Projection Exercise, a team of six senior staff economists known as the Projection Secretariat uses the Quarterly Projection Model (with technical support from three other staff economists in what is called the Projection Group) to consolidate and analyze information provided by a number of 'sector specialists,' junior economists who, on an ongoing basis, monitor and analyze particular areas of the economy using 'satellite models,' smaller adjuncts to QPM.[10] The members of the Secretariat, the Projection Group, and the sector specialists form a network of differentiated expertise, with their shared understandings of QPM (as a symbol-based representation of the Bank's paradigm of the Canadian economy) providing a common, intersubjective framework for their discourse and intellectual collaboration.

Photograph 2: A sector specialist's workstation (Photo: William P. McElligott / Bank of Canada)

Over the month-long course of the Projection Exercise, the Secretariat, with the technical help of the Projection Group, 'runs' QPM on a Sun-SPARK computer a dozen times or more, using various 'settings' that combine different assumptions about the behaviour of the Canadian economy (assumptions negotiated within the Secretariat) with the most recent available statistical data. A department chief describes the process:

> [*The members of the Secretariat*] *play with QPM, introducing different sets of assumptions, until everyone is more or less happy with what you get. There's always a complete set of data used; it's just that you're imposing different assumptions:* 'Ah, I don't like that; let's try it again. We'll do this – what if the exchange rate went this high instead? What would the results look like then?.' *(Chief 4)*

After each substantively different run of QPM on the computer, and there are typically a half dozen or so of these during the month, the Projection Group distributes the resulting 'outputs' to the members of the Secretariat and the sector specialists in the form of numerical tables and graphs available both on paper and in electronic hypertext, a practice that is called a 'round.' Each time, after some preliminary discussion with the sector specialists, the members of the Secretariat gather to discuss the results.

As the rounds with their 'outputs' proceed, and interpretations of successive results are negotiated within the Secretariat, a consensual 'story' is gradually developed regarding the current state of the Canadian economy, its likely future performance, and given this, the most effective path of interest rates for achieving the Bank's inflation-control targets for the national economy. According to the Projection Coordinator, the economist responsible for orchestrating the *White Book* 'write-up':

> *It's a staff exercise, and you're trying to develop a common story. That's not to say we don't have quite different views at times, but what we try to do is bring these views together as best we can.* (Staff Economist 1)

The Coordinator goes on to underscore the narrative impulse driving the production of the *White Book*:

> *As the Projection Exercise goes on, the Secretariat has to interpret the results from QPM. And that's the key thing: you have to be able to tell a story out of the numbers. That's what our jobs are, to make sure there's a story, and that there's sound economics behind it. That's what my job is as Coordinator, is to make sure that there's a good story that we can put in the White Book to explain things.*

Given our concern in this study for the interplay between written and spoken discourse on the one hand and the technology of economic modelling on the other, the translation of numerical output from the Quarterly Projection Model into a narrative conveyed in (relatively) plain written English is an important aspect of the activity of economic knowledge-building and policy-making. A staff economist explains:

> *No matter what great theory you've got in the model, or what wonderful new technology it uses, if you can't write the results down in terms of standard economic concepts described in plain English – aggregate demand and supply, things like that – you'll get dismissed by the [senior executives on the Governing Council]. They'll say, 'Well, this is just techno-mumbojive – what does it mean? You may have this fancy system of complicated non-linear equations in your model, but if you can't describe and justify the results in a simple coherent argument that can be understood intuitively, I'm just not going to believe it.' If you want to get the senior people's attention and convince them, you've got to be able to say, 'Here's the story in straightforward English.'* (Staff Economist 2)

To come back to the Projection Exercise itself, the 'story' that is gradually constructed during the projection rounds, first orally and then in writing, draws on both numerical output from the Quarterly Projection Model and a large measure of what Bank economists refer to as 'professional judgment.' This judgment appears to encompass what we might think of as sub-theoretical ideas (in the sense of existing at a less well-defined and established level than formal disciplinary theory) – intuitive understandings on the part of the Bank's economists regarding how different economic variables (e.g., consumption, investment, exports and imports) tend to interact in the Canadian economy.

As the story to be told in the *White Book* is progressively developed, professional judgment comes into play in two ways. First, in assessing what is currently happening in the economy and in predicting how it will evolve over the next two quarters, the Secretariat relies heavily on the individual views of the sector specialists. This is because in constructing the story, input from QPM only comes fully into play from the fourth quarter into the future and beyond. A department chief elaborates:

> *In the Projection Exercise, we rely more on [professional] judgment in the short run, where we have information that informs the specialists' sense of things. But the further out in the future you get, the less information we have; and so once you get a year out and further, we rely more on the properties of QPM to tell us how things are likely to evolve. For example, what effect is fiscal policy going to have on the economy? When we do our analysis, we'll say, 'There are some things the specialists are aware of that we'll want to take into account in the first couple of quarters, and we'll rely on their judgment there; but after that, we'll let the model tell us.'* (Chief 1)

And second, in gradually developing the story over successive projection rounds, the members of the Secretariat apply their own professional judgment in assessing output from QPM regarding how the major variables in the economy will evolve in the longer-term future, bringing to bear their sense of the inter-relationships among different variables.

These instances of professional judgment are interesting from the perspective of distributed cognition, recalling Roy Pea's (1993) view of the relationship between people and their computer technologies. The interface of human judgment and computer-run economic model can also be seen as a point where 'private spaces of cognition' (Bazerman, 1994b) meet the organizationally-achieved 'intelligence' embodied in the public and intersubjective space provided by a shared representation of the economy.

But what does the story that emerges from the Projection Exercise look like? Below, a department chief describes the broad thrust of the narrative:

> *As the Projection Exercise moves along, they build their story. For example: 'The economy's still adjusting to that rise in interest rates last fall, so that's why there's less activity than we thought there would be' or 'We think investment's going to do this, and housing's going to do that, so it all adds up to something along these lines.' So, anyway, that's the magic part; that's the art. They bring everything together and then say, 'With all of this, to move towards our inflation-control targets, monetary policy has to look like this.'* (Chief 3)

However, in addition to describing current and expected future developments in the national economy and, on the basis of this account, recommending a path for the country's interest rates, the members of the Secretariat also assess the various 'risks' associated with the assumptions underlying their prediction of how the world will unfold. From this 'risk analysis' – another cultural tool, one that is conceptual and analytic in nature – the Secretariat develops several 'alternative scenarios' based on different feasible assumptions regarding factors such as, for example, the future world price of oil, U.S. interest rates, and the growth of the economy. As a deputy governor explains, the Secretariat's risk analysis (including the attendant implications for monetary policy) is then integrated into the story to be presented in the *White Book*:

> *The writing part of the Projection Exercise, producing the White Book, involves putting a storyline together. And this means describing a 'base case,' but it also involves looking at alternative scenarios that say, for example, 'Well, what if the U.S. economy were to be substantially weaker than we think it will be?' or 'What if there was a significant unexpected change in U.S. fiscal policy?.'* (Executive 3)

This practice of considering risks and producing alternative scenarios reflects an acknowledged uncertainty about predictions of future economic events. In a comment that reflects a self-reflexive awareness of the tentative nature of the Bank's knowledge-building, a department chief explains why this aspect of the Projection Exercise is important for monetary policy:

> *Forecast accuracy is of course desirable. However, it's well known that large margins of error exist around the analyses of economists, given the state of the science. What's important here, from the point of view of policy, is that the risks of each prediction be carefully identified, and a thorough assessment of those risks be conveyed. This helps to ensure that the [Governing Council] can react to unforeseen developments in a manner consistent with the Bank's longer-term objectives.* (Chief 3)

(This approach to dealing with uncertainty is reflected in the economic theory built into in the Quarterly Projection Model, a point that will be discussed later in the chapter.)

The end product of the Projection Exercise is the *White Book*, a document of approximately 50 pages that conveys economic analysis and policy advice – in the form of a recommended path for interest rates – to the Governing Council. The official title of the *White Book* is *The Staff Economic Projection*, and the executives on the Governing Council are adamant in claiming that the document represents the independent views of the staff economists. According to one deputy governor:

> *We don't intervene in the Projection Exercise. In fact, we don't see the*
> *White Book until it arrives from the staff. Nobody comes to us and says, for*
> *example, 'Here's the set of assumptions we're using in our analysis. What*
> *do you think?"* (Executive 4)

Another deputy governor describes the situation this way:

> *What we have in the Bank is an exercise where the White Book is produced*
> *without any input from [the Governing Council], because what we want is*
> *the staff's objective view, without them trying to second-guess what I might*
> *be thinking or someone else might be thinking. We want their best effort in*
> *terms of putting together a consistent view, given the issues as they see them*
> *and given the tools they have to work with.* (Executive 3)

Contrary to the claim of these senior executives, however, several of the staff economists that I interviewed see a strong tacit influence at work in the preparation of the *White Book*, with the staff inclined to shade their story to accommodate their sense of the executives' expectations. Here is how one staff economist put it:

> *The staff working on the Projection Exercise tend to want to give [the*
> *Governing Council] the picture [that the staff] think they're looking for.*
> *[The senior executives] tend to send out certain signals about the way they'd*
> *like the story in the White Book to turn out.* (Staff Economist 3)

Another economist adds:

> *What comes out of the Projection Exercise isn't always what goes into the*
> *White Book, because the staff have to temper the analysis that's generated*
> *so it will 'sell' to the executives. We have to mettre de l'eau dans vin [put a*
> *little water in our wine] sometimes. They have certain views, assumptions,*
> *and biases that condition what they're willing to accept.* (Staff Economist 5)

Given that the members of the Governing Council, like any group working closely together, are bound to share *'certain views, assumptions, and biases'* (quoted earlier), one might wonder whether there is any real possibility of the Bank's staff economists influencing the executives' way of looking at the world. A deputy governor, asked at an orientation session for junior economists the question, *'how we can convince [the Governing Council] about changes to the Bank's paradigm [of the economy]?,'* replied:

> *You do it through the force of logical argument, with propositions and*
> *supporting empirical evidence. And you need to develop an intellectual*
> *critical mass around your point of view by persuading people and getting*
> *your colleagues on side. [The members of the Governing Council] do*

happen to believe certain things, and we're stolid, but we're willing to
change, if the evidence is there. (Executive 1)

He went on to mention several occasions where an important change in the
Bank's approach to monetary policy, such as, for example, the use of a variable
known as the 'monetary aggregates,' had originated with staff economists
who had succeeded in convincing the executives of their view.[11] However, I
will leave the last word to an economist who says that, given his experience
in the Bank:

I have to take the idea that the executives are open to rational argument
from the staff with a grain of salt. (Staff Economist 5)

In the quotations above, we can see certain signs of the 'normalizing' influence
of an organization on individual thought and expression – as, for example,
in the view of the two staff economists that the Projection Exercise is really
about producing a story that will accommodate the senior executives' view of
the economic world. However, at the same time, conversely, one could take
the disagreement between the staff economists and the senior executives on
this same issue as evidence that Mikhail Bakhtin's (1981) 'heteroglossia,' the
give-and-take of contending perspectives and voices, thrives in the discourse
of this professional organization as it does in others.

At this point I want to begin looking more closely at the roles and social
interactions associated with the monetary-policy process. As we have seen,
activity theory suggests that conventionalized collaborative arrangements – as
one type of cultural tool – can play an important mediating role in the complex
reasoning and knowledge-building accomplished within a community-of-practice. Viewed from this perspective, the Projection Exercise and the production of
the *White Book* can be seen to be organized around a number of oral genres – a
sequence of scheduled formal meetings that mediate the economists' intellectual collaboration. And while this study is particularly concerned with written
discourse, we will see here that spoken language also plays a vital role in the
Bank's knowledge-building and policy-making. In this respect, the Projection
Exercise – and, more generally, the monetary-policy process – corroborate
the observation of discourse theorists that within organizations, written and
oral genres of discourse are intertextually connected and mutually supporting
(Loos, 1999; Piazza, 1987; Spilka, 1993; Witte, 1992).

Below I describe the series of formal meetings held during the Projection
Exercise and explain their respective functions in the production of the *White
Book*, also noting the various documents read prior to and discussed in the
meetings. As we will see, the rhetorical impulse – the need to persuade others of
the validity of one's views – runs like a thread through this written and spoken

discourse. Before beginning a close examination of this series of meetings, however, it would be helpful to look at a diagram representing the chain of oral genres (meetings, in this case), with their associated documents, which mediates the Projection Exercise. (Here as in Chapter Five, it is useful to think of 'chains' of oral genres and written genres connected in activity.)

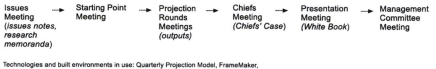

Issues Meeting (*issues notes, research memoranda*) → Starting Point Meeting → Projection Rounds Meetings (*outputs*) → Chiefs Meeting (*Chiefs' Case*) → Presentation Meeting (*White Book*) → Management Committee Meeting

Technologies and built environments in use: Quarterly Projection Model, FrameMaker, FAME, Sun-SPARKS computers, economists' workstations, meeting rooms

Diagram 3: The chain of oral genres (meetings) associated with the Projection Exercise

Issues Meeting

The Issues Meeting is the first major event in the Projection Exercise and is attended by the chiefs of the economics departments (Research; Monetary and Financial Analysis; Financial Markets; and International), the members of the Projection Secretariat, the sector specialists, and other economists involved in research to enhance the Quarterly Projection Model (of which, more later). Two kinds of issues are discussed: significant (i.e., usually unexpected) economic developments over the last quarter and proposed changes to QPM. In the first quotation below, a member of the Secretariat describes how changes to QPM are negotiated with the department chiefs; the second quotation presents the view of one of the chiefs, the final arbitrators of any proposed changes.

> *At the Issues Meeting, the staff presents the changes they want to propose for improving QPM, along with the supporting research work, to the chiefs. So, for example, if we wanted to make a change to one of the equations in the model, we'd have to convince all the department chiefs that it's an appropriate thing to do. And that would involve writing a paper explaining the change and providing supporting evidence, as well as showing what the implications would be for the model as a whole.* (Staff Economist 1)

> *People who want to bring issues to the table write background papers. They'll say, 'Hey, you know, we've finally got this issue licked and what we'd like to do is build this assumption into the mathematics of the model, and this is why.' And the whole group that's involved in the Projection Exercise will kick the idea around, and in the end the chiefs either accept the proposed change to QPM or they don't.* (Chief 3)

These two quotations suggest the degree to which the written discourse and the spoken discourse associated with the Projection Exercise are linked. In the context of the Issues Meeting, for example, when a change to QPM is being proposed, an 'issue note' is circulated prior to the meeting, often accompanied by a longer 'research memorandum' describing background research work. Then at the meeting, the author or authors provide an oral overview of the note. Discussion of the proposed change follows, with the department chiefs accepting or rejecting it, or possibly asking for further research to be carried out and documented.

Starting Point Meeting

The Starting Point Meeting, attended by the Secretariat and the sector specialists, occurs shortly after the latest version of an extensive body of economic data officially titled the National Income and Expenditure Accounts (and more commonly known as the National Accounts) is released by Statistics Canada.[12] Earlier, I mentioned Latour and Woolgar's (1986) inscription theory (further developed in Latour, 1990). A key idea in this theory is that scientific 'facts,' or accepted statements about the world, are socially constituted within research communities. Indeed, according to Latour and Woolgar, even empirical data, the basis for scientific statements about the nature of reality, are socially constituted. The National Accounts provide a good example of this. Guided by formal categories of economic theory as well as by the methodological needs of public-sector organizations such as the Bank of Canada and the Department of Finance, Statistics Canada has, over time, identified a particular range and configuration of information that serves as a statistical representation of economic activity in Canada. And of course in gathering and processing this information and then presenting it in numerical tables, Statistics Canada applies its own particular organizational procedures. Thus, in a sense, the economic data available to the Bank in the National Accounts are already socially-constructed entities (as with the biochemical data discussed by Latour and Woolgar), even prior to their analysis by the Bank economists monitoring the Canadian economy.

Parenthetically here, I want to look at an interesting illustration of the constructed and potentially mutable nature of the data provided in the National Accounts, and the potential effects of this on the work of Bank of Canada economists. Below, a staff economist describes a case in which Statistics Canada changed one aspect of a procedure for defining and assembling data related to the 'terms-of-trade,' with the result that a body of information that several Bank economists had been using to argue for a newly-developed model of Canadian exchange rates shifted beneath their feet.[13]

*We'd been writing a series of papers on the exchange rate. Now, there
wasn't a whole lot of theory behind the model we were proposing: it was
just a case where we said, 'Well, the model fits the data and it seems to be
really robust.' Then at a certain point we found ourselves in an awkward
situation – things that we thought were robust seemed to be changing. What
happened was that we got revised data from Stats Canada. They'd gone
and changed the base year for the terms-of-trade-indices, so ten years of
historical data suddenly changed on us. Now originally, we'd sold people
on the equations in the model [of Canadian exchange rates] saying, 'Well,
you know, here are the data, and the model fits the data.' But then suddenly
things changed, and the model no longer fit the data. We would have
expected history to remain constant, and in this case it didn't, which came
as a rude reminder that things we take as immutable facts sometimes aren't.*
(Staff Economist 6)

At the Starting Point Meeting, the members of the Secretariat consult with the
sector specialists to negotiate an accepted view about what has recently been
happening in the Canadian economy. As a deputy governor points out, '*Setting
out the starting point assumptions is a key area where professional judgment
must be brought to bear, in this case the judgment of the sector specialists*'
(Executive 3). In another display of intellectual self-reflexivity regarding the
Bank's knowledge-building, he goes on to explain how such judgment is a
necessary complement to the Quarterly Projection Model:

*The judgment of the sector specialists usually involves something that QPM
can't capture – like, for example, certain aspects of the behaviour of the
housing sector. There will always be events that won't be properly captured
by the model. We all realize that the models don't replicate the real world
because there's more that goes into deciding individuals' behaviour than
those key variables that you tend to capture in a macro-economic view of
the economy.*

In the following interview excerpt, the Projection Coordinator describes the
events of the Starting Point Meeting, emphasizing the focus on 'shocks,' or
surprises, appearing in the National Accounts data (vis-à-vis the economic
outlook presented in the previous *White Book*) and explaining how the Quarterly
Projection Model is used as a reference point for predictions of future economic
developments:

*Shortly after the National Accounts come out, [the members of the
Secretariat] hold a meeting with the sector specialists. The specialists try to*

explain the shocks in the National Accounts and say how they interpret the implications of these shocks for the future. And we also ask them to say how their interpretation differs from QPM's. So, for example, if we [had been] expecting consumption growth of, say, 3%, and consumption came in at 1% [in the National Accounts], we'd ask the sector specialist who's responsible for looking at consumption to explain – 'Well, this is why it came in at 1%, as opposed to 3%, and I think these factors are very transitory,' or else, 'I think these factors are going to persist for a while, and though the model says that they should die out within two years, I think the factors will persist for ten quarters or more.' (Staff Economist 1)

This emphasis on 'shocks' in the National Accounts data recalls Thomas Huckin's (1987) observation regarding the need in scientific discourse to balance the 'factuality' derived from well-established quantitative methods and rules of evidence with 'surprise value,' or newsworthiness.

In their oral contributions at the meeting, the sector specialists are encouraged to focus and distil their comments about their particular area of the economy. Several years ago, a memorandum containing guidelines was distributed to the specialists describing the kind of analysis required. A member of the Secretariat explains: '*The meetings used to take two hours when they should have taken one; so we created these written guidelines. And they seem to be working*' (Staff Economist 7). Once again we see the rich network of intertextual links connecting spoken and written discourse in the accomplishment of intellectual work.

After the Secretariat and the sector specialists have come to agreement on a common perception of the 'starting point,' that is, of the present state of the economy, the numerical values in the Quarterly Projection Model's equations are adjusted, or 'set,' to reflect this view. And the Projection Exercise proceeds.

Projection Rounds Meetings

During the following two weeks, the Quarterly Projection Model is typically run numerous times on a Sun-SPARK computer, each time with a different set of assumptions and the most recent available economic data. The output from each round is primarily in the form of numerical tables and graphs, with a small amount of written text. This material is communicated via a local computer network to all the people involved in the Projection Exercise, who print out that part of the output that is specifically relevant to them. After each substantively different round of results from the model, the Secretariat meets for a discussion. Typically, this occurs two or three times a week. During these meetings the six members of the Secretariat negotiate how the results should be interpreted and collaborate in developing the 'story' that eventually will be written up in the *White Book*.

Chiefs' Meeting

After the projection rounds are completed and the members of the Secretariat have agreed on the broad outline of the story that is to be told in the *White Book*, the Secretariat and the sector specialists meet with the four chiefs of the economics departments to discuss this story, as summarized in the 'Chiefs' Case,' a document including several introductory paragraphs of text and a dozen or more pages of numerical tables and graphs. At the meeting, also attended by the sector specialists as observers, the Projection Coordinator presents an overview of the story orally and then the members of the Secretariat add detail and respond to questions from the chiefs. (See Appendix F for a sample agenda from a Chiefs' Meeting.) According to one department chief, '*the purpose of the meeting is to thrash out the results, to critique them, and recommend any changes prior to the creation of the White Book*' (Chief 4). A secondary, implicit function of the meeting is to provide the sector specialists with some important professional training – an example of Lave and Wenger's (1981) situated learning – in that they are able to see the larger organizational context to which their work contributes. Indeed from all reports, this meeting is viewed by the sector specialists as a key learning opportunity.

Once the Secretariat has negotiated the story intended for the *White Book* with the chiefs, the Projection Coordinator proceeds with the final 'write-up.' As a chief describes it,

> The chiefs having said, '*OK, we accept the story*,' *the staff then go and write it up in the White Book. [The Projection Coordinator] holds the pen, but often he farms out sections to [staff economists in the economics] departments and they prepare a first draft. He pulls them together, smoothes out the links, and then gives us a copy for comment, usually in bits. And then when it's done, it's printed.* (Chief 3)

Presentation Meeting

Once completed, the *White Book* is sent on to the executives on the Governing Council. Several days later, the executives meet with the Secretariat to discuss the story presented in the document, with the sector specialists and other interested staff economists also in attendance. The Presentation Meeting appears to follow an unofficial but well-established protocol, with the seating arrangements, the participants' order of arrival, and the sequence of speakers conventionalized to a large extent. This brings to mind Anne Freadman's (1994) notion of the 'ceremony' – the ritualized setting, situation, and practices associated with a written genre.

The Presentation Meeting offers the Secretariat the opportunity to position the *White Book* in terms of how they hope it will be read, in another example of the intermeshing of written and spoken discourse. According to one deputy governor:

> *The meeting permits the economists to show where they want to put the emphasis. They write the White Book under pressure and then afterwards have an opportunity to reflect on it, on 'What's the broad message?' So at the meeting there's a summary presentation of the broad features of the document, which is presented with an emphasis or slant on one aspect or another.* (Executive 2)

On the other hand, the meeting also gives the Governing Council the opportunity to examine the quality of the 'surrogate thinking' (Smart, 1999) that the staff economists have performed on their behalf in producing the *White Book*. Another deputy governor explains:

> *The head of the Secretariat chairs the meeting; and therefore they have full flexibility to emphasize what they think is important. But we in turn have full flexibility in terms of probing, asking questions, making sure that we understand what's there. They're presenting a product, and what's important for us is that we understand the thinking and judgment that went into it, so that we can then discuss and debate that among ourselves later.* (Executive 3)

According to the first of the two deputy governors quoted above, an important part of the 'probing' involves the 'risk analyses' included in the *White Book*. He explains:

> *We ask questions about how they've assessed the risks. And if we feel that the balance of risks is different than they do, then we may want to shade our policy actions differently over the next two or three months, relative to what the staff are recommending as a path for interest rates. That's because the staff's recommendation depends on everything else in the White Book, including the risks to the analysis.* (Executive 2)

A sector specialist provides a 'supply-side' perspective of the executives' scrutiny:

> *What happens at the meeting with the executives is that they're there to test and prod your story, to say 'OK, here's the story, and what would happen*

if I told you that I don't believe this part. How does it work now?' A large
part of it has to do with the risk analysis, where they say, 'What if this
were to happen, rather than what you're assuming; how would your story
accommodate that, or how would you have to change it?.' (Staff Economist 8)

Here we see a further depiction of the Bank as an 'extremely disputatious
place,' to recall an earlier quotation, where knowledge-building is a highly
rhetorical activity.

As a deputy governor points out, the meeting also has a training dimension,
in that it again helps the sector specialists to understand the larger organizational
relevance of their particular contribution to the Projection Exercise:

The meeting is an opportunity for people to feel that they're part of a
process, and gives them a chance to see how their work is channeled and
conveyed to the executives. It's good training, to see what the executives'
concerns are, what sort of questions they ask the staff. (Executive 2).

Management Committee meeting

Immediately following the Presentation Meeting, the Management Committee
(comprising the executives on the Governing Council, the chiefs of the four
economics departments, and six senior staff economists) gathers to discuss the
implications for monetary policy of the discussion that occurred there. As one
deputy governor describes it:

The meeting is specifically meant to discuss monetary policy proper. We
say, 'OK, we know where the staff is in terms of the outlook for the economy
and their recommendation for interest rates. Now, how do we assess their
analysis, and what strategy are we going to follow in the next six weeks or
so?.' (Executive 2)

Stepping back once more to view the monetary-policy process as an activity
system, we can see that the diversity of perspectives and expertise described
above is essential to the Projection Exercise. This multi-vocality is an important
aspect of distributed cognition within an organization, ensuring that a variety of
views and understandings are brought to bear on complex questions or problems
(Cole & Engeström, 1993). The division of intellectual labour inherent in the
Projection Exercise operates through an organizational structure of differentiated expert roles and regularized social interactions that enable the production
of the specialized knowledge about the economy that is instantiated in the
White Book. At the same time, the Projection Exercise can be seen to embody
historically-achieved organizational wisdom about the most effective way to
accomplish a particular type of complex economic analysis.

Before turning to a more detailed discussion of the *White Book* itself, I want to look at several ways in which the knowledge-building activity of the Projection Exercise has changed in recent years as a result of enhancements to the Bank's computer technology. First, the pattern of collaboration associated with the Projection Exercise has been altered by advances in computer-enabled communication. One such change involves the increased interactivity accorded by the networked Sun-SPARK computers used by the staff economists. For example, during the successive 'rounds' of the Projection Exercise, electronic mail now allows for frequent back-and-forth exchanges among the members of the Secretariat and the sector specialists regarding how numerical output from the Quarterly Projection Model is to be interpreted. Then later on, during the 'write-up' of the *White Book*, the Projection Coordinator receives textual contributions from colleagues and distributes his drafts for comments via the computer network, so that there is considerably more negotiation over the document-in-progress than occurred previously. In both cases, the 'fund of expertise' (Moll, Tapia, & Whitmore, 1993) distributed across the participants in the Projection Exercise is more readily brought into play as a continuously available resource.

Second, during the 1990s, two new computer softwares altered the preparation and textual form of the *White Book*. Using FAME, a data-base management software, writers working on different segments of the document can simultaneously access data-bases and create graphs, charts, and tables; and then using FRAMEMAKER, a documentation software, they can combine these graphic elements with prose to achieve a more effective presentation. As a consequence, the rhetorical structure and visual presentation of the *White Book* have changed in ways that have been well-received by the Governing Council.

The *White Book*

According to genre theory, a written genre can be viewed as typified socio-rhetorical action that encompasses regularities in texts, composing processes, reading practices, and social interactions and that is enacted within a professional organization to regularize writer/reader transactions and so enable the reliable, consistent construction of specialized knowledge (Paré & Smart, 1994). Adding in the perspective of activity theory, the genre of the *White Book* can be seen as cultural tool employed by the Bank's staff economists (as writers) and executives (as readers) to create, on a consistent basis, a particular kind of knowledge about the Canadian economy and the appropriate direction for the country's monetary policy.

In its textual aspect, the *White Book* is a representation – in the form of prose text, graphs, and numerical tables – of the negotiated meanings and consensual knowledge that emerge from the QPM-supported analytic work performed by the members of the Secretariat and other staff economists during the Projection Exercise.[14] As mentioned earlier, the document – which is typically about 50 pages in length – describes current and expected future economic conditions in Canada, and, given this, recommends a particular path of interest rates to guide the Canadian economy towards the Bank' inflation-control targets. Also included are several risk-related 'alternative scenarios' for the future, described by a department chief as *'qualifications to the conclusions of the argument in the White Book'* (Chief 3). As described below, the *White Book* serves a three-fold function: as an end-of-quarter input to policy-making, as a benchmark for the ongoing work of 'current analysis,' and as a reference point for a series of meetings during the quarter.

End-of-quarter input to policy-making

A staff economist offers his perspective on the *White Book*: *'What it does is lay out a view by the staff of where the economy is today, where it's going and, given that, what it's going to take to get to our [inflation-control] targets'* (Staff Economist 9). Another staff economist adds this comment:

> The *White Book* tells [*the Governing Council*] a story: *'Given everything that's happening outside Canada and inside Canada and given what we know about how the economy works, this is the path of interest rates that we believe is required if our objective of achieving the inflation-control targets is to be met at a particular point in the future.'* (Staff Economist 5)

A third staff economist elaborates on the 'story' communicated in the *White Book*:

> The 'story' focuses on the bottom line, our policy advice: *'Here's what you should do to achieve our inflation-control targets.'* That's really the crux of it, the path of interest rates we're proposing. But then of course we've got to explain how we got there: We don't just say that you should set interest rates at 5%, or whatever, and that'll get us to our targets, because we'd leave too many questions unanswered. We need to say what factors we think will affect the output of the economy, and how we think the exchange rate is going to react and the impact that'll have on interest rates, and so on. (Staff Economist 8)

The executives on the Governing Council use the economic knowledge inscribed in the *White Book*, along with other sources of information available to them, to make strategic (long-term) and tactical (short-term) decisions intended to influence Canadian interest rates, the Bank's primary method of guiding the country's economy.[15] As one executive puts it, '*We look at the White Book as a framework for thinking about the economy and about policy*' (Executive 2).

The *White Book*'s forward-looking view of the Canadian economy and its recommended path for interest rates together represent a knowledge claim specifically designed as input for the Bank's decisions on monetary policy. A department chief characterizes its 'story' as *the* quintessential piece of policy advice that the Bank's staff economists have to offer the executives: '*It's a summary of everything we know, the best advice we can give them*' (Chief 3). A staff economist points to the professional understanding and confidence that this writer-reader relationship implies:

> In the White Book, we focus on getting to the key points as quickly as possible, presenting them as simply as possible, and with as little excess baggage as possible, so that people who are pressed for time can see the story. They in turn have to rely on us having done the professional work that has to lie behind that kind of simplification. (Staff Economist 4)

The genre of the *White Book*, then, is a cultural tool that functions as the primary medium for the 'surrogate thinking' performed by the staff economists for the benefit of the executives on the Governing Council. Once again to view the monetary-policy process as an activity system, the knowledge inscribed in the *White Book* is the product of an 'intelligence' distributed across the people, built environments, technology, symbol systems, and collaborative arrangements that constitute the Projection Exercise, a product that subsequently feeds directly into the executives' policy discussions and decision-making.

Benchmark for current analysis

In addition to its use as an end-of-quarter input into the executives' decision-making on monetary policy, the *White Book* serves another important function in the Bank: its forecast component gives the staff economists, in particular the sector specialists, a benchmark for doing 'current analysis' – the process of monitoring and interpreting economic developments (as primarily reflected in statistical data) during the following quarter. Says one department chief:

> It gives us a framework for evaluating new information, weighing it appropriately, and thinking about its implications for policy. (Chief 3)

A staff economist notes the key question that the sector specialists who monitor ongoing developments in their particular areas of the economy need to ask: '*What's new in the data and how does it affect our view of what's going on in the economy?*' (Staff Economist 11). A department chief elaborates, suggesting that current analysis is concerned with four questions:

> '*What significant events occurred, and why? Were these events in accordance with what theory, our models, and past trends would predict? Were they in accordance with the forecast in the last White Book? And what are the implications of the events?*' (Chief 1)

Another staff economist describes the process of current analysis in more detail, again accentuating the role of the *White Book*:

> *The White Book tells a story. And then as information comes in each week during the quarter, it's interpreted relative to that story. So the White Book also provides the benchmark. When you're getting new information, it's only useful if you have a view of where you thought you were going to be. You need something to interpret it, relatively. And that's what the White Book does: it helps us interpret new information as it comes out over the quarter.* (Staff Economist 2)

He goes on to explain that the relationship is reciprocal, with the incoming data also potentially exerting an influence on the economists' perception of the soundness of the story contained in the previous *White Book*:

> *If the numbers coming in don't fit the story – say the economy doesn't seem to be doing as well as we thought it would – then the story doesn't look as good. But time will tell. If the numbers come back in line, then the story will stay intact; we'll say, 'Well, the story is OK.' But if we start to see more out-of-synch numbers, we'll say, 'Well, we're going to have to reconsider the story.'*

The *White Book* story, then, is an evolving representation of economic knowledge carried forward in time and repeatedly revised through written and spoken discourse. (Later in the chapter I will elaborate on this notion in discussing the narrative known in the Bank as the 'monetary-policy story.') As the quarter continues, and new incoming economic data are analyzed, the story that was presented in the *White Book* is gradually updated, first through informal spoken exchanges and then through written texts (such as the 'inter-projection information package,' to be described later). The process continues throughout the quarter, with the most recent version of the story becoming the foundation for the next Projection Exercise.

Reference point for sequence of meetings

Here we will turn once more to the conventionalized roles and social interactions associated with the knowledge-building and policy-making dimensions of the monetary-policy process, another type of cultural tool mediating this activity. Earlier, I described the sequence of formal meetings associated with the production of the *White Book* during the month-long Projection Exercise. Once the Projection Exercise is completed and the *White Book* has been presented to the Governing Council, the document becomes a key point of reference in another set of conventionalized social interactions during the following quarter, a series of regularly-scheduled meetings in which department chiefs and other senior staff economists brief the Governing Council on the results and policy implications of the ongoing 'current analysis' performed by the sector specialists. The Projection Coordinator provides an overview of these meetings, describing the role of the *White Book* story:

> *The White Book provides a basis for the discussions that take place between the staff and the Governing Council during the quarter about how to interpret incoming information. We do the White Book and present it four times a year; so we think of our work as involving a thirteen-week cycle. Every week during the cycle the chiefs meet twice with the Governing Council; and there's a discussion of economic developments that's carried out using the White Book as a reference point. And then in the seventh or eighth week there's the Inter-Projection Meeting, which looks at all the information that's been received to date, to see how it would affect what was said in the previous White Book.* (Staff Economist 1)

Below I describe the meetings individually (along with the documents involved), looking at how each meeting contributes to knowledge-building and policy-making, an account that will help us better understand the organizational functions of the *White Book*. Once again we will see the intermeshing of written and spoken discourse that characterizes the Bank's monetary-policy process.

Friday Presentation and Tuesday meeting

Every Thursday the members of the Governing Council receive a 'weekly information package' from each of the economics departments (Research; Monetary and Financial Analysis; Financial Markets; and International), reporting economic data that has come in during that week. The packages contain a sheaf of numeric tables and graphs, along with some text. Then on Friday morning the four department chiefs meet with the Governing Council to present an analysis of this information, voicing their respective *'judgments about the state of the economy,'* as one chief puts it (Chief 4). There are also regularly-scheduled meetings within each department before and after the Friday morning presentation, as described by a deputy governor:

> *On Friday the chiefs report to us on the week's economic developments. And in order to make a presentation, each chief has to be briefed. There'll be a*

large subset of people within each department involved – and they may have
sub-meetings among themselves – in order to get that briefing prepared. And
then after the meeting with us, typically later the same day, the department
chiefs will have departmental meetings where they'll report back to their
staffs about the discussion. (Executive 5)

Another deputy governor offers his perspective on the Friday Presentation, underscoring the benchmarking role of the previous *White Book* story:

In the end-of-week session, all the current information is summarized by the
chiefs. It goes something like, 'Yes, the White Book said this, but here's the
analysis from the most recent week's monitoring.' Actually, quite often they
may just give the analysis without explicitly going back to the White Book
at all, but in our minds it's always in the context of, 'Well, the economy
is weaker or stronger than the White Book predicted, and that implies
something.' (Executive 4)

The following Tuesday morning, with everyone having had time to reflect on the Friday Presentation, the department chiefs meet with the Governing Council again to discuss the implications of the previous week's monitoring and analysis of the economy for monetary-policy 'tactics.' These tactics involve '*decisions about how to implement policy in the short term, that is, over the next week,*' in the words of one deputy governor (Executive 3). Here we see the discursive interface between the staff's knowledge-building and the policy-making of the Governing Council.

A staff economist describes how the story presented in the previous *White Book* serves as a backdrop for the two weekly meetings:

The White Book story defines the point of reference for all these policy
discussions. When the department chiefs go to the Friday morning wrap-
up meeting, that's the whole point, to talk about what's happened that
week and its interpretation in the light of how we understood things
before. And then the Tuesday meeting reassesses it all in a slightly less
rapid way, with a focus on, 'What should we do in the very short term
in our monetary policy interventions in markets?' But always then, in
the background, there's this base, the story about how we thought things
would unfold. (Staff Economist 4)

From the perspective of activity theory, we once again see a case of knowledge-building and policy-making organized around and mediated by cultural tools – in this instance the conventionalized social interactions of regular meetings and the genre of the *White Book*.

Governing Council meetings

There are two other regularly-scheduled meetings involving the executives on the Governing Council. Every day, at 11:00 a.m. and 5:00 p.m., the Governor and the five deputy governors meet to discuss policy actions. At these daily meetings, the executives consider questions of 'strategy,' i.e., the broad, longer-term orientation of monetary policy, the staying 'on track' mentioned earlier, as well as questions of 'tactics,' the short-term actions taken to implement policy. These short-term actions are a daily 'cash setting,' involving transfers of government monetary reserves back and forth between the Bank of Canada and the Canadian banking system and a weekly decision on the selling price of ninety-day treasury bills, which influences short-term interest rates.

Inter-projection monitoring exercise and meeting

Half way through the quarter, the Projection Secretariat and the chiefs of the four economics departments gather to discuss the significance of the statistical data received since the last Projection Exercise and to reconsider the *White Book* story, focusing attention on the economic outlook for the next two quarters. One of the chiefs describes this 'inter-projection monitoring exercise,' as it is known:

> *Mid-way through the quarter we take stock of all the developments that have happened up to then, and we say, 'Well, based on this, how should we be rethinking what was in the White Book?' Because, we've already learned enough that if it were to be redone, we know that it would have some new properties. We wouldn't know exactly what they were, because we wouldn't be using QPM, but we'd have an idea of where things were going.* (Chief 1)

Once the department chiefs and the Secretariat reach agreement on the updated story, they meet with the members of the Governing Council in the Inter-Projection Meeting. In the quotation below, one of the chiefs speaks of the 'inter-projection information package' prepared for the executives prior to the meeting:

> *The idea is to diagram the old [White Book] story, and indicate how we'd modify it now. In our department, we do three notes: one on the major industrial economies, one on the U.S. dollar and current account balance, and one on Canada's exchange rate, trade and current account balance. Each of these is a two-page note with graphs, tables, and some text. And the other departments have their input as well.* (Chief 4)

A deputy governor describes the discussion that occurs at the meeting:

> We take stock of where we are relative to the last Projection Exercise and White Book – what new information has been incorporated into the picture – and how this shades the outlook for the short term. And then we discuss what this means, in the context of our inflation-control targets. (Executive 2)

Management Committee meeting

Immediately after the Inter-Projection meeting, the Management Committee (the Governing Council, the chiefs of the four economics department, and six senior staff economists) meets to discuss the implications for monetary policy. At this point, one of the executives explains:

> a decision will be taken about the interest rate track to be followed over the next six to eight weeks, unless new developments were to call for an obvious change. (Executive 1)

In describing the meetings that regularly occur during the quarter, I have mentioned two supporting background documents – the 'weekly information package' and the 'inter-projection information package.' In addition to these documents, there are a number of other written genres in play. For example, every day each of the economics departments sends the executives on the Governing Council a 'daily information package': one or two pages of tables and graphs, with a brief prose text. As well, throughout the quarter, the sector specialists report on their current analysis work to their department chief as well as, in certain cases, to one or more of the executives on the Governing Council in 'analytic notes' of varying frequency. Below, a deputy governor comments on the extent to which the *White Book* story influences readers' expectations for these notes:

> 'Analytic notes' are of interest to executives for their broad-brush connection to the White Book story. Any information suggesting that the story is at risk should be communicated. Notes of this type should be structured as follows: 'What's happening? Is this a surprise or not, vis-à-vis the White Book? If so, how would you explain it? And are there any forward-looking implications?' (Executive 3)

A staff economist adds an interesting nuance here. When writing 'analytic notes' to the Bank's executives, he says, one has to understand that the executives tacitly adhere to a 'hierarchy of information,' in which different types of analysis have a different value with respect to monetary policy. A writer needs to become aware of this hierarchy. The economist recounts an experience earlier in his career when he was a sector specialist responsible for monitoring and reporting on world oil markets:

> *As a sector specialist, you tend to have your own hierarchy of value for incoming data. But as part of your initiation in the Bank, you have to learn about the relativity of this hierarchy vis-à-vis the hierarchy held by the [executives]. Sometimes this means learning not to get overly excited about 'big' events in the sector. For example, when I started, I thought a billion-dollar discovery of oil in Saudi Arabia was big news; while actually, in the grand scheme of things, for the [executives] it wasn't such a big deal. After all, what impact would this have on the Canadian Consumer Price Index? And the [executives'] hierarchy of information changes over time. For example, the monetary aggregates are no longer considered as significant as they once were, while at the same time developments in the financial services industry have become much more important.* (Staff Economist 12)

The same economist sees a connection between the executives' 'hierarchy of information' and the stylistic conventions for the 'analytic note': *'The Bank's preference for non-journalistic, non-colourful language relates to this hierarchy of information. You need a transparent, neutral style so the executives can immediately assess the value of information presented in 'analytic notes' in terms of their own hierarchy.'* This quotation suggests something of the way that the executives' expectations for documents derive from contextual influences. As Charles Bazerman (1988) points out, an individual reader's transactions with texts are at the same time both idiosyncratic and conventionalized: 'Readers make their own readings, each for their own purposes and by their own lights. Yet, although each reading is a personally constructed event, the individual reading is embedded in communally regularized forms, institutions, practices, and goals. The reading is part of the historical realization of a communal project' (p. 235). In the Bank, the 'communal project' of directing monetary policy exerts a shaping influence on the reading practices and expectations of the executives, and in turn these practices and expectations elicit a particular kind of discourse from the staff economists in genres such as 'analytic notes.'

In Chapter One, I referred to theorizing on activity and discourse genres in professional organizations. Before concluding this section, I would like to come back to these ideas and consider four related points. First, I want to consider the nature of the knowledge-building performed through the genre of the *White Book*. As socio-rhetorical action, the genre of the *White Book* has a dual function: as a discursive site for the joint analytic practices of modelling and writing, the genre contributes to the intersubjectivity that the Bank's staff economists need in order to collaborate in producing specialized, policy-relevant knowledge about the Canadian economy; and, as well, the genre provides the key medium for communicating this knowledge to the institution's decision-makers (with this communication involving the rhetorical element of persuasion, of course).

Second, as support for the view that an organization's larger goals shape its activity and discourse, I will quote the Governor of the Bank, who gives us a sense of how the exigency of directing monetary policy influences the expectations that he and his senior colleagues, as readers, have for the *White Book*, expectations that shape the genre: '*We always look at the story* [*in the White Book*] *in the context of monetary policy: What does it suggest about the kind of policy we should be following – does it suggest something different from what we're doing?*' The Governor leaves no doubt about his view of the organizational motive for the *White Book*: it exists to help the Bank's senior decision-makers direct monetary policy. And should one wonder how clearly this objective is understood by the Bank's staff economists, here is a comment from one of them:

> *Institutional economics is all about advancing practical economic thought in a way that goes beyond what an academic would be doing. It goes beyond just knowing it for its own sake: with the White Book, for example, there are policy implications that come into play and they're extremely important.*
> (Staff Economist 9)

Third, I want to suggest that organizational exigencies shape not only writing but also the related intellectual practice of mathematical modelling. In the Bank, this overlap of exigency is reflected linguistically in the dual use of the word 'projection' to refer both to the modelling performed in the Projection Exercise and to its ultimate product, the 'story' contained in the *White Book*. One staff economist, when asked about this duality of meaning, and about what the term 'projection' means for him, replied,

> *Well, that's a hard question. When people think about the 'projection,' what it is depends on where you sit. As a co-designer of [the Quarterly Projection Model] and the person who's most in charge of everything to do with its technical execution, I tend to think of it more as working with a mathematical model of the economy. However, if you were to ask [the Projection Coordinator, the person responsible for orchestrating the production of the White Book] what he thinks of it, for him it's more like the story. (Staff Economist 9)*

I would argue, then, that both the writing and the mathematical modelling associated with the monetary-policy process originate in and are shaped by a single, fundamental organizational exigency: that of providing the Bank's executives with knowledge about the Canadian economy needed for making decisions on policy actions intended to guide the economy towards price stability and enhanced performance.

Finally, we need to recognize that the needs of an organization change with time, and thus evoke different kinds of discourse. While social processes tend to reproduce genres as fairly stable entities, writers enacting the genres may choose to modify them in response to social or technological changes (Yates & Orlikowski, 1992). The *White Book* provides us with a good example of such a modification to a genre, in this case as a response to the demands of the readership in the light of innovations in desktop publishing technology. One of the executives comments on recent changes to the *White Book*:

> *We asked the staff to try and simplify the White Book, and they've responded quite nicely. It used to have an awful lot of detail, much more than we really needed. But what the White Book is now – and in part this comes back to the new technology, because now the staff can integrate charts and tables into text much more effectively – is more of an overview, the big story, along with the risks and so on. It no longer focuses on details such as 'consumer durables' or 'nondurables,' like it used to.* (Executive 4)

This example of a significant change to the *White Book* reflects something of the dynamism and flux that discourse theorists ascribe to genres (Miller, 1984; Bakhtin, 1986). We will see further examples of this later in the chapter as well as in Chapter Five.

The monetary-policy story

Here I want to look at the Bank's activity of economic knowledge-building and policy-making from another angle and consider the nature of the narratives constructed by the organization's economists for generating, embodying, and communicating knowledge about the Canadian economy. In particular, I wish to look at a narrative referred to in the Bank as the 'monetary-policy story.'

First, though, we need to consider some theoretical concepts relevant to this account. Earlier, in discussing activity theory, I mentioned the role that symbol-based representations play in knowledge-building within professional organizations. Now I want to consider a particular kind of representation – the narrative. Several theorists have pointed to the epistemic, or knowledge-generating, role of narrative in professional discourse. Debra Journet (1995), for example, refers to 'the powerful heuristic value narratives have for science [as] an interpretive and rhetorical strategy' (p. 446), while for Susan Jarratt (1987), 'narrative [is] a vehicle for the serious tasks of knowledge creation, storage, and use…' (p. 22). Jarratt also addresses the persuasive dimension of narrative, pointing out that as a medium for knowledge it can also serve as a way of making arguments: narrative can be used not only to 'shape knowledge,' but also to 'effect action' (p. 10). For his part, Ivor Goodson (1993), cautions us about the situated, political, and ideological nature of narrative. As a way of 'producing, collaborating, representing and knowing,' narrative is 'far from socially and politically neutral.' Narratives are 'located [and] fully impregnated by their location within power structures and social milieux' (pp. 1, 8, 16).

In a similar vein, in what follows we will see how narratives, or 'stories' in the Bank vernacular, are employed in the collaborative work of knowledge-building and policy-making, first as conceptual devices for analyzing economic data and subsequently as discursive vehicles for communicating economic analyses in acts of rhetorical persuasion. We will also see that these stories have an ideological dimension, embodying particular aims, values, and assumptions regarding the Canadian economy.

Frequently in this chapter I have referred to the 'story' told in the *White Book*, just as the economists quoted here repeatedly used the term in interviews. And indeed, we can think of the knowledge about the Canadian economy generated through the Bank's monetary-policy process as a form of narrative representation – a particular kind of 'story' derived from combining empirical data, mathematical logic, technology-supported analytical methods, and professional judgment.

Shortly, I will describe in some detail how the narrative known as the 'monetary-policy story' is constructed. First, however, I want to look at the way the term 'story' is used within the Bank to refer, in a more general way, to the kind of economic analysis produced by staff economists to support the members of the Governing Council in their decision-making. Below, quotations from the Governor and three deputy governors describe the nature of this discourse and suggest some of the concerns and attitudes associated with it. (All four quotations are taken from presentations the executives made as guests in writing seminars that I designed and presented for staff economists.)

> *When reporting on their work, the staff are being asked to tell a 'story' – an explanation for events – rather than neutral description, and all in the context of the job we do here at the Bank. Now on the other hand, of course, we don't want just opinion; we want factual analysis – a story based on evidence.* (Executive 3)

> *What I look for is the staff's assessment of their respective areas [of the economy]. How do you explain what's going on? The crucial thing is to have a coherent story. The story should describe the underlying economic forces, offering an explanation of why key events occurred and suggesting causal linkages among events.* (Executive 4)

Develop a story about what's happening in the world and why, rather than just mentioning a series of events or presenting a bunch of numbers. Don't be ashamed to tell a simple story – and tell it in a clear and forceful fashion so that people will remember it. It gives me confidence to know that someone has a story to tell me. I know they've thought about things. (Executive 1)

We need to know the broad economic story underlying the data – what's going on in the economy and why, and what's the outlook. What we're interested in is your interpretation of developments in your sector [of the economy]. What can you say about the data you're looking at? What do the numbers tell you? What economic processes are at play? And does this lead you to revise your view of what's been happening in the current quarter, and what the outlook is? And to the extent that you can be brief, by all means be brief. Your job is to make us as aware about specific developments in your sector as we need to be to make policy decisions, and that doesn't require highly detailed information. (Governor)

As the term is used above, a 'story' appears to address these questions: What of significance has been happening in the economy, is happening now, or will likely happen in the future? Why is this the case? (i.e., what are the underlying economic forces at play?) And what are the implications for 'the job we do here at the Bank' – directing monetary policy? Another question that is implicitly addressed – one that reflects the central importance of acts of persuasion within the Bank's discourse – is this: 'Why should we believe your perception and explanation of what's happening in the economy?' In this guise, we can see the 'story' functioning as a key cultural tool mediating the economists' discourse and knowledge-building.

We will also look at the views of two staff economists regarding this type of narrative discourse. In discussing the 'stories' that she and her colleagues produce, the first economist describes them as the result of bringing together economic theory and statistical data. She begins by talking about theory as a lens for interpreting data:

We're always trying to see whether the data fit into what economic theory tells us. You know, should this be occurring now in the business cycle? We know that during business cycles this sort of event should occur – and is this what we're seeing? And if not, why aren't we seeing it? (Staff Economist 10)

In another instance of self-reflexive professional awareness, she then goes on to point to the constructed, and necessarily partial, nature of economic stories:

We often use the word 'story' when we look at some numbers and say how

> *we interpret them. But we know the story isn't reality, it's just our best*
> *guess. Of course you want to believe that you're able to look at the data*
> *and understand what's going on with the economy, and to some extent you*
> *probably can; but you can only see through to a certain layer of what's*
> *really going on – there are always underlying factors that just can't be*
> *quantified, such as feelings in the market and political factors.*

Interestingly, a second economist, when asked to explain the meaning of the term 'story,' replied in a similar way regarding the merging of economic theory and statistical data, bringing in the specific influence of QPM:

> *Well, when you look at a bunch of data, what does it mean? What's it telling*
> *you? That's the 'story.' And underlying that process, you've got to have*
> *a theoretical framework, implicit or explicit. And with QPM it's explicit.*
> *You've got your data, the numbers, and you're saying, 'Well, how do these*
> *numbers coincide with the framework in the model? Do they match or don't*
> *they match? And if not, why?' And that's your starting point for developing*
> *the story.* (Staff Economist 8)

Constructing the monetary-policy story

Apart from this more generic meaning, the term is also employed within the Bank in a more specific, qualified way in the phrase the 'monetary-policy story.' This particular narrative, used in the Bank as a discursive medium for generating, negotiating, communicating, and applying specialized knowledge about the Canadian economy relevant to monetary policy, is developed in three phases, over time and across a number of discourse genres, with each successive variation building and elaborating on the previous one. In the first phase, the narrative emerges as a cluster of what we might think of as 'sector-stories' – sector specialists' analyses of developments in their respective areas of the economy (e.g., consumption, government expenditure, business investment, employment, importing/exporting); in the second phase a more encompassing, though still somewhat circumscribed, narrative about the Canadian economy as a whole is developed by the Secretariat during the Projection Exercise and inscribed in the *White Book*; and then in the third phase a fully-elaborated version of the story is constructed by the executives on the Governing Council from the *White Book* and other sources of information.[16] A staff economist provides an overview of this process of narrative development:

> *The sector specialists all have their little stories, that they create using*
> *satellite models. Then in the Projection Exercise, the Secretariat uses QPM*
> *to pull all these stories together and make them interact with one another*

to produce a larger story. And then there's the presentation of the White
Book to the executives, where they test and prod your story. And then they
take it from there, themselves, and decide on their own view of things. (Staff
Economist 8)

As a narrative representation used to create, communicate, and apply knowledge needed by the Bank for carrying out its mandate of directing Canada's monetary policy, the 'monetary-policy story,' with its three phases of development, functions as a pivotal cultural tool for the organizational activity of knowledge-building, policy-making, and external communications. The story serves several purposes: first, it serves to focus and coordinate collaboration among the Bank's staff economists, ensuring that their work is aligned with the organization's mandate and goals; second, it gives the Bank's senior executives access to the staff's ongoing analyses of economic developments; third, it provides the members of the Governing Council with a discursive frame for interpreting the staff economists' input in relation to other knowledge and sources of information in making decisions about monetary policy; and finally it is used by the Governing Council to explain and justify monetary policy to audiences outside the Bank.

In the pages that follow I elaborate in greater detail on the development and application of the 'monetary-policy story' – how it is produced and what it is used to accomplish. I will begin with events inside the Bank and then move to the organization's external communications. As described earlier, throughout each quarter the sector specialists monitor and analyze incoming statistical data, using 'satellite models' (described by one department chief as *'little models, equations, that explain how a sector works'* [Chief 3]) as well as a large amount of professional judgment. Each sector specialist is expected to, as the same department chief puts it, *'tell a story'* about his or her assigned area of the Canadian economy. In effect, each specialist is required to construct and maintain what I have referred to as a 'sector-story,' identifying and explaining significant developments – past, current, and future – in his or her sector of the economy, and continuously updating the narrative as new data arrive. These evolving sector-stories must be available for the telling, and are reported regularly, both orally and in writing, to more senior staff economists, including the chief in the specialist's own department. Then in the Projection Exercise – at the Starting Point Meeting, specifically – the specialists confer with the members of the Secretariat, and the most recent versions of the sector-stories are factored into the initial 'setting' of the Quarterly Projection Model. From this point on during the Projection Exercise the sector-stories fall away as they are absorbed through the medium of QPM into the broader narrative about the economy as a whole contained in the *White Book.*

As we have seen, the *White Book* describes and accounts for what has been happening in the Canadian economy over the last few quarters, what is likely to occur in the future, and given all this, what path of interest rates is required to move the economy towards the Bank's inflation-control targets. A staff economist describes the story presented in the *White Book*'s in this way:

> *In the White Book, everything is brought together into a coherent view of what's been happening in the Canadian economy and what's likely to happen in the future. The White Book also tells a complete macro[economic] story about why things have turned out differently than we thought they would when the last White Book was done. And then there's the policy advice: 'OK, given all this, this is what we need to do to achieve our inflation-control targets – and here's why, the rationale.'*
> (Staff Economist 4)

This quotation calls to mind way in which discourse theorists have characterized narrative. According to Debra Journet (1995), the narrative device of plot 'allows the storyteller to draw a boundary around a subject, select a beginning and an end, place events or action in causal connection, and see the movement from beginning through middle to end as part of the meaning of the sequence' (p. 449). Journet evokes Paul Ricoeur's (1981) contention that a key feature of narrative is the tension created by the meaningful and coherent movement of 'narrated time' from the past, through the present, and on to a significant ending. This description of narrative time clearly applies well to the 'monetary-policy story.' With its focus on the goal of steering the Canadian economy to the Bank's inflation-control targets at a specific point in the future, the story has a definite end point that gives shape and meaning to selected economic developments – past, present, and future.

Once the *White Book* version of the story has been conveyed to the members of the Governing Council, it is incorporated into a larger narrative elaborated by the senior executives themselves. We might see this narrative as the full organizational story about the state of the Canadian economy and the appropriate monetary policy to be followed – the complete 'monetary-policy story.' In elaborating on the story presented in the *White Book*, the senior executives bring to bear other sources of information as well as their own professional judgment. This judgment reflects both a recognition of inherent limitations in the Quarterly Projection Model and the fact that the senior executives' views on certain issues may differ from those of the Projection Secretariat. One deputy governor describes the situation this way, pointing to a particular limitation of QPM that needs to be offset with professional judgment:

> *What we ask the staff to do in the White Book is to give us their best sense*

*of the policy actions required to achieve the inflation-control targets
six to eight quarters down the road. They aren't asked, though, to make
adjustments for what they think the [financial] markets will allow. QPM
doesn't deal with the state of market confidence; it's something we factor
in it afterwards. For example, there's nothing in QPM that says we can't
bring our interest rates below the U.S. rates, and so the staff may well come
up with a story which has future Canadian interest rates below those of the
U.S. Now there's nothing inherently wrong with that, and some day we'll
arrive there if our inflation rate continues to be below the American. But,
in the present circumstances, we may judge that this isn't possible. So one
thing QPM can't deal with – and I don't think any model can – is market
nervousness in certain circumstances.* (Executive 4)

Below, the same senior executive goes on to give several other examples of
areas where he and his colleagues on the Governing Council may look at the
world differently than the staff economists. He explains that in certain cases,
the senior executives may simply apply their own judgment as an 'overlay'
on the story in the *White Book*; while in other cases, they may feel there are
unidentified 'risks,' or uncertainties, associated with particular assumptions
underlying the depiction of future economic events in the *White Book*, and
so will ask the Secretariat to do a follow-up 'risk analysis' examining the
implications of these risks:

*For example, we may have a different sense than the staff of what's
happening overseas, or what the outlook for the U.S. economy is, or what
the implications of the next federal budget will be. For some of these
different assumptions, we can just put an overlay of our own thinking on
things. But for others, the staff may be asked to go back and do a formal
risk analysis, and produce an alternative scenario for the economic outlook:
'If a different assumption is used, what's the outcome?' Then they put the
results into the back of the White Book.*

Once the Bank's executives have developed their own fully-elaborated version
of the 'monetary-policy story' through discussions among themselves, they use
it as a communal resource for making decisions about policy. Unlike the earlier
version of the story presented in the *White Book*, this larger version is nowhere
fully articulated in written form in an internal document; rather, it surfaces in
oral discussions and underlies certain assumptions and lines of argument in
documents produced by the senior executives.

I have been describing the pivotal role of the 'monetary-policy story' in
the creation and use of economic knowledge in the Bank. From the perspective
of activity theory, this narrative can be viewed, in its successive versions, as a

cultural tool – a knowledge-bearing representation – deployed by the bank's economists to create a shared symbolic-based intellectual locus that, to once again quote Charles Bazerman (1994b, p. 146), 'mediate[s] between private spaces of cognition and public spaces in which intersubjectivity is negotiated.' Seen this way, the 'monetary-policy story' is an evolving knowledge-bearing representation, generated through collaborative activity, that both emerges from and influences the technology-mediated intellectual work of the Bank's economists. As mentioned earlier, theory on representations also points to the linkages among the various representations and analytic methods used within a research community; later in the book we will see that this holds true for the Bank, when I discuss the interplay between the economists' discourse and the Quarterly Projection Model.

Apart from its internal use in knowledge-building and policy-making within the organization, the members of the Governing Council also draw on the 'monetary-policy story' as a rhetorical resource for communicating the Bank's monetary policy – both the 'what' and the 'why' of it – to the Canadian public and other external audiences. Various aspects of the 'monetary-policy story' appear in a number of written genres employed to convey the Bank's view of the world, including speeches by the Governor and other senior executives (these speeches are usually accompanied by published texts), the *Annual Report of the Bank of Canada*, the twice-yearly *Bank of Canada Monetary Policy Report*, the 'Commentary' section of the quarterly *Bank of Canada Review*, as well as *Bank of Canada Technical Reports* and *Bank of Canada Working Papers*.

These Bank genres are part of a larger public-policy genre system that encompasses the written and spoken monetary-policy-related discourse of the Canadian financial and business community, various levels of government, academics, the media, and so on. In a sense, then, the Bank is engaged in an ongoing 'conversation' with other organizations and with the public. The 'monetary-policy story' serves as a foundation for the Bank's 'turns' in this conversation. A deputy governor explains:

> *In communicating with [outside audiences], you always have the broader picture in the back of your mind about what's happening in the economy. Rather than specific numbers, it's the storyline you talk about. This shows up, for example, in the Monetary Policy Report; and aspects of it will be in the 'Commentary' section in the Bank of Canada Review, and in the Governor's speeches. When I go out to give a speech myself, I try to be quite clear in my mind about what kind of story we have. And even when a speech isn't directly related to that, it'll certainly come up in questions afterwards.* (Executive 4)

(In Chapter Five, I expand on this theme, providing a more detailed account of the Bank's use of discourse in its external communications with other groups in Canadian society.)

I have been suggesting that the Bank's senior executives draw on the 'monetary-policy story,' in its full organizational form, not only as an epistemic resource for making decisions about monetary policy but also as a rhetorical resource for communicating policy to outside audiences, with different parts of the narrative being used according to audience and occasion. Here is the broad schema of the narrative, as described by another deputy governor:

> *Well, we have inflation-control targets that are the anchor to the story-line. So the story is, first, to repeat what the target is, to make it very clear that people understand our objective and the government's objective. Then, 'What is inflation today? Where are we relative to those targets?', and, based on our assessment of trends in the economy, 'What's the explanation for where we are?' For example, 'Inflation is, let's say, 2 % today, and that's a reflection of all that's gone on over the last year or two. So much of it is our exchange rate depreciation, so much of it is aggregate demand relative to supply, and so on.' And, then, the story also includes – given our interpretation of the economy and our sense of where we're going on the inflation front – what that implies for the Bank's future monetary-policy actions to ensure we get to where we want to go.* (Executive 3)

The Bank's twice-yearly *Monetary Policy Report*[18] follows the full schema more explicitly and completely than any other single published text. Below, excerpts from the April 2004 *MPR* provide a sense of the elements in the larger story. The *MPR* itself goes into detail about each of these elements. (The *Summary of the April 2005 Monetary Policy Report*, with its similar narrative line, can be seen in Appendix I.)

> In February 1991, the federal government and the Bank of Canada jointly announced a series of targets for reducing total [Consumer Price Index] inflation to the mid-point of a range of 1 to 3 percent by the end of 1995. That inflation-control target range was extended a number of times, most recently in May 2001, in this last case to the end of 2006. Monetary policy will continue to aim at keeping future inflation at the 2 percent target midpoint of this range, both to maximize the likelihood that inflation stays within the target range and to increase the predictability of inflation over the longer term.

> The Canadian economy continues to adjust to developments in the global economy. These include stronger world demand, higher commodity prices,

the realignment of world currencies – including the Canadian dollar – and the intensified competition, together with new trading opportunities, coming from emerging-market economies, such as China and India...

At the end of 2003, the Canadian economy was operating at a lower level than the Bank had projected in the October *Monetary Policy Report*... This came about despite stronger global economic activity, particularly in the United States but also in Japan and other Asian economies, and strong increases in commodity prices. Preliminary indications are that growth in the first quarter of 2004 was marginally below 3 per cent at annual rates. As expected, core inflation has generally been below the Bank's 2 per cent target since the October *Report*. Against this backdrop, the Bank lowered its key policy rate by a total of 75 basis points, reducing it by 25 basis points on each of the last three fixed announcement dates, to bring it to 2 per cent (Chart 1).

The Bank's outlook for economic growth and inflation in Canada is essentially unchanged from that of the January *Monetary Policy Report Update*. The Canadian economy is expected to grow at an annualized rate of about 2 3/4 per cent in 2004, picking up to about 3 3/4 per cent in 2005. Such growth would return the economy close to its production potential by the third quarter of next year. Core inflation is expected to average about 1 1/2 per cent for the rest of 2004 and to move back to the 2 per cent target by the end of next year. The main uncertainty for the outlook continues to relate to how the Canadian economy adjusts to global developments.

Earlier I mentioned the concept of the 'genre set' – the full repertoire of genres employed by the members of a professional organization to accomplish their work (Bazerman, 1994a; Devitt, 1991; Yates & Orlikowski, 2002). As we have seen, the economists at the Bank of Canada have developed a set of written and oral genres to enable their knowledge-building and policy-making and to communicate with audiences outside the organization. Internally, this genre set includes, for example, the *White Book*; 'issue notes; 'analytic notes'; 'research memoranda'; the 'outputs' of tables and graphs circulated, both on paper and in hypertext, after each round of the Projection Exercise; the 'Chiefs' Case'; the 'inter-projection package'; and the daily and weekly 'information packages.' As well, there are the externally-published genres, including speeches by the Governor, the *Annual Report of the Bank of Canada*, the *Monetary Policy Report*, the *Bank of Canada Review*, *Bank of Canada Technical Reports*, *Bank of Canada Working Papers*, as well as conference papers and journal articles produced by Bank economists. Linked to these written genres are a number of conventionalized social interactions. Examples include, most visibly, the series of meetings held during the Projection Exercise, the meetings held during the quarter to convey the results of the staff's 'current analysis' work to the executives, and press conferences for media representatives following the release of the *Annual Report of the Bank of Canada*, the *Monetary Policy Report*, and each issue of the quarterly *Bank of Canada Review*. These meetings can be viewed as oral genres, and, as I have suggested, the genre set associated with the Bank's monetary-policy process can be seen to comprise both written and spoken discourse.

Variations on genre conventions

Here I would like to return to a point made earlier in discussing recent modifications to the *White Book*. While the set of genres used to develop and apply the monetary-policy story is a 'stabilized-for-now' (Schryer, 1993) site of knowledge-building, policy-making, and external communications, variations in individual instances of a genre certainly do occur. As writers, the Bank's economists continually look for new ways to accomplish their rhetorical goals. To illustrate this point, we will look at three different situations in which writers produced innovative and unconventional texts within normally stable genres. In each case, the writer consciously departed from the conventions of the genre to achieve a particular rhetorical effect.

The first instance, which dates back a number of years, involves a staff economist who had been involved in a debate with colleagues in the Projection Secretariat and with the department chiefs over the trade sector of the model RDXF, the forerunner of the Quarterly Projection Model. The economist had been collaborating with others in his department to condense the set of trade-related equations in RDXF and, at the same time, to ground the equations in more recent economic theory. During a Projection Exercise, prior to an Issues Meeting, the economist wrote an otherwise conventional 'issue note' intended to persuade the chiefs of the economics departments of the advantages of the revised equations. What was unusual about the 'issue note' was that it began with an epigraph taken from a song by the Rolling Stones (see Appendix G for the first page of this 'issue note'):

> *You can't always get what you want*
> *But if you try sometimes*
> *You just might find*
> *You get what you need.*

Asked about the rhetorical context for the note, and about why he chose to employ this unusual epigraph, the economist explained:

Well, there are three things. One, I wanted an eye-catcher to get people's attention, so we'd get the approval we needed [from the department chiefs]. Second, there was a stress-release motive. In a very short period of time, a number of people in the department had worked very hard, under pressure, on this issue. And so it was a way of relieving pressure – saying, 'Yes, it's been a hard situation, but we're all kind of rocking and rolling away.' I was trying to muster some enthusiasm among the troops, because it was a difficult period. And the third thing is that it really did convey the message I wanted to give. Through tradition, in the Projection Exercise people had been using [the complex set of trade-related equations in RDXF] for quite a while – big thing, high cost, low value. In redesigning the trade sector, we used a Gordian knot sort of strategy: cut as much as you can. And so the idea [in the 'issues note'] was: Because of the cost, 'You can't always get what you want. But if you try sometimes, you just might find you get what you need' – the type of information you actually require. (Staff Economist 5)

With his epigraph, the writer apparently caught the bemused attention of his audience, the effect he was seeking, and the 'issue note' went on to make a persuasive, and ultimately successful, argument for the proposed change to the trade sector in RDXF. I should note, however, for the annals of genre theory, that despite the rhetorical power of Mick Jagger and friends, the genre of the 'issue note' has not morphed into a rock-lyrics/issue-note hybrid.

A similar case of innovation in a genre involves a staff economist who also included an epigraph at the beginning of a 'research memorandum.' The economist had been working with a colleague to develop and 'sell' a mathematical model of the exchange rate. At a certain point, Statistics Canada complicated the issue by revising a series of trade-related data for a recent ten-year period. The economist then wrote a paper with the epigraph,

'*Facts are stubborn things.*' John Adams (1770)
'*Not!*' [name of the writer's supervisor] (1993)

He explains the circumstances and his decision to include the epigraph:

Suddenly things changed, and the model no longer fit the data. So we had to come up with a paper that brought people up to date on what the situation was, what had changed, and to what extent we had to revise our thinking. And we wanted a hook – to try and grab the readers' interest. Also, we were trying to think of a good way to express the feeling you get when something like that happens. We would have expected history to remain constant, and in this case it didn't, which came as a rude reminder that things we accept

> *as immutable facts sometimes aren't. And so that led to this quote, 'Facts are stubborn things.' Well, not necessarily!* (Staff Economist 6)

Interestingly, the same economist describes another situation where he considered breaking with convention and giving a document an unusual title, but decided against it:

> *There was another paper I gave a very snappy title to as I was writing it, but finally changed to something I thought would be less controversial. I was writing a piece on measuring the 'output gap.' There were some conceptual problems in how we were going about measuring the gap, and I felt that people needed to think more carefully about some of the issues involved. But I was having a real hard time trying to get anyone to take me seriously. So I wrote a paper saying what I thought the logical problems were in our way of going about this. Now, I'd spent a lot of time thinking about the output gap, so I tried to make sort of a double entendre out of the title and called the paper 'Thinking Gaps' – both thinking about output gaps and gaps in our thinking. Finally, though, I felt the second sense of the title would rub some people too much the wrong way, and in the end I wound up changing the title to 'Why Is It So Hard to Measure the Current Output Gap?'*

A third and quite striking example of innovation in a genre involves one of the economists who participated in building the Quarterly Projection Model. With a colleague, he had been in a running debate with a number of other staff economists who appeared to be resisting the new model. He and the colleague had written, and presented at in-house seminars, a number of 'research memoranda' attempting to explain what they were trying to do in QPM. After these memoranda failed to persuade enough people to win the day, the economist wrote a paper that took the form of a two-act play set in the Bank cafeteria and in a pub, in which one character asked another a series of questions about economic modelling theory in general and about the new model in particular. (See Appendix H for the first page of this text.) With the approval of the writer's department chief, the paper, titled 'PAQM – Q & A,' was distributed among the Bank's economists. (At an early point in its development, QPM was called the Policy Analysis Quarterly Model, or PAQM.) The writer explains his motivation:

> *I wrote the piece in about a day and a half. At that point in the history of the model, one of our problems was that we were trying to explain answers to people who didn't understand the questions. And what we needed was a real simple paper that not only gave the answers, but also gave the questions. So that's when I conceived 'PAQM – Q & A.' It gave questions and answers in a way I thought everybody would be likely to read, because it's format was*

> *so unusual. And in retrospect I really think it had a big impact, because the ball started to roll our way after that.* (Staff Economist 9)

One of the recurrent motifs in this account of the Bank's monetary-policy process has been the joint use of the Quarterly Projection Model and a set of discourse genres to construct specialized knowledge about the Canadian economy. In the next chapter, we will focus in on the interplay between discourse and mathematical modelling viewed as two intermeshed analytic practices used to interpret the meaning of data and build economic knowledge.

Methodological reflections: research questions, data collection, and data analysis

Here we will continue the discussion of methodology begun at the end of Chapter Two, first considering the evolving focus of my research at the Bank and then looking at the range of data I gathered and the approach I used to interpret these data and produce the ethnographic account presented in this book. With regard to the research questions that focus and guide scholarly inquiry, Gary Anderson (1990) points out that 'ethnographers tend to go looking, rather than go looking for something' (p. 150). According to Martyn Hammersley and Paul Atkinson (1995), this approach has important implications for the design of research: 'Ethnographic research has a characteristic 'funnel' structure, being progressively focused over its course. Over time the research problem needs to be developed or transformed, and eventually its scope is clarified and delimited...' (p. 176). Consequently, the researcher may be well along the path of inquiry before discovering 'what the research is *really* about' (p. 176).

These observations apply very well to my own study. At the outset, I was guided by the broad question of how the Bank's economists employ discourse in transforming large amounts of statistical data and other, more qualitative information into specialized knowledge about the Canadian economy and applying this knowledge in directing national monetary policy. In exploring this issue, I began to see the economists' activity as being structured by a set of discourse genres, and new questions arose. Then as I went further, I was struck by the centrality of mathematical models in the economists' work, and decided to investigate the nature and use of these models, in particular the Quarterly Projection Model. This in turn led to a consideration of the relationship between written and spoken discourse on the one hand and computer-supported economic modelling on the other. At each step along the way, as I gathered and analyzed data, new angles of vision on the economists' discourse and intellectual collaboration opened up and additional research questions presented themselves.

This brings us to the issue of how I gathered and analyzed data in the study. As Clifford Geertz (1973) points out, ethnographers' accounts are their 'own constructions of other people's constructions of what they are up to' (p. 9). Producing such an account involves two levels of work. The first is to collect a particular kind of data: what John Van Maanen (1979) refers to as 'first-order constructs,' the informants' own observations and interpretations of events in their world, gathered 'as they arise from the observed talk and action of the participants in the studied scene' (p. 542). (I understand Van Maanen's 'first-order constructs' and Geertz's 'experience-near concepts' to refer to the same phenomena, and from this point on I will use Van Maanen's term.) The second level of work for the researcher involves interpreting these collected data: identifying significant themes in the informants' first-order constructs and bringing these themes together into a 'theoretical scheme' (Hammersley & Atkinson, 1995) which provides the basis for developing a textual representation of the conceptual world of the group under study. However, these two levels of research, gathering informants' first-order constructs and interpreting them, are not sequential. Rather, data-gathering and interpretation are performed concurrently in an ongoing dialectical process of meaning-making (Hammersley & Atkinson, 1995). As Michael Agar (1980) explains:

> In ethnography … you learn something ('collect some data'), then you try to make sense of it ('analysis'), go back and see if the interpretation makes sense in light of new experience ('collect more data'), then you refine your interpretation ('more analysis'), and so on. The process is recursive, not linear. (p. 9).

Accordingly, while below I discuss the collection of data and my interpretation of these data separately, in reality these are intertwined aspects of a single research activity.

During my years working at the Bank of Canada as a writing consultant and trainer (1984–1996) and in the time since I left the organization (1996–2005), I have collected and analyzed a wide variety of qualitative data for this study. These data were selected for their potential as first-order constructs casting light on the Bank economist's discourse and intellectual collaboration, as well as for their compatibility with the evolving 'theoretical scheme,' to borrow Hammersley and Atkinson's phrase, that provided the basis for the emerging textual account I was producing. In order to ensure a range of perspectives, I included informants at three different levels in the Bank hierarchy: junior staff economists, senior staff economists (including department chiefs), and senior executives. (I also collected data from four other Bank employees, including two editors and two chiefs of the Communications Department, as well as from ten economists outside the organization.) My assumption here was that an individual's role in an organization determines both his or her access to information and pattern of social interactions, and thus strongly influences the individual's perspective on the organizational culture (Anthanases & Heath, 1995). As well, this approach mitigated against the tendency to assume a 'hierarchy of credibility' (Becker, 1970, cited in Goodson, 1993), with the views of the most senior people in an organization taken as defining reality.

Much of the data I collected consisted of different forms of recorded talk, since speech is the primary medium of expression for people in ascribing meaning to events. As Michael Agar (1980) puts it, '[attending to] the details of informant talk [provides] a way to get at their interpretation of the world around them' (p. 103). Accordingly, interviews were a major source of spoken data. Following Eliot Mishler's (1986) conception of interviews as 'speech events or activities [involving] the joint construction of meaning' (p. 66), I approached my interviews with the Bank's economists and other employees as opportunities for dialogue where they might be encouraged to give voice to first-order constructs regarding their professional work-world. After experimenting with different formats, I eventually settled on the tape-recorded, semi-structured interview (Merriam, 1998; Winsor, 1996) as the norm.[19] Typically, I would send an informant a list of questions several days prior to a scheduled interview, a practice consistent with the writing-intensive nature of the Bank culture. The questions varied somewhat from one interview to another, depending on the individual's role in the organization, as well as on the particular aspect of the Bank's knowledge-building, policy-making, and external communications that I was exploring at any given phase in the research. (As an example, see Appendix D for a list of interview questions used with a department chief at a point when I was starting to examine the relationship between writing and economic modelling.) The opportunity of seeing the questions in advance seemed to foster reflection on the part of informants, who often prepared detailed notes in response. Following Anthony Giddens (1984), I suspect that the questions acted as a stimulus to prod the economists' 'practical consciousness,' tacit understandings related to their everyday work activity, thus expanding their 'discursive consciousness,' those matters they could articulate in conversation.

While the questions sent to an informant provided a starting point for an interview, they by no means limited its scope. To borrow from Mishler (1986), 'respondents [were] invited to speak in their own voices, allowed to control the introduction and flow of topics, and encouraged to extend their responses' (p. 69). According to Mishler, 'when the interview is opened up in this way … respondents are likely to tell 'stories'' (p. 119). And indeed, this frequently occurred in the interviews I conducted, with informants offering narrative accounts of various aspects of their work.

In addition to interviews, I also collected a large number of reading protocols (Waern, 1979; Dias, 1987; Haas & Flower, 1988) in sessions where I observed and tape-recorded a reader responding aloud while going through a work document. While the document at hand provided the point of departure for these sessions, they generally took on a conversational tone, ranging over different topics in much the same manner as the interviews. To complement the interviews and reading protocols, I also gathered spoken data in a number of other contexts, including writing-training sessions with economists (both individual 'tutorials' and writing seminars for groups); presentations by department chiefs and senior executives appearing as guests in writing seminars; discussions between employees (writers) and supervisors (reviewers) during the preparation of documents; presentations by staff economists and senior executives at orientations sessions for newly-recruited employees; work meetings involving groups of economists; and informal conversations (e.g., over coffee or lunch, in people's offices, with a jogging partner). I transcribed tape-recorded material (interviews, reading protocols, presentations, discussions between writers and reviewers) as I proceeded. Using an approach suggested by Agar (1980), I began by transcribing entire tapes, and then became more selective as significant patterns began to emerge.

In addition to the spoken data, I recorded extensive field-notes and gathered a wide variety of work documents (drafts, with reviewers' annotations, as well as final versions of both internal documents and texts intended for distribution outside the Bank). As well, over a number of years I collected a large number of newspaper and magazine articles concerning the Bank, monetary policy, and related economic issues.

The approach I followed in interpreting this data can best be characterized as that of 'analytic induction' (Glaser & Strauss, 1967; Goetz & LeCompte, 1981; LeCompte & Preissle, 1993; Lincoln & Guba, 1985; Strauss & Corbin, 1998). Analyzing transcripts, field-notes, and work documents as they were collected, I looked for themes in informants' first-order constructs that seemed to point to significant aspects of the Bank economists' discourse and intellectual collaboration. As such themes emerged, I would feed them back to informants for a reaction, generating additional related data. Working in this way – 'using the data to think with' (Hammersley & Atkinson, 1995, p. 210) – I gradually extended my 'interpretations of interpretations' (Van Maanen, 1979, p. 541) into an increasingly detailed and complex portrait of the economists' professional work-world.

In Chapter Two I outlined four research strategies proposed by Clifford Geertz that I used in interpreting my data and developing an ethnographic account of the Bank economists' discourse and intellectual collaboration: probing 'key terms' in the economists' vernacular; examining 'life-cycle' narratives; identifying converging perspectives; and applying disciplinary theory. Below I describe these strategies in more detail and explain how I employed them in my study.

Probing key terms

According to Judith Goetz and Margaret LeCompte (1984), 'reconstruct[ing] the specific categories that participants use to conceptualize their own experiences and world view' (p. 6) is a major part of ethnographic interpretation. One way of gaining entry to a professional organization's conceptual categories is by exploring its vernacular, as Hammersley and Atkinson (1995) explain:

> The actual words people use can be of considerable analytic importance. The 'situated vocabularies' employed provide us with valuable information about the way in which members of a particular culture organize their perceptions of the world, and so engage in the 'social construction of reality.' (p. 153)

In examining the data I was gathering, I tried to achieve a sense of the 'situated' meaning of terms that appeared frequently and seemed central to the economists' knowledge-building, policy-making, and external communications – terms such as 'the monetary policy process,' 'stories,' 'professional judgement,' 'logical rigour,' 'current analysis,' 'strategic' and 'tactical' decisions, and 'transparency.' As I gradually developed a sense of what these and other key terms signified to the economists, I used interviews and informal conversations to confirm this understanding and to probe further. Acquiring a working knowledge of this 'situated vocabulary' was an important part of developing a quasi-insider's sense of the organization's conceptual world.

Examining life-cycle narratives

I also explored the 'life-cycle' dimension of intellectual life in the Bank, as expressed in informants' narratives about historical developments in the profession of economics and in the organization itself (though these overlap, of course). As have other researchers (Ledwell-Brown & Dias, 1994; Goodson, 1985; Mishler, 1986), I found such narratives to be a rich source of first-order constructs regarding the economists' professional work-world. For example, as described later on in Chapter Four, in examining the economists' narratives I found perspectives on the profession's transition in the 1960s from a field known as Political Economy into a 'scientific' discipline grounded in mathematical models and statistical analysis; on the evolution in macroeconomic modelling from large-scale models derived from historical data, representing the various sectors of the economy in great detail, to more highly-aggregated, theory-driven models; and on the development of the Quarterly Projection Model by three of the Bank's staff economists.

Identifying converging perspectives

Another interpretive strategy I employed was to look for converging perspectives in the data – commonalities across the economists' first-order constructs. I assumed that these would point to aspects of intersubjectivity underlying the economists' discourse and intellectual collaboration. Eventually, I was able to discover significant areas of intersubjectivity and place them in a larger configuration, mapping out features of the economists' economic ideology. A key example of such intersubjectivity involved shared beliefs about the particular features and functioning of the Canadian economy and the appropriate role for monetary policy. (In Chapter Four I describe how I attempted to safeguard against over-identifying with the economic ideology of the Bank's economists.)

Applying disciplinary theory

According to Van Maanen (1988), 'weav[ing] the reported facts into the framework of theory that is used and developed in the text' (p. 29) is an important part of ethnography. Disciplinary theory provides the researcher with conceptual frames for integrating perceived themes in informants' first-order constructs into larger patterns that eventually evolve into the ethnographic account. Keith Basso and Henry Selby (1976) describe this process as one in which 'the ethnographer must step back, turn analyst, and, using concepts and principles alien to the culture he is studying, perform an act of interpretation.' In doing this, the researcher 'translates a collection of native representations from one system of meaning (theirs) into another (his own), thereby transforming them into a new and wholly distinct representation' (p. 4).

As I began to interpret the data I was gathering from the Banks' economists, I was broadly oriented by the theoretical assumption, mentioned earlier, that professional organizations create, through their discourse practices, the specialized forms of knowledge needed for accomplishing their work. At the same time, I was guided by theoretical notions regarding the knowledge-generating function of discourse genres and by ideas from activity theory regarding the way that technologies, symbol systems, and conventionalized patterns of interaction mediate intellectual collaboration. Using this initial theoretical framework to analyze the data, I began to develop a written ethnographic account of the work-world of the Bank's economists. As I proceeded, however,

I realized that I needed to draw in additional conceptual frames to develop my interpretation, and so I looked to theories of inscription, narrative, modelling, organizational change, the social production of information, and ITexts (i.e., the fusing of texts and technology in media such as websites, intranets, e-mail, and on-line instructional systems). And in crafting the text of the ethnographic account itself, I found myself working back and forth between my evolving theoretical framework and my analysis of the data – these two aspects of the text seemed to 'talk to one another,' with one acting as a heuristic for the other as I developed the account.

At the end of Chapter Five, we will look at another important consideration for a researcher wishing to employ interpretive ethnography to examine discourse and intellectual collaboration within a professional organization: the need to maintain a balance of *engagement with* and *detachment from* the conceptual reality constructed and inhabited by the study's informants.

Chapter Four

The interplay of discourse genres and economic modelling

According to one Bank staff economist, discourse – specifically writing – and mathematical modelling are inextricably linked:

> *Most of our work leads to writing. Anything that we want to survive, and that includes all our analytic work, leads to a document of some kind. And a lot of this writing is associated with models. We do economics by doing models, simple or big. There's always some framework – and usually that means a model – to allow us to discuss about what's going on.* (Staff Economist 4)

Here we see how one type of symbol-based representation – used within a community-of-practice to generate, embody, and communicate economic knowledge – is linked to another form of symbol-based, knowledge-bearing representation, with the two combining to play a key role in an organization's knowledge-building, as theorized by Bruno Latour (1990), Steve Woolgar (1990), and Michael Lynch (1990). This merging of texts in different symbol systems within the activity of knowledge-building can be viewed as a particular form of intertextuality (Bauman, 2004; Bazerman, 2003; Fairclough, 1992; Witte, 1992).

This chapter examines in some depth the interplay between written and oral genres of discourse on the one hand and the technology of mathematically-based economic modelling on the other, highlighting the social and epistemic role of the Quarterly Projection Model, seen as a mathematical instantiation of the Bank's paradigm of the Canadian economy. Once again bringing together what Clifford Geertz calls 'experience-distant' concepts – in this case, theoretical ideas about discourse, activity, distributed cognition, and knowledge construction – and 'experience-near' concepts embedded in commentary from a number of the Bank's staff economists and senior executives, the chapter explores the following question: what are the reciprocal lines of influence between written/spoken discourse and mathematical modelling within the activity of the monetary-policy process?

I will begin this examination of the interplay between discourse and mathematical modelling by considering what QPM is – the nature of the model, as seen by the staff economists who use it to produce knowledge about the Canadian economy and by the executives who apply this knowledge in making decisions on monetary policy. Next, taking up a prompt from activity theorists (Cole & Engestrom, 1993; Pea, 1993; Resnick, 1991) to view a professional organization's legacy of inherited cultural tools as carrying traces of the organization's intellectual history, I present a narrative of the construction and 'selling' of QPM and describe the ongoing process through which it is enhanced. This leads into a consideration of what QPM does – the different ways in which the model mediates the activity of knowledge-building and policy-making in the Bank. Here I consider two broad functions associated with QPM: I look at the model first as a 'tool of reasoning' (Resnick, 1991) used to analyze statistical data, and then as an 'organizational tool' (to quote a bank staff economist) that engenders the social organization and intersubjectivity necessary for productive intellectual collaboration. Finally, I describe three ways in which QPM influences the written and spoken discourse of the Bank's economists.

What is the Quarterly Projection Model?

According to one deputy governor, *'QPM is a tool, not an end in itself. It's really used as a tool around the place'* (Executive 4). But just what kind of tool is the Quarterly Projection Model? Another deputy governor points us towards an answer in describing QPM as *'a tool for organizing our thoughts and doing our analysis'* (Executive 3). In the pages that follow I build on this view of the model, drawing extensively on commentary from the bank's staff economists and senior executives.

First, we will look at five characterizations of QPM from two staff economists, two department chiefs, and a deputy governor. As we will see, there is a striking similarity in their perceptions of the model as a representation of historically-achieved consensual knowledge and an intellectual tool.

We look at the [Canadian] economy through the eyes of the model.[1] (Staff Economist 13)

You can look at the model several ways. On one level it's simply some code in the computer. On another level, though, it's a set of ideas, a way of thinking about the economy. (Staff Economist 14)

You can think of the model as bringing together most of the understandings we have about the economy and connecting them in a coherent way. (Chief 1)

QPM is a kind of storehouse of knowledge. It represents our best guess as to how the economy functions. (Chief 3)

QPM has to be able to deal with the key questions that arise every day in doing monetary-policy analysis. So it's very much an embodiment of views that have been built up over time in the Bank about how to characterize the economy and the impacts of monetary policy. (Executive 3)

These quotations converge in a view of the Quarterly Projection Model as an embodiment of the Bank's '*paradigm [for] how the [Canadian] economy works*,' to recall the words of a department chief quoted earlier. This perception of the model reminds one of Janet Giltrow and Michelle Valiquette's (1994) description of a written genre as 'a system for administering communities' knowledge of the world – a system for housing knowledge, producing it, practicing it' (p. 47). The parallel here with QPM invites us to see writing and economic modelling as closely interconnected intellectual practices central to the Bank's knowledge-building activity, a theme I will be pursuing in this chapter.

While QPM can be viewed, similar to a written genre, as a symbolic structure for 'administering' the Bank's knowledge about the Canadian economy, this knowledge is expressed mathematically in the model, not linguistically. (This is not to ignore the fact, of course, that the model does not speak for itself; to be meaningful, its output must be talked or written about.) A staff economist explains:

In economics, we often theorize about economic behaviour and then try to translate this into mathematics. With a macro-economic model [i.e., a model representing an entire national economy], you've got a theoretical view about how the economy as a whole functions, and you're trying to express it in mathematical form. (Staff Economist 8)

Another staff economist expands on this idea:

A model is a formalized expression of how the economy works, in terms of variables and equations and numbers. Let's say you have a view of the economy, and you've convinced yourself and your colleagues that it's valid. The next challenge is to say, 'Well, what we need to do is formalize this view based on economic principles,' and so you write down the view in a bunch of mathematical equations. And then you say, 'OK, the structure of equations in this model reflects my view of the real-world relationships in the economy; now I need to put some numbers into the equations and quantify the relationships numerically.' (Staff Economist 2)

A computer-run model such as the Quarterly Projection Model, with its inscribed network of mathematical equations, allows economists to represent, and employ as a tool of analysis, a conception of the economy that is much more elaborate and complex in its structure and dynamics than any purely mental representation could be. As a result, the economists' ability to think about the economy and its functioning is considerably extended. This recalls the claim by activity theorists that people in professional organizations invariably create knowledge-bearing tools that allow them to think together in ways that are significantly more powerful than would be possible without such tools. A deputy governor describes the utility of QPM in very similar terms:

> *Why do economists use models like QPM? Well, quite simply because the relationships in the economy are sufficiently complex that we don't have the capacity to deal with all those relationships in our heads. With the model, you can analyze extremely complex relationships.* (Executive 3)

If QPM is a mathematically-expressed representation of the Bank's paradigm of the Canadian economy, what kind of economic ideology, or notion of economic reality, does the model embody? The interview excerpts below describe some of the main theoretical assumptions built into QPM. As background for this discussion, some readers may at this point wish to refer to Appendix B, which contains a text situating the Bank of Canada's economic ideology within the larger disciplinary field of economics, with particular reference to the opposing Neo-Classical and Neo-Keynesian views of how economies function.

First, the model represents an economy constituted of different 'markets' and characterized by particular relationships among key economic variables:

> *QPM reflects a view of the world that's broadly shared in the Bank, and it's largely a market-driven view. We see the economy as made up of different markets – labour, financial, agricultural, commodity markets. And we think that, within these markets, there are structural relationships among different variables. For example, we believe prices are determined by supply and demand relationships.* (Executive 3)

Second, QPM incorporates a view of the economy as a 'self-equilibrating' system:

> *We see the world as made up of markets that function, not of markets that fail; and so QPM reflects what we call a Neo-Classical view, where policy intervention has a role and is necessary for some purposes, but isn't central to the functioning of the economy. Other people have very different views about that and see the world differently. But here at the Bank, we wouldn't build a model where government spending was necessary to keep the economy from collapsing. So QPM has natural self-equilibration mechanisms built into it, based on the theory of a functioning market system.* (Staff Economist 4)

Related to this 'self-equilibrating' view of the economy is the notion of a 'steady-state':

In QPM, the economy tends towards a 'steady state' of no change – that is, toward a certain constant growth rate of output, and a certain level of inflation, and so on. So that if a 'shock' [i.e., an unexpected development] is introduced into the economy, it'll eventually 'run off' and things will move to the steady state. Now all of this is only a tendency, of course; we know that the steady state won't actually ever be reached. (Staff Economist 10)

Third, QPM embodies an assumption about what causes inflation in an economy and what central banks can do to control it:

There's a basic view that's become widespread across policy institutions around the world; it's common to the OECD [Organization for Economic Cooperation and Development], the IMF [International Monetary Fund], the central banks. This view is that it's the level of excess demand that determines inflation. And that the monetary authority [i.e., the central bank] can control inflation by using interest rates to affect spending. That view is essentially built into the model. (Staff Economist 2)

This assumption is an important point of contention in the debate between Neo-Classical and Neo-Keynesian economists:

Certain Neo-Classical ideas about relationships among prices and output and inflation and monetary policy are, in a sense, built right into the mathematics of the model through what's called the Phillips Curve. And this is linked to a key assumption of Bank policy – that there are large costs involved in having inflation run at high levels, and therefore it needs to be controlled. This relates to one of the big questions in the debate between the Neo-Classicists and the Keynesians: Is it acceptable to have high levels of inflation over the longer run? The Keynesian view is that the costs aren't as big as it might seem and there are some definite benefits. Whereas the Neo-Classical view, the one we tend to believe in, is that there are high costs and no significant benefits. (Staff Economist 8)

Finally, QPM reflects certain assumptions about human behaviour, in regard to how people form expectations about future economic events.

When it comes to expectations, QPM is both forward-looking and backward-looking. This has to do with the debate between the Neo-Classicists and Neo-Keynesians about how people look at where the economy is going, when they make decisions. Do they look backwards and say, 'This is what happened before so therefore it's going to happen again?'

That's what the Neo-Keynesians believe. The Neo-Classicists believe in 'rational expectations' – that people are more forward-looking and tend to say, 'I've got this information about what's going to happen in the future and my information is perfect, and so therefore it's going to occur' – a kind of self-fulfilling prophecy. QPM has aspects of both notions included it. (Staff Economist 10)

Earlier I suggested that the professional site where economists are located influences the nature of the particular conceptual economy they construct to do their work. And indeed, the mathematical structure of the Quarterly Projection Model – and the economy it embodies – are directly influenced by the Bank's mandate for conducting monetary policy and, more specifically, by its commitment to achieving price stability. As a deputy governor explains:

You can build different types of models, depending on your focus of interest. At the Bank the focus is on monetary policy, so that, for example, the issue of the consequences of debt accumulation is a big concern. And so QPM has been built along these lines: it takes into account people's expectations about monetary policy, the price-level implications of interest rates and exchange rates, and what we call stock-flow dynamics, the interaction between debt and spending. What we did was to design the model to highlight the major relationships we feel are important for our purposes, for our work here at the Bank. (Executive 2)

A staff economist elaborates on this dimension of QPM's structure:

QPM incorporates certain linkages – relationships we believe exist among the key economic variables – that we think are important for controlling inflation. For example: the relationship between aggregate demand and aggregate supply, and the role that interest rates and exchange rates play in the transmission mechanism.2 And so what we have is a powerful tool that represents those linkages the Bank thinks are important to consider in conducting monetary policy. (Staff Economist 2)

Another executive describes a related property of the model:

QPM allows us to understand the longer-run implications of things that are developing in the economy at any time, from the point of view of monetary policy. This is possible because we've incorporated our policy objectives into the model, so that if the economy is subject to a particular shock, the model enables us to say, 'All right, given our inflation-control target two to three years out, and given this shock, these are the actions that are required.' (Executive 3)

As a department chief observes, in addition to reflecting certain theoretical assumptions, QPM's structure is specifically designed to allow the kind of 'storytelling' the Bank needs as a basis for decision-making:

> *The question we want the model to answer requires it to be the way it is:*
> *'What interest rate path do we need to achieve our inflation-control target?'*
> *QPM is about as abstract as it can be and still have the elements you need*
> *to tell a story. It's purpose is to allow us to get an internally consistent story*
> *we believe can be used to tell the executives, 'Adjust policy this way or that*
> *way, and this is what we think you'll get.'* (Chief 3)

These perspectives on QPM recall the point made earlier in the book that a professional organization's discourse practices are evoked and shaped by the aims and exigencies of the organization can be extended to other related intellectual practices. Indeed, it would appear that QPM is shaped by the same organizational aims and exigencies that prompt and shape the economists' discourse.

We have been looking at the Quarterly Projection Model as a representation of the Bank's paradigm of the Canadian economy. If indeed the organization can be characterized as having a consensual view of the economy, is there not a danger that this could result in a kind of 'group think' constraining intellectual practice? When asked this question, here is how one deputy governor responded:

> *Yes, there's a danger. Do you have a consensual view because of a process*
> *of discussion and debate that's occurred over time? Or do you have an*
> *institutional view that's been forced on people because they're afraid of*
> *speaking their minds? It's hard to know. They're what economists would*
> *call 'observational equivalents': the end result looks the same in both bases.*
> *But while one is positive, the other is very dangerous. In my view, what's*
> *happened here at the Bank is that there's been a process of trial and error*
> *over the years that's led to some consensus. The competition of ideas has*
> *helped us to converge on the truth – the 'truth' as we know it now, but which*
> *obviously will change over time.* (Executive 2)

This observation once speaks to the tension between an organization such as the Bank's tendency to impose a deterministic 'normalization' of discourse and thinking on their members and a recognition of the need for intellectual creativity, reflexivity, diversity of perspectives, and lively debate among the organization's economists.

In a similar vein, we might also ask what epistemological status the Bank's economists accord the Quarterly Projection Model. As it turns out, they appear to have a decidedly social-constructionist view of QPM. As one staff economist puts it, with a model such as QPM, '*you can never describe anything like the reality you see out the window*' (Staff Economist 9). A department chief adds, '*The model is a way to organize and bring our knowledge together; but we recognize that it's not the truth*' (Chief 1). An executive expands on this perception:

> *Reality is complex; models are always simplistic. A macro-economic model isn't reality; it's only a caricature of reality. A model is like an artist's sketch, very impressionistic. But it isn't a like a Cannaletto (a Renaissance landscape artist), where you try to convey every detail, like in a photograph. A model isn't a photograph of the economy; it only depicts the major features and relationships of particular interest to policy-makers, the users of the model.* (Executive 2)

A particular example of constructionist skepticism comes up in a staff economist's comments about the extent to which QPM reflects actual human behaviour, specifically regarding the way the model represents people's expectations of future events:

> *The model helps you think about people's behaviour, assuming of course that the model actually corresponds to reality. And that's a huge assumption; in fact, there's no guarantee that it does. There's really no way for us to measure people's actual thought processes. When they have an expectation, what are they basing it on? It's very difficult to know for certain.* (Staff Economist 8)

A deputy governor expresses a similar view:

> *We all realize that these models don't replicate the real world because there's more that goes into deciding individuals' behaviour than those key variables that you would tend to capture in a macro-economic view.* (Executive 3)

One of the economists who built QPM discusses his view of the relationship between economic model and reality:

> *I've changed my views since I came here from school ten years ago: I used to believe there's a truth out there, and that modelling is all about finding the truth. Now I no longer believe that. I've become much more of a Bayesian: somebody who thinks you're not likely to ever find the truth, so that if you're building a model what you want to do is consider a range of possible truths and then embody them in a view of the world in a way that'll minimize your errors.*[3] (Staff Economist 9)

He goes on to link this rather postmodern notion to the pragmatic influence of the policy-oriented ends for which the Quarterly Projection Model was constructed:

> *In the model, we were writing down structures (i.e., mathematical equations) that we can't say we know to be the truth, or even close to the truth necessarily – but that are features we think will best keep us out of trouble in terms of monetary policy. For example, we might not know there are risk premiums on government debt, but we think our possibilities of giving the right policy advice are better if we assume this to be so than if we say it isn't – because it can be dangerous to assume it isn't true. So we were working back from the Bank's objectives to the pieces of the tool – quite an instrumentalist approach.*

One of the economists from outside the Bank whom I interviewed for this study would take this constructionist skepticism much further, contesting the soundness of the 'mythic structure' or 'belief system' that I have been referring to as the Bank's paradigm of the Canadian economy. In the spirit of multi-vocality that characterizes interpretive ethnography, I want to give this critic of the Bank's economic ideology an opportunity to present his perspective:

> *Although you make it clear enough that the White Book and the monetary-policy [process] are built around a 'mythic structure,' a general belief system that the structures of practice [of the Bank's economists] tend to reinforce, and although [your use of the term] 'stories' makes that clear enough, [nevertheless] you don't – for my money – make as much as I thought you would of the degree to which the coherence of the institution and its function depends upon that contestable belief system embodied in the QPM. As you can see, my thoughts take me in the direction of urging you to lay greater emphasis on the matters discussed in [Appendix B] on economic theory, or at least to acknowledge more explicitly that different belief systems lead to different stories, and [also] lead to different institutions and different structures and practices. … While relative price stability is clearly desirable, it seems to me to be achievable by much less costly means than is embodied in NAIRU [Non Accelerating Inflation Rate of Unemployment] doctrine. Indeed the willingness to tolerate present levels of unemployment, and levels of income inequality, in order to achieve price stability is, in my view, far too high a price to pay (no matter how successful your external communications are in persuading the world that it must be so!). But it is the single-mindedness of the belief in price stability that, again, fundamentally underlies the institution, the practices, and the role of the technologies you describe.*

We have seen, then, that the Bank's economists view the Quarterly Projection Model as a mathematical expression of their paradigm of the Canadian economy – of the sectors and markets that constitute the economy and how these components interact with one another. In addition to serving as a repository of knowledge, however, QPM also serves as a tool for collaborative intellectual activity – it is, as a staff economist puts it, both *'a way of thinking and a way of doing'* (Staff Economist 5). But what is it that the model is used to do? What are its functions in the Bank's work? And what are the reciprocal lines of influence between QPM and the discourse practices of the Bank's economists, as joint elements in knowledge-building? As a first step in addressing these issues, I turn now to describing how QPM was constructed and implemented in the Bank and how the model continues to evolve over time. This account reveals significant aspects of the relationship between discourse practices and economic modelling, for, as we shall see, the construction and 'selling' of QPM were, in large measure, achieved through particular genres of written discourse, as is its ongoing enhancement.

Building, 'selling,' and enhancing QPM

Activity theorists point to the historically-accrued nature of knowledge within professional organizations, with much of this knowledge embodied in an organization's cultural tools and work practices (Cole & Engestrom, 1993; Pea, 1993). It has also been suggested that we can learn much about an organization's intellectual life by considering the social history of its primary cultural tools (Gee, 1992). An examination of the Quarterly Projection Model as one such primary tool – a 'socially constructed tool of reasoning [embodying the organization's] intellectual history' (Resnick, 1991, p. 7) – will cast light on the activity through which knowledge about the Canadian economy has been and is created in the Bank. To this end, I want to consider QPM as a socially-devised analytic tool with its own rhetorical history. I shall describe, first, how QPM was built (including the efforts of the model's designers to persuade their colleagues that it should replace RDXF, its predecessor), and second, how QPM is continually modified to incorporate new understandings about the economy. We will see how the model emerged out of writing-intensive negotiation, debate, and eventual consensus (or at least acquiescence) among Bank economists, how it has achieved a large measure of intellectual orthodoxy, and how it continues to evolve over time to reflect advances in disciplinary theory and the results of ongoing empirical work. In all of this, we will attend to the key role that written and oral genres of discourse have played in the construction and 'selling' of QPM, as well as in its ongoing enhancement.

The Quarterly Projection Model was built over a four-year period beginning in 1989, was first used in the Bank during the September 1993 Projection Exercise, and continues in use today (May 2005). As background for discussing the development of QPM, I want to present two accounts of disciplinary history: first, a deputy governor describing how economics originally developed as an empirically-oriented discipline; and then a department chief recounting how the use of macroeconomic models representing national economies evolved over the three decades preceding the construction of QPM.

The deputy governor describes the shift in economics that occurred in the 1950s and 1960s as the field evolved from its origins in the field of Political Economy into an independent discipline with an empirical, 'scientific' orientation:

> *There was a basic shift in the discipline through the '50s and '60s. Prior to that, economics was really part of Political Economy, a much more general framework including, at the University of Toronto for example, Political Science, Economics, Commerce, and Sociology. But following Samuelson's publication of The Principles in 1947 and then with computers and technology, economics got very much into the scientific method approach, where one established a hypothesis, determined a means of testing it, and tested it against available data.*[4] (Executive 5)

Part of the shift in economics towards greater empiricism and analytic rigour came from the innovation of using mathematical models as tools for interpreting economic data. For the discipline, this shift meant crossing over from the tradition of 'moral philosophy' (to use Kant's term) into the realm of the sciences with its emphasis on, as Stephen Toulmin (1985) puts it, 'harness[ing] the power of mathematics to the empirical description of nature' (p. 6).

Next, we will hear a department chief describe how macroeconomic models – models of entire national economies – evolved over the three decades prior to the construction of QPM. As he recounts, the early approach employed in the 1960s and 1970s involved taking historical data on different sectors of the economy as the basis for inductively creating, or 'estimating,' a large structure of mathematical equations:

> *In the late '60s and early '70s, there was tremendous enthusiasm in the profession for the construction of large, very detailed models of the economy. There was a sense that if you looked out the window at the world and then thought long and hard enough to come up with equations for what you saw, you could adequately represent almost every little sector in the economy, and then use this with confidence to forecast future developments. This led to the creation of huge, 'blunderbuss' models.* (Chief 4)

However, in the 1980s, finding that these large data-based models of the economy were not working particularly well, economists generally took a different tack: they moved to smaller, more highly-aggregated models, relying more heavily on economic theory to 'calibrate,' or assign numerical values to, equations, and thus define the models' properties. He explains:

> *Model-builders soon realized that the size of the models would have to be scaled back, since they were too large and awkward and threw up very odd results, especially as you looked out into the longer term. In part, this was because we realized the structure of the economy wasn't nearly as stable as we'd hoped. As well, and this is in part a reflection of the state of technology, we weren't able to give adequate representation to the importance of 'rational expectations,' people's expectations about the future, or to some of the dynamics we know underlie the economic process. All of this caused a major rethinking in the discipline, and the result has been a move to much smaller models that are more consistent with economic theory, more accurately reflect long-run properties of economies, and give more attention to the role of expectations.*[5]

In the Bank, for example, RDXF had by the late 1980s fallen significantly behind the organization's state of economic knowledge so that, according to a deputy governor, '*the model was giving us results that were, quite frankly, impossible, given what we knew*' (Executive 4). Through the 1980s, there had been ongoing attempts to adapt RDXF to new theoretical insights arising in the profession. However, this effort had faced fundamental constraints, as described by a staff economist:

> *It's as if you had a really old car and were trying to put a brand-new piece in it. You can't put a fuel injection in a 1940 DeSoto – it just won't work. Well, there were two big problems with RDXF that patching it up couldn't remedy. First, it lacked inter-relationships among the different sectors in the economy. So you couldn't go and, for example, put some long-term properties in a sector, because they wouldn't be reflected anywhere else in the model. And the other problem was with the way people's expectations were modeled. Everything was what we call 'backward-looking': all people's anticipations of the future simply keyed off the past. This created tremendous instability problems; it was like driving your car by looking in the rear-view mirror.* (Staff Economist 2)

Eventually, something had to be done. As one deputy governor recalls,

> *Our views on the economy had evolved at the Bank, and we'd tried to introduce some of the new ideas into RDXF. But at a certain point we*

realized that we needed another model that fully reflected our way of thinking. (Executive 2)

This recognition that a new economic model was needed to replace RDXF was reinforced by a significant change in the Bank's approach to directing monetary policy. In 1988, for the first time, the Bank explicitly declared its primary goal to be controlling inflation in the Canadian economy, and in 1991 (in conjunction with the Department of Finance) it announced a series of inflation-control targets for the coming five-year period. This reorientation of the Bank's mandate in turn meant a subtle change in the nature of the knowledge the executives needed from the staff economists in the Projection Exercise and the *White Book*. The question became, in the words of one department chief, '*What interest rates do you need in order to meet your inflation-control targets?*' (Chief 1). Another Chief elaborates:

> *Ultimately, you're now working back from the end objective, saying, 'This is the range within which we want to keep inflation.' We want to ensure, to the extent we can, that inflation as measured by the CPI (Consumer Price Index) stays within that specified range. So the question becomes, 'What path of interest rates will ensure that outcome, based on what we think we know about economic activity in Canada? What sort of policy is required so that inflationary pressures are held in check?'*. (Chief 4)

And as explained by one of the economists who built QPM, this change in the objective of the Projection Exercise, and in the particular kind of knowledge to be produced for policy-making, led to demands that the old model, RDXF, could not accommodate:

> *You wanted to know, 'Given where we are today, and where we want to be, say, two or three years from now, what do we have to do to get there?' Now, that put a great deal of strain on a model like RDXF, which wasn't built to answer policy analysis questions, and so it became a constant headache for the people running the thing. If you're trying to pick a path to hit some target in the future, your model has to have certain properties; in particular, it has to be stable. And RDXF wasn't stable. As circumstances changed, and the demands on the model changed, it just couldn't handle things.* (Staff Economist 9)

As another of the economists involved in building QPM puts it, '*Trying to use RDXF in the new policy environment was like trying to get a dinosaur to jump through hoops*' (Staff Economist 14).

Unlike the old model, the Quarterly Projection Model was designed specifically to produce the new type of knowledge about the Canadian economy

– knowledge related to the inflation-control targets – that the executives needed from the staff economists. One of the model-builders explains this difference, referring to the highly-aggregated, theory-driven 'top-down' approach used with QPM:

> *If we were going to send the senior people simple, straightforward messages*
> *about what the Bank had to do to hit our inflation-control objectives*
> *at a point in the future, the Projection Exercise couldn't be about the*
> *consumption of automobiles and re-sales of housing. It had to be about*
> *macro-economic things and that meant 'top down'; it meant more of a*
> *policy analysis [i.e., theoretical] orientation than the summation of a*
> *thousand little tiny bits of information about the economy. So, we built a*
> *policy analysis model that was intended to do what needed to be done in the*
> *Projection Exercise.* (Staff Economist 9)

Once the two staff economists given the task of constructing a new macro-economic model to be used in the Projection Exercise and for other analytic work began their project in 1989, certain genres of discourse, particularly written genres, played a major part in their work. (There were two economists involved at the beginning of the project and a third joined part way through). In describing the part that discourse genres played in the development of the Quarterly Projection Model, I will focus on two themes: first, that the project was extremely writing-intensive and that the relationship between written discourse and the model-in-progress involved a reciprocal influence; and second, that the construction of the model was a thoroughly rhetorical endeavor.

The model-builders wrote continuously as they worked to create the complex configuration of mathematical equations that would define QPM's structure. As one of them recounts:

> *We wrote constantly. It's just staggering how much writing we did. I*
> *think there were something like thirty-five research papers written.* (Staff
> Economist 14)

And, as we shall see, these 'research memoranda' and other texts played a central role in the construction of the model.

There was, of course, as in any bureaucratic organization, the concern for accountability and the need for a written record of the work carried out in the project. Initially, this involved producing several 'research memoranda' to solicit management approval to proceed with the project, as one of the model-builders recollects:

> *With QPM there was a fair amount of up-front planning, decisions taken, as*
> *to 'OK, we're going this way and here are the reasons'.* (Staff Economist 14)

Then as the project moved forward, writing was necessary to provide the required 'paper trail' of actions and events. However, there were other motives for the ongoing documentation as well. Writing, supported by word-processing technology, was intrinsic to the technical research work involved in building QPM. According to one of the model-builders, the complex process of developing QPM's extensive body of mathematical equations was carried forward through texts:

> *Since the introduction of word processors, writing has become very much a part of the process of developing a model. Building models twenty years ago, when they had major technology constraints, was very different. Now we use FRAMEMAKER [a software that facilitates combining written text and graphic forms such as equations, numerical tables, and graphs], and it really helps you do the two together. For example, if you decide you need change your assumptions, FRAMEMAKER goes through the document and makes the changes to the equations almost automatically.* (Staff Economist 14)

As I have been implying, the relationship between written discourse and the model-in-progress was characterized by a mutual line of influence. '*The causality ran both ways,*' as one of the model-builders puts it (Staff Economist 14). On the one hand, from time to time, as he and his colleagues worked on some property of the model, developing and 'calibrating' equations, an unanticipated but significant issue would arise. He explains:

> *We'd be doing modelling work, developing some of the mathematics, and an interesting implication of the modelling would come out, and then we'd write a ['research memorandum'] around that.*

On other occasions, the model-builders would outline a plan for a 'research memorandum' intended to demonstrate certain properties of the envisioned model, committing themselves to presenting the piece at a departmental seminar on a given date, and then, working to this deadline, would proceed to build a mathematical prototype of that particular part of the model, composing the 'research memorandum' as they went along.

Another of the economists involved describes this process:

> *The project was designed to get us to deliver products at certain times, though it was flexible enough that we had some latitude about exactly what the product was to be at a particular time. Often the schedule meant, 'We want to deliver a ['research memorandum'] at a certain date, and here's the aspect of the model we want to describe in it; so let's go and construct a prototype that exhibits these properties.' So the objectives of the written piece would drive the model.* (Staff Economist 9)

As the project proceeded, the model-builders increasingly took this latter tack:

> *As we got smarter, not about modelling but more about marketing, we*
> *ended up doing more of the building around the [research memoranda']*
> *instead of the other way around – we'd move from an objective in a paper*
> *back to the modelling needed to achieve it. We worked the way that any*
> *producer of a product would do – we went from the market back to what you*
> *have to do to get it.* (Staff Economist 9)

In a sense, then, we could say that the written discourse and the modelling served as reciprocal prompts for technical and rhetorical invention.

As the last two quotations above suggest, the economists involved were not writing *only* for themselves, to support the technical work required to develop the structure of the new model. They were also thinking rhetorically, about a particular audience: other Bank economists who had to be convinced that QPM was a significant improvement on the older model, RDXF.

According to Nigel Gilbert (1976), the construction of a new model within a research-oriented organization is invariably a collaborative and rhetorical process. And given the relationship of models to the 'paradigm' guiding work in an organization, that is, to the organization's 'construct of the world and … the methods [it] uses to study it,' researchers building a new model 'may find that radical changes are … resisted' (p. 284) and, therefore, that their best rhetorical skills are required to move events forward. The experience of the Bank economists who built QPM appears to bear out Gilbert's claim. Indeed, as they describe it, the construction of QPM was, from beginning to end, a thoroughly rhetorical affair.

The model-builders knew their audience would be concerned about two issues: first, the kind of tool QPM would be and the functions it could perform, and second, the nature of the economic paradigm that would be instantiated in the model. One of the model-builders comments on this rhetorical dimension of the project:

> *People were basically saying, 'Prove to us that this is a good thing to do.'*
> *And so we kept writing and writing and writing, on the marketing of the*
> *theoretical ideas in each little bit of the model and why they were important,*
> *and, towards the end of the project, on what the model as a whole could do.*
> (Staff Economist 9)

The economists knew full well that this aspect of the project would not be an easy matter, given the epistemological stakes for the organization as a whole. As one of them explains:

A model is really a way of thinking. So, if you're trying to persuade people about a different way of thinking about things, you've got to have a good understanding about who they are and what's important to them. You need to understand your audience in intimate detail. There's a lot at stake for everybody. (Staff Economist 14)

This concern for convincing colleagues who would be reading the papers produced during the development of the model had a marked influence on the technical work of building up the structure of equations that would eventually become the Quarterly Projection Model, so that in a sense the two converged. As the same economist recalls:

When I sat at my computer, I'd think about the message I was trying to convey to people, and that interacted a lot with the actual research. You think, 'OK, I think we should put this property into the model, for these reasons.' So then you write that down, sort of mapping out your argument. And at the same time, you're mapping out the research that has to be done; and then you go and do it. Well of course, often the research won't turn out exactly as you'd planned. And then you go back to your paper and revise it. So you're using the writing to think about the convincing process, and also to advance the research.

As negotiations over the mathematical structure of QPM continued, the model-builders made certain compromises in order to ensure its eventual acceptance. One such compromise involved rendering the model somewhat less complex than originally planned, as one of them explains:

And so, in terms of our own standards, we made an incredible amount of sacrifices, theoretically and technically. In the end, we designed the model so that a student coming from university would be able to operate it. In other words, a student from Queen's [University] who'd just finished doing an M.A. would be able use the model and maintain it and improve it – that's the level of sophistication we felt we could get away with. (Staff Economist 14)

Another aspect of the negotiations involved keeping QPM close enough to the Bank's existing conception of the Canadian economy so that staff economists could apply aspects of the model in their heads or on paper, in an informal, *ad hoc* way, to think about issues.

A lot of things that QPM does in response to specific shocks [i.e., new economic developments] you can trace through in your mind. And that's important: We could never have foisted something on the Bank that was at such violent odds with people's priors that they had to simulate everything [i.e., 'run' the model on a computer] before they could get an answer to a

question. We couldn't have pushed them off the old paradigm too far. (Staff
Economist 9)

A comment from another of the economists involved in the project underscores
the extent to which QPM was, literally, a socially-constructed tool, a product
of ongoing negotiation among members of a professional organization:

> *We slipped a lot of things into the model that people initially didn't like
> very much at all, and we managed to, convince may be too strong a word,
> but managed to get them to acquiesce. Because it's a staff model, the staff
> have to at least acquiesce to it. They don't have to all sign off on it, and in
> fact if they did and everybody had a veto, you'd never finish a model. But
> through some strange process of consensus, by picking up enough of the old
> Bank paradigm and somehow getting people to buy in, it went through and
> became the staff model.* (Staff Economist 14)

From the perspective of the economists developing QPM, there was also a
pronounced political side to the negotiations over the model's structure and
properties. This involved resistance from certain Bank economists who, over
time, had developed a high degree of expertise related specifically to RDXF,
along with the personal influence that this expertise brought, and who were
naturally reluctant to relinquish their *'investment of human capital,'* as one
of the model-builders refers to it.[6] (This resistance recalls Pierre Bourdieu's
[1991] reference to knowledge as a form of 'symbolic capital'). The model-
builder explains:

> *It took support from some important people at high levels in the Bank,
> fighting off other people – some of whom had legitimate questions about
> why we were doing this, and just didn't understand our explanations, and
> others who stood to lose from replacing the old model with the new model
> and were acting to protect their own investment of human capital. If you've
> invested a lot in developing an understanding of an existing model and
> somebody comes along and replaces it, they've destroyed your human
> capital in that technology. And to the extent that you're able to protect your
> investment you'll do so. And a bunch of people did that – so there were a lot
> of battles.* (Staff Economist 9)

The same economist explains that the seminars at which the model-builders
presented papers on the emerging mathematical structure of the new model
(or more accurately, the 'corridor conversations' that followed these seminars)
offered adversaries a forum for resistance:

> *The most distressing part was, the opposition was never public. We'd
> present a ['research memorandum'] at a research seminar and a few*

questions would be asked. And afterwards we'd say, 'Well, that went well;
there was maybe something a little uncomfortable about it, but it went pretty
well.' And then later we'd hear a grapevine discussion about the spin other
people were putting on it, mostly – at least from my point of view – people
who had something to lose from implementing the model. They'd engage in
corridor conversations with other people, interpreting what they'd seen in
the seminar, saying that our paper was about was 'this' – which would be
a gross distortion of what it was really about – to make us look bad. (Staff
Economist 9)

Of course, recalling Gilbert's point that introducing a new model into a research
setting often involves challenging the prevailing paradigm, it comes as no
surprise that the economists working on QPM encountered resistance from
certain colleagues. For in effect, implementing the new model meant modifying the Bank's working paradigm of the Canadian economy to include recent
disciplinary theory. As one of the model-builders puts it, *'We weren't just trying*
to sell the model, we were trying to sell the paradigm behind the model' (Staff
Economist 9). And as a member of the Secretariat explains:

> *Since the model we use for the Projection Exercise represents the Bank's*
> *paradigm of the economy, and since this paradigm involves fundamental*
> *questions and assumptions central to how we do our work, any change will*
> *involve a lot of debate among the people affected.* (Staff Economist 5)

During the course of the project, resistance from adversaries led the economists
building QPM to adapt their rhetorical approach in several ways. At the beginning, their seminar papers tended to describe the complexities of the in-progress
model's properties in great detail. As one of the model-builders explains, this
failed to work:

> *We learned a lesson about how much information people could absorb. We*
> *used to pack the ['research memoranda'] we were presenting at research*
> *seminars full of information. Eventually, we realized the papers were just*
> *too packed – we'd been saying so many things that the key points didn't*
> *come through. And that left room for the spin doctors: we were making*
> *it easy for our opponents to put negative spins on what we were doing.*
> *Finally, we also learned that people, well-meaning people, can only absorb*
> *a certain number of things at one time.* (Staff Economist 9)

Learning from experience, the economists started to write papers that their
readers could deal with more easily, as well as give the 'spin doctors' less room
to operate. Another of the model-builders elaborates:

> *For a long time what we did was write twenty- and forty-page ['research*

*memoranda'] dealing with the details of how the model worked. I think it
took us at least a year see that that wasn't working. We finally figured out
that because our audience had lots of demands on their time, we had to give
them something short and focused, highlighting just what the model could do
– something they could read on the bus and get excited about. I'm thinking
of one time, for example, when we wrote a two-page piece on the role of the
monetary authority [i.e., the central bank] in QPM. You could read it in five
minutes, and understand everything. So, eventually it turned out that a lot
of the stuff that really had an impact on people, was really short: two- and
three-page papers that would say, :This is what this part of the model will
do' – pieces that crystallized the idea in people's minds, so they'd say, 'Yes,
good, let's continue with this. Now go write the forty-page paper.' Because,
of course, this being the Bank, they would say, 'Well, OK, I've got the gist
of it, now tell me more about what it all means. Give me the ['research
memoranda'].' And so we would go ahead and write it. But getting the
message out in a boiled-down form first was really important countering the
spin doctors and getting people on board.* (Staff Economist 14)

Along the way, the model-builders also learned another rhetorical lesson,
gaining a particular kind of local genre knowledge. Originally, their approach
was to write 'research memoranda' promoting the features of the new model-
in-progress, rather than attacking RDXF for its inadequacies. As one of them
recalls:

*We tried to take the high ground saying, 'This is how we should be thinking
about modelling in the Bank: the best kind of modelling is done like this,
and this is what it can do.'* (Staff Economist 9)

He goes on to explain why this approach failed to work, drawing on game
theory:

*Often, when you're doing something different in an organization, nobody
wants to be associated with it 'til they know it's going to be a success.
And so it was hard to find allies. Game theory explains a lot of this: for
whatever reason, the loss function of doing research is often asymmetric in
the following way – if a project succeeds and you're associated with it, you
get +1; but if it fails you get -10. Therefore it pays to play it safe and aim for
zero. I don't think the Bank is unusual that way, but we were naive. We tried
to take the high road initially and were surprised, genuinely surprised, that
it just didn't seem to be working.*

Consequently, the model-builders decided they needed to go on the offensive
and attack RDXF's weaknesses in their 'research memoranda':

When we realized the high ground wasn't going to work, we started trashing RDXF and criticizing that whole paradigm very directly. But, really, we had no choice. So at least at that point, we had two competing paradigms going head to head, and the choices became quite distinct. And that was a good thing.

In addition to convincing other staff economists of QPM's superiority over RDXF, the model-builders also faced the task of communicating their ideas upward in the hierarchy to the executives on the Governing Council, who in the end would need to approve the new model and the modified paradigm of the Canadian economy that it embodied. To catch the executives' attention, the model-builders employed an interesting strategy, as one of them recalls:

We put out a lot of [Bank of Canada] 'technical reports' on QPM. The reason was because if you write a 'technical report,' and this is different from an internal 'research memorandum,' [the members of the Governing Council] have to read it and approve it before it's published outside the Bank. So we'd write a report not because we were necessarily all that concerned about it going out, but to get [the members of the Governing Council] to read it. This was our way of going around all the spin doctors among the staff. The reports were about ideas we were building into QPM – notions about how to think about monetary-policy targeting in an economy, for example. So we did a fair amount of that kind of writing, and it worked pretty well, because the executives realized that whatever it was we were doing, we seemed to know what we were talking about. (Staff Economist 14)

We can see that there was a great deal at stake, then, given the impact QPM would have on the Bank as an organization. As one of the model-builders puts it:

You have to realize that when you're working in a bureaucracy, bringing in something like QPM, because it's an organizational device, means changing people's work lives. (Staff Economist 14)

And indeed, as another remembers: '*It was a hard sell, I can tell you*' (Staff Economist 9). In a counterview to the model-builders' perspective on their experience, however, a deputy governor offers another perception:

They tended to over-dramatize things a little, depicting themselves as martyrs; and at times they also tended to rub people the wrong way, unnecessarily. (Executive 2)

Again, this multi-vocality provides us with differing views on reality, a familiar feature of organizational life.

In addition to leaving a 'paper trail' of the project's activities, advancing the technical work on the mathematical structure of the new model, and 'selling' their ideas to colleagues and senior executives in the face of skepticism and resistance, there was another motive for the ongoing writing done by the model-builders. They assumed that in documenting the research as they proceeded and eliciting colleagues' responses to their papers, they would benefit greatly from other people's ideas. One of them explains:

> *If you respect your peers, professionally, you want to get your work out to them and get their comments. You're going to have a far greater chance of success from giving them an idea about where you're going and having their input. It certainly turned out that way with QPM.* (Staff Economist 14)

Overall, then, the research and writing involved in developing the new model converged as part of a technical, rhetorical, and political process. This process involved collaboration that included not only the three economists working to construct QPM but also colleagues who responded to (and, it was felt, in some cases tried to subvert) documentation describing and explaining the model's properties. One of the model-builders emphasizes to degree to which the final version of the model was a product of this larger collaboration:

> *I don't view QPM as our model. I mean despite the fact that we argued, one way or the other, for the direction the model should take and the hands-on role we had in actually calibrating the equations, I don't think of it as our model. Ultimately, we were doing it because we wanted people around here to use the model, and that meant getting them involved and bringing them onside.* (Staff Economist 14)

In the end, then, the three model-builders did succeed in 'selling' the Quarterly Projection Model to the other staff economists and to the Bank's executives, and it was implemented as a replacement for RDXF. As one of the executives comments:

> *They [the model-builders] had a hard time, what with the skepticism of many of their colleagues, but they really fought for it. And thank God for their stubbornness! QPM is by far the best model the Bank has had. In fact, it's the best model of its kind in Canada, and one of the best in the world. And the results with it have been very good.* (Executive 2)

Once QPM had been 'sold' and implemented inside the Bank research community, there was still further rhetorical work to be done. At this point, the discourse moved beyond the Bank's internal genres out into the public domain. Another of the model-builders explains:

Once we implemented QPM in the Bank we turned our focus outside. The Bank of Canada Review article is one attempt to communicate with the outside world about what we've done, and we've also published three Technical Reports describing the model in more detail for a professional audience.7 With this external audience, the job isn't so much to persuade, in the same way it was inside the Bank, although we are trying to convince people that this is an interesting and useful way to think about the world. (Staff Economist 4)

This description of the building and 'selling' of QPM begins to suggest something of the mutually-constituting relationship linking the practices of written discourse and mathematical modelling. There is a further point to be drawn from the description: it provides support for the claim that professional organizations advance in their work by building achieved knowledge into their tools, which are then in turn used to engender new knowledge. Theorist Roy Pea (1993) elaborates on this idea:

> [R]epresentational tools ... carry intelligence *in* them, in that they represent some individual's or some community's decision that the means thus offered should be reified, made stable, as a quasi-permanent form, for use by others. (pp. 53–54)

This notion is similar to Latour and Woolgar's (1986) suggestion, noted earlier, that the 'inscription devices' used within research communities are not only material objects, but also reifications of prior intellectual activity and accepted knowledge, with such knowledge often having emerged from lively debates among community members. From this perspective, the Quarterly Projection Model's mathematical structure can be seen to embody knowledge in the form of new economic theory and innovative methodology. Viewed this way, QPM is a knowledge-bearing tool endowed with achieved 'intelligence,' constructed for the purpose of developing further knowledge. And its development and implementation was certainly a highly contentious episode in the organization's history.

This narrative of the construction and implementation of the Quarterly Projection Model can also be seen as a prime example of learning taking place on an organizational level (Orlikowski, 2001; Wenger, 1998; Wenger, McDermott, & Snyder, 2002). As an organization develops new cultural tools, building recently achieved knowledge into these shared tools, it is in effect learning to manage its activity and accomplish its collaborative work more effectively.

In the preceding pages, we have been looking at the Quarterly Projection Model as a socially-constructed tool with a significant rhetorical history. We have considered how the model was built and how its designers went about persuading other Bank economists that it should replace its precursor, RDXF. However, the history of QPM continues: as time passes, it is constantly being enhanced to reflect new disciplinary theory, in-house research, and ongoing empirical monitoring and analysis of developments in the Canadian economy. And as we shall see, while the ongoing enhancement of QPM is a highly technical procedure, it is also a rhetorical process, with particular genres of discourse, particularly written genres, once again playing a key role. In examining how enhancements to QPM are accomplished, we will encounter a further example of newly-achieved knowledge becoming embedded in a cultural tool.

As Nigel Gilbert (1976) explains, models in widespread use within a research community typically evolve:

> [M]odels act as 'maps' to guide the course of research.... But during the course of research, models are frequently changed to improve their 'fit' with empirical data. Concepts may be sub-divided, combined, added to the model or rejected; inter-relationships may be made more precise or altered. Sometimes the model is expanded to cover additional features such as a new aspect of the phenomena being studied, or the mode of operation of a new piece of apparatus. (pp. 283–84)

Similarly, the Bank's Quarterly Projection Model undergoes continual change. It is '*a living, changing model* [*with*] *improvements constantly being made to it…*' (Duguay & Longworth, 1997, p. 17).[8] According to one department chief, the need for this is inevitable:

> *If we see that the model is repeatedly letting us down during the Projection Exercise in some way – and because it's an abstraction, by definition it always will – we know we have to deal with it. So we'll work on it until we think we've got that particular aspect of it nailed down.* (Chief 3)

Indeed, from its very inception, the Quarterly Projection Model was foreseen as a tool that would evolve over time. '*QPM was fully intended to be organic,*' according to one of the model-builders (Staff Economist 9). As he explains, the idea was to build a model that would be relatively easy to enhance:

> *We designed the model so that it was very flexible. One of the problems with RDXF was that it wasn't adaptable enough, and as the Bank paradigm changed or as circumstances changed, or, most importantly, the way we did the Projection Exercise changed, the model just couldn't handle it. And so we worked hard to insure that that wasn't the case with QPM.*

A department chief talks about the process of enhancing the model:

> *QPM isn't static; you're always trying to improve things. Every half-year, if*

*not every quarter, changes are put into it. We know some areas of the model
are weaker than others, and so we keep working on those, considering
new theory or trying to refine the theory that's in there on the basis of new
empirical evidence.* (Chief 1)

Another chief describes several of the various types of enhancements that
QPM may require:

*You might say, 'Well, we don't like the way exports behave in the model,
because it's saying this, which was true before the Free Trade Agreement
[with the U.S.], but now things look more like that.' As well, QPM is a
highly-aggregated model; and so there are some disaggregations we'll likely
be building in over time. For example, at present 'housing' isn't separate in
the model; it's part of 'investment.' And similarly, 'inventories' aren't built
into the model separately; and yet inventories are responsible for most of the
big swings in the economy. So we're working on those things, to articulate
the model further and make it more logically complete.* (Chief 3)

Another way of viewing such ongoing enhancements to QPM is once again to
consider the model in the context of the monetary-policy process, viewed as
an activity system with a natural capacity for adaptation (Cole & Engeström,
1993). The most visible part of this adaptation occurs through the Issues
Meeting, the first major event in the Projection Exercise. A department chief
describes the procedure: '*If you've got research to back up a proposed change
to the model, fair enough. You present it at the Issues Meeting and say, 'We
want to change the model this way*'' (Chief 3). As he explains, this is a highly
rhetorical, writing-intensive task:

*The discipline we impose on people is: 'If you want to propose a change to
QPM, go do your research, present it, and we'll judge it and then possibly
change the model.' But it's got to be carefully-reasoned, well-documented
research. Some people have spent the two years since we brought in QPM
saying, 'I don't like this or that.' And I've spent two years telling them,
'OK, go do your research, write it up, show it to us, and we'll be happy
to change the model, as long as the idea is sound.' So people who want
to propose changes do a longer 'research memorandum' and then, on the
basis of that, write an 'issue note' of a couple of pages and present it at an
Issues Meeting.*

Here again we see an example of the intertextual links that connect written and
oral discourse genres in the accomplishment of the Bank's work.

An economist wanting to propose a change must start by convincing people
in his or her own department, as a staff economist explains:

> *The Issues Meeting is the final, formal part of getting new ideas into QPM. But first you've got to do careful research and write up a 'research memorandum,' to convince your colleagues that this is important and is something we should consider putting in QPM.* (Staff Economist 2)

Once colleagues in the economist's home department are on side, the negotiation broadens out to include economists in other Bank departments. A department chief comments on the reason for this:

> *Initially, the discussion is within your department. But usually major changes aren't made in the model without getting everybody's approval. There's so much simultaneity and interaction in the model that we want to make sure that we're not putting something in that's going to disrupt something that somebody else thinks is important for their work.* (Chief 1)

An economist describes the final step in the process:

> *Then at the Issues Meeting, people present a note outlining the proposed changes they want to make and the supporting arguments to the chiefs. So, for example, to make a change to one of the equations in the model, you'd have to do a good job of convincing all the department chiefs that it's a reasonable thing to do. And that would involve providing evidence about why your view is sound, and showing what the implications will be for people using the model.* (Staff Economist 1)

Another department chief elaborates on the different functions served by the writing involved in the process of enhancing the model:

> *There's this tradition of writing. It's time-consuming, but it's beneficial because it provides a written trail, a history you can go back and look at. For us [the department chiefs] it's also important in another way: you usually get notes a day or two in advance, and so you don't come to the meeting cold and have people talk to you about changes they're proposing; you get a chance to think about it beforehand. As well, it also imposes a certain discipline on writers: when they write up the paper presenting the research behind a proposed change they'll end up saying: 'Well yes, I was going to propose that, but the more I struggle to organize my thoughts and write it up, the more I realize it's kind of a bonehead idea,' or 'Yes, the model really does need to be changed this way.'* (Chief 4)

Here again we can see an instance of organizational learning. In this case, the learning occurs as the Bank's economists enhance an existing cultural tool in order to better manage the activity of knowledge-building.

Above we have begun to examine the interplay between discourse and economic modelling, viewed as intermeshed intellectual practices that are central to the knowledge-building activity of the Bank's monetary-policy process. Having looked at what QPM is – the nature of the model – I now want to elaborate on the question of what QPM does – the various ways in which the model, as a cultural tool, mediates collaborative knowledge-building in the Bank.

What QPM does

I have suggested that the Bank's monetary-policy process can be seen as an activity system designed to produce and apply specialized knowledge about the Canadian economy. Within this activity system, the organization's staff economists generate, and convey to its senior executives, '*views, judgments, and ideas*' (quoted earlier) – or put another way, 'stories' – about current and future economic developments, with the executives using this knowledge in making decisions about monetary policy. The Quarterly Projection Model enables and shapes this collaborative intellectual work within the community-of-practice. The model, together with a set of discourse genres, makes possible a pattern of social interaction and a style of collective thinking that allow the Bank to construct the particular type of economic knowledge it needs to accomplish its mandate for directing monetary policy.

In this section we will examine two broad functions of the Quarterly Projection Model, again drawing extensively on the perspectives of Bank economists. First, we will look at QPM as a 'tool of reasoning' (Resnick, 1991) – a tool for producing, negotiating, communicating, and applying organizational knowledge. Here we will explore several different angles: how QPM functions as a representation of the Bank's paradigm of the Canadian economy, how the model supports research intended to develop this paradigm of the economy, and how it is employed to interpret statistical data and to carry out policy analysis. Second, we will consider the model as a tool of social organization that contributes to the intersubjectivity needed within a professional organization for productive intellectual collaboration. In this guise, QPM will be seen to contribute to creating a domain of shared focus, perception, and understanding among the Bank's economists and, as well, to act as a similar bridge to academics outside the institution. Finally, we will examine QPM's influence on the economists' discourse practices, specifically in terms of the 'QPM vernacular,' 'logical rigour,' and the *White Book*.

QPM as a tool of reasoning

A staff economist describes the model's overall impact in the following manner:

> *With QPM, there's a big difference in the way people talk about issues, compared to RDXF. And a lot of it has to do with the QPM paradigm: once you introduce a new paradigm, it changes the way people think. Overall, QPM has added more theoretical sophistication to the way people view the economy.* (Staff Economist 9)

Below, I discuss various ways in which the model, as 'a tool of reasoning,' supports the Bank's knowledge-building.

Representing the Bank's paradigm of the Canadian economy

The Quarterly Projection Model has had a major influence on the Bank's paradigm of the Canadian economy, the organization's '*working understanding of the economy*' (quoted earlier). While QPM was under development and after the completed version of the model had been introduced in the Bank, the staff economists who built it wrote a number of papers explaining particular aspects of the model to the executives on the Governing Council. One of these executives talks about the effect of the model on the Governing Council's thinking about the economy:

> *Getting used to the way QPM works has required a lot of rethinking of things. Its dynamics are much more complex than with RDXF – for example, with the question of debt accumulation. So there's been a period of learning, and as we've learned about the model, we've added to our stock of knowledge about the economy.* (Executive 2)

At the same time, however, as the staff economists developing QPM wrote papers about the model, this also influenced the way they themselves viewed the economy. As one of them describes it:

> *Writing papers explaining QPM to [the senior executives] was a really good exercise. Among ourselves we'd have a tendency to look at the equations, and say, 'Well, technically, this equation does this, which gives us that, which does this.' But, really, the equations themselves don't matter; what matters is the underlying economic logic. So when you were writing to [the senior executives], they didn't want to hear, 'Well, in this sector, this equation does that, and this other equation does something else.' That would have been useless to them. You had to step back and say, in straightforward English, 'Well, this is the view that's encoded in that*

part of the model.' And explaining the logic inherent in the model actually enhanced our own understanding. (Staff Economist 2)

QPM continues to exert a strong influence on the way the Bank's economists think about the economy. Says one deputy governor:

QPM has made people in the Bank look at the economy differently than before; it's not linear thinking – it's dynamic. (Executive 2)

A key factor here is the model's 'general equilibrium' structure – a feature reflecting the theoretical notion that *'everything in the economy simultaneously interacts with everything else'* (Staff Economist 10). According to a department chief, QPM has raised the level of awareness across the Bank about the ways in which the complex dynamics at work in the economy play out over time:

With its structure of highly-integrated equations and its coherent long-term properties, QPM has forced economists here to think about the economy more globally than they did in the past. They're more sensitive to how things interact and evolve over the longer term. (Chief 4)

Here we have a further example of Roy Pea's (1993) observation that human cognition may be qualitatively altered through interaction with a cultural tool such as the technology of a computer-run economic model.

For the sector specialists, working in the context of the Projection Exercise, taking this larger perspective means looking beyond economic developments in their individual area of responsibility to view the economy as an interconnected whole:

QPM helps you understand what's going on outside your particular sector. It gives you an idea of the whole economy, its interactions and dynamics. (Staff Economist 10)

A department chief talks of the more specific influence of QPM on how the staff economists view monetary policy:

In the structure of the model, you've got half a dozen or so major variables to describe the economy, with monetary policy being one of them. And so having the model in your mind forces you to consider those other variables, before saying something about what monetary policy should be doing. The model reminds you that, as a policy institution, you're part of a general equilibrium system, not a stand-alone entity. (Chief 3)

Another way that QPM has influenced the thinking of the Bank's economists is through its assumption that people's expectations regarding future economic developments are, to a large extent, 'rational' or 'forward-looking,' rather than conditioned solely by past events. A staff economist explains:

*I think one of the biggest influences of QPM comes out of its orientation
as a forward-looking model, in terms of rational expectations. It's forced
us to start looking at the implications of this view on a very detailed level,
quantitatively. And there have been times when we've been very surprised
with the results. Before, we may have bought into the concept of forward-
looking expectations, theoretically, but never had to work it through to the
details and the numbers.* (Staff Economist 8)

He goes on to describe how the notion of forward-looking expectations takes
on a particular degree of complexity within the general equilibrium structure
of QPM:

*If people are modeled as forward-looking, then you've got to consider
this in terms of the various parts of the economy working interactively
and simultaneously. It's one thing to look at an isolated element, let's
say consumption behaviour, and say, 'This is how the idea of forward-
looking expectations affects consumption.' But it's very different to say
that we've got forward-looking consumption, a forward-looking labour
market, a forward-looking monetary policy authority [i.e., central bank], a
forward-looking government, and so on – and that these are all interacting
simultaneously. And that's been a major contribution of QPM: it's helped
us think of people's behaviour, as it relates to expectations, in a more
sophisticated way.*

A further illustration of how the mathematical structure of the Quarterly
Projection Model, serving as a common point of reference, influences how
Bank economists understand and think about the Canadian economy relates
to the issue of 'uncertainty.' One of the model-builders explains:

*One of the things we've brought on board with QPM is some attention to
uncertainty. We wanted people in the Bank to think more deeply about, not
just what we know about the economy, but what we don't know; and to take
the implications of this seriously. Because the concept of uncertainty is built
right into the model, people now tend to recognize that the world's a very
complicated place. Now people knew this before, of course, but they more
or less ignored it because it was hard to deal with quantitatively.* (Staff
Economist 9)

While QPM has clearly had a major influence on how Bank economists think
about the economy, we need to acknowledge several qualifications. First, learning about the complex dynamics of the model is a gradual process. According
to one staff economist:

*QPM is still something of a black box to lots of people around here, who
don't really understand all its properties. It's only through working with the*

*model in the Projection Exercise a number of times or using it frequently
to do policy analysis that you gradually get really familiar with it.* (Staff
Economist 10)

A second qualification relates to the question of how closely QPM, as a 'public
[cognitive] space' (to use Bazerman's phrase), corresponds to the 'private
spaces' of individual economists – that is, the extent to which their personal
beliefs about how the economy functions match the paradigm embodied in
QPM. Here once more we see the tension between, on the one hand, the influence of organizational 'normalization,' and on the other, individual perceptions
and intellectual multiplicity. A staff economist reflects on this issue:

*Does QPM reflect the ideas about the economy that people around the
Bank have in their minds? To a degree, I suppose. But it really depends
on what views of the economy you subscribe to. There are lots of different
economic theories out there in the literature, with their own strengths and
limitations. And every economist evaluates those theories and decides
which ones best describe the dynamics of the economy. Now what QPM
does is bring together a particular set of ideas into an explicit working
model. But the question is how much the model represents or influences
the views people have in their minds, given that these views can be quite
strong.* (Staff Economist 8)

In the end, however, he concludes that the model has, in fact, had a widespread
influence on thinking within the Bank:

*I think I'd say, though, that, to a fairly large extent, QPM has brought
people to a common view of important aspects of the economy.'*

Enabling research to develop the Bank's paradigm of the economy

In addition to its central place in the Bank as a representation of achieved
knowledge, or 'knowledge-already-made,' to use Bruno Latour's (1987) term,
the Quarterly Projection Model also serves as a tool for engendering new
insights into how the Canadian economy functions, a form of 'knowledge-
in-the-making,' as Latour calls it. Thus the model is at the same time both an
embodiment of the Bank's current paradigm of the economy and a tool for
further developing this construct. (Earlier, I described the process of enhancing
the model, with the Issues Meeting as a forum for presenting, debating, and
deciding on proposed changes.)

One instance of the ongoing development of the Bank's paradigm of the
economy occurs when the economists who are 'running' QPM on the computer during the Projection Exercise encounter unanticipated results. As a staff
economist observes:

After a while the model starts to teach you new things: you put data in and get surprising outcomes. (Staff Economist 4)

A department chief elaborates on why this happens:

QPM is a reflection of how we think the economy behaves, but it's also instructive: sometimes when you run it, you get unexpected results that point towards particular kinds of interactions in the economy that would otherwise be overlooked. And so you have to think about these. (Chief 4)

QPM is also used outside the Projection Exercise as a vehicle for research that probes and extends the Bank's paradigm of the economy. A staff economist explains:

QPM is used as a tool for asking questions about the nature of the economy. In the model you've got a series of equations that embody our best ideas about how to characterize the economic process; but none of that's known with absolute certainty: there are always questions about whether you're using the right theory or what the right mathematical structure is. So every year, when we're planning our research program [for the coming year], we identify a number of these questions to work on. And QPM has been built so that you can do interesting thought experiments with it. (Staff Economist 4)

A department chief gives an example of such research:

We're interested in the response of the economy to different kinds of shocks [i.e., unexpected economic developments] – for example, price shocks, fiscal shocks, monetary policy shocks. So we might say, 'OK, let's look at this kind of shock. Is it permanent or temporary? Let's make an assumption about that.' Then we'd introduce the shock to the model, and see what the model tells us about the way the economy would react and what the implications for the future would be. (Chief 1)

As described by the same Chief, while this research sometimes involves working with the full structure of the model, on other occasions a smaller version is specially constructed:

We often do research using the full version of QPM, but sometimes to deal with a particular issue we'll build a stripped-down version of the model and deal with that. QPM has certain theoretical properties and we'll try to replicate them in the small model. Then we use it to ask the questions we're concerned about. Eventually, the results might feed back into the dynamics of the full model, in an enhancement. One example of this would be work we've recently done on the 'terms-of-trade.'

QPM also offers the Bank's economists a testing ground for new theoretical arguments in the larger economics literature regarding the behaviour of economies. A staff economist explains:

> *If somebody in the field comes up with some new argument for why something is the way it is, we can recast it in the paradigm we understand, and that opens things up to debate from all sides here in the Bank. Sometimes that means actually having to translate the argument into the mathematical structure of the model; other times you can just say, 'Well, if I modeled that in QPM, this is what would happen, and therefore it makes sense or it doesn't make sense.' Often it's a matter of attenuating the hegemony of fashion. Lots of fashionable arguments come up in the literature, and it's important to avoid getting too caught up in them prematurely.* (Staff Economist 9)

Once consensus is reached within the Bank on the validity of a new theoretical idea that has arisen in the literature, it may then eventually be built into QPM and incorporated into the organizational paradigm of the economy.

This consideration of the ways in which QPM serves as a tool for enabling research in the Bank brings up an issue of synergy: the mutually-prompting relationship between the mathematical structure of the model and the computer technology used to run it. A staff economist describes this relationship:

> *With the new computer technology QPM uses, you can do certain kinds of research involving advanced mathematical techniques that you couldn't do in the past, things that weren't really worth even trying with a model like RDXF. Back in the RDXF days, we had some of these ideas in our minds – for example, the forward-looking expectations, the stock-flow dynamics, the nonlinearities – and they were being talked about; but nobody could see a practical way of modelling them with the computers we had. But then when the new technology came along, people got down to working on the mathematics of it, which then allowed us to do new research, to do modelling experiments. But then, as well, doing these experiments provided the impetus to try to further improve the software programs we use.* (Staff Economist 3)

In this discussion of QPM's role as a vehicle for research in the Bank, I should mention a caveat: the perceived importance of maintaining a sphere of ongoing research that is entirely separate from QPM, to act as a check against the model and the way of thinking it represents. One of the model-builders explains:

> *When you build a macro-economic model like QPM, you can never describe anything like the reality you see out the window. You're faced with forcing*

a complex world into a relatively simple mold; and inevitably you have to make a lot of choices and compromises. And therefore, as an institution, you wouldn't want all your research to be limited by the choices you've made in the model; you have to be doing other things too. So, while you want a lot of your research to be done in the context of the model, to benefit from the framework it provides, there should also be a healthy amount of research going on that's got nothing to do with the model, that's looking at things from outside it. (Staff Economist 4)

A department chief gives an example of this latter kind of research:

I have people doing work on smaller models with maybe only four or five variables. They're strongly empirical models, without nearly as much theoretical structure as QPM. We use them, at least in part, to say, 'Well, do we get substantially different answers from these models than we do from QPM? And if we do, what does it tell us?.' (Chief 1).

We can see, then, that the Quarterly Projection Model functions as both a representation of the Bank's current paradigm of the Canadian economy and a tool for research intended to advance the institution's understanding of how the economy functions. As well, however, in the context of the Projection Exercise and the ongoing activity known as 'current analysis,' QPM also serves another essential purpose: it operates as a device for bringing the Bank's paradigm of the economy to bear on empirical data – *'interpreting the events of the day'* (quoted earlier).

Interpreting economic data

In employing the Quarterly Projection Model in the Projection Exercise and in 'current analysis' work, the staff economists are able to apply the Bank's paradigm of the Canadian economy to large amounts of statistical data and produce 'stories' about recent and future developments in the economy, knowledge needed by the executives on the Governing Council for making monetary-policy decisions. According to one staff economist:

The model reflects what we believe about the economy. So we allow the data to speak through it and give us an idea of where the economy's been, where it's going, and what effect monetary policy is having. (Staff Economist 10)

In this function, as a department chief explains, the model helps to orient the staff economists' ongoing analytic work towards the Bank's monetary-policy goals:

Basically, QPM is there to help us meet the inflation-control targets the Bank has identified. As the framework for the Projection Exercise, it ties the analysis being done right into the objective of achieving the targets. And then in addition to that, as a framework for current analysis, QPM helps us to bring together all the information we get on the economy, as it comes in, and to think about what it means for policy in a coherent way. (Chief 1)

A staff economist elaborates on QPM's role as a 'framework' for the Projection Exercise and for current analysis:

You can characterize our support for monetary policy on two different levels, and QPM was designed to serve both. First, there's the Projection Exercise. Four times a year we produce a systematic story on the economy, with the White Book as the vehicle for communicating that story. And QPM is used as the analytic framework for that. Then as well, there's the other support for monetary policy – current analysis, which is tracking what's going on in the economy during the quarter and interpreting it, with some of that getting reported orally and some getting written down in the form of short notes, often with a graph or table. QPM also provides a framework there. (Staff Economist 4)

The two interview excerpts above again illustrate how a professional organization's discourse is evoked and shaped by its goals. And we can see how QPM, in its influence on the *White Book* and on 'analytic notes' reporting on current analysis, acts as a key mediating tool for aligning the staff economists' thinking and written work with the organization's larger policy aims.

So far in this discussion I have been depicting the Quarterly Projection Model as an intelligence-bearing cultural tool – one combining disciplinary theory and insights derived from empirical experience in a complex mathematical structure – used for interpreting statistical data. For a fuller understanding of QPM as an intellectual tool, however, we need to consider another factor. The model is not simply an algorithmic instrument that is employed mechanically to perform economic analysis. In using it, the Bank's economists apply a considerable amount of professional judgment.

As mentioned earlier in my description of the Projection Exercise, 'professional judgment,' in the specific context of the Bank, refers to its economists' intuitive understandings of how a range of economic variables interact in the Canadian economy. A staff economist speaks of this as it relates to the Quarterly Projection Model:

We've got a model that's been written down in the form of equations. But a model is only an abstraction: it captures the major relationships you expect to see among economic variables, but it's a simplification of reality. So when we talk about 'professional judgment,' we're referring to our feeling for factors that aren't captured in the model but which could affect these relationships, as well as to our sense of how long a given factor will persist – two quarters, three quarters, whatever. (Staff Economist 2)

A sector specialist explains how 'professional judgment' comes into play in his work:

You've got an implicit model in your head that includes things going on in your sector that you just can't measure, like political uncertainty, consumer confidence, things that you know affect people's behaviour. And that's where judgment comes in. Applying judgment means factoring in assumptions from your own implicit model and merging them with results you get from QPM. The model in your head influences and attenuates things, telling you, for example, that QPM is a little bit off track or is giving results that are a little too strong or too weak. (Staff Economist 8)

In this interface of mathematical model and human judgment – the meeting of tool and mind – we once again see an instance of the dialectic between a socially-constructed and sanctioned tool and individual cognition and agency.

Performing policy analysis

The Bank's staff economists also use QPM as a tool for applying the organization's paradigm of the Canadian economy in carrying out 'policy analysis' for the executives on the Governing Council; that is, responding to questions 'sent up' by the executives, questions that have arisen out of their ongoing discussions about monetary policy. A staff economist explains:

QPM is also a great vehicle for analyzing monetary-policy issues for the senior people. The issue of government debt is a good example: they might ask, 'What would happen if the market's perception of the sustainability of our debt suddenly falls and big risk premiums get built into interest rates. How would that affect the economy? And what would be the impact of such and such a policy response?' When a question like that comes up, we'll say, 'OK, how can we use QPM to address this?' And we'll try to formalize the scenario in the mathematics of the model. QPM is a very useful tool for this, because when questions come up, you have to answer them fairly quickly, and it's good to have a model that's sitting there running. Now it may take a little time to decide exactly how to approach a question, because you have to fit it into the context of the model as best you can, but in a day or so you can usually get an answer you're comfortable with. (Staff Economist 2)

There appears to be a certain tension associated with this use of QPM, at least in some people's minds – a tension between, on the one hand, the staff economists' inclination to qualify output from QPM, given the model's theoretical complexity and, on the other, the executives' preference for clear, unequivocal answers to questions. A staff economist explains:

> *We constantly wrestle with what I'd call a 'rule-of-thumb mentality.'*
> *The executives will ask something like, 'If the dollar drops by one cent,*
> *how much will prices go up by in two quarters? In four quarters? Six*
> *quarters?' And a QPM answer is, 'Well, it depends,' because with a general*
> *equilibrium model, where everything interacts, it almost always depends.*
> *And they hate that – they hate 'it depends.' Instead, they want rules-of-*
> *thumb. So when you're asked to do some analysis on a particular economic*
> *variable, there's a constant friction between this reduce-the-world-to-*
> *a-rule-of-thumb attitude and the fact that when you're using a general*
> *equilibrium model, you have to know what all the other variables in the*
> *system are doing before you can respond. So what we do is use an approach*
> *where the answer does indeed depend, but, subject to a long list of caveats,*
> *we can give them a rule-of-thumb answer.* (Staff Economist 9)

This tension is not unique to the Bank, of course. Many research-and-policy organizations display a similar conflict between the technical specialist's appreciation of theoretical and methodological nuances and the policy-maker's mandate for unequivocal pragmatic action in the world. (See, for example, Shore & Wright, 1997, and Hofstede, 2003.)

QPM as a tool of intersubjectivity

In addition to its use as an analytic tool, a macroeconomic model (i.e., a model of an entire national economy) such as the Quarterly Projection Model offers another kind of support to intellectual collaboration within the community-of-practice: on the social plane, QPM also serves to foster intersubjectivity – a domain of shared focus, perception, and understanding – among the Bank's economists in a way that enables them to 'think in partnership' (Salomon, 1993).

An economist specializing in model-building and monetary policy whom I interviewed at the Brookings Institution in Washington, D.C., offers a starting point for considering this facet of QPM:

> *To do monetary policy, you've got to answer questions like, 'What would*
> *happen if we changed policy in the following way? Or, how would things*
> *be different if we did B instead of A?' To make progress on such questions,*
> *you've got to have an analytic framework of some kind, to reflect your*
> *view of the economy. Now, without an explicit model, you don't know what*
> *framework people are using. You don't know what its strengths are, or its*

weaknesses; and so you can't critique it very well, or improve it. With a
model, though, you can examine the thinking and logic involved in analysis,
and discussion tends to move forward.

The view expressed here is that economists, even those working closely together
in the same professional setting, may hold very different tacit assumptions
about the way economies function; and that a macroeconomic model, in rendering its theoretical assumptions explicit, affords its users a greater degree of
intersubjectivity in their collaborative analytic work, as well as the collective
self-reflexivity needed to evaluate and broaden their field of knowledge over
time. The Quarterly Projection Model can be seen to operate in just this way:
as a symbol-based representation of the Bank's paradigm of the Canadian
economy, the model serves as the basis for a relatively well-defined and stable
locus of intersubjectivity within the organization's discourse, allowing the
economists to render explicit, reflect on, negotiate, and extend their shared
understandings.

I have referred to Charles Bazerman's (1994b) observation that
'[r]epresentations mediate between private spaces of cognition and public
spaces in which intersubjectivity is negotiated [among] numbers of people
engaged in coordinated activities' (pp. 146–147). Taking up this theme, in the
pages that follow I examine in some detail, first, QPM's role in creating a realm
of intersubjectivity within the Bank's community-of-practice, looking at how
the model provides a common ground for intellectual collaboration among
the organization's economists and, second, the way in which QPM acts as an
intersubjective bridge to academics outside the Bank.

Within the Bank, '*QPM brings cohesion and mutual understanding to the*
work of a large number of people,' says one staff economist (Staff Economist
4). According to a deputy governor, the model began this function even as it
was being developed:

> *The people collaborating in building the model had to formalize [i.e.,*
> *translate into mathematics] their individual views of the economy, and*
> *this created the opportunity for them to talk about these views. And, also,*
> *they had to discuss what they were doing with other members of the staff*
> *and with [the executives], to negotiate what the model should look like.*
> (Executive 2)

And according to a department chief, QPM continues to serve this purpose:

> *QPM gives people a common base to operate from, and so it facilitates*
> *work and cooperation. There's less confusion about what's in play and*
> *what's intended, because with the model's mathematical structure, there's*
> *something explicit: this is the model; and people know where they're*

starting from. So you don't get, or at least you limit, the unhelpful sorts of discussions that go, 'Oh, all along I thought you meant this, that, or the other thing.' (Chief 4)

On the other hand, when disagreement arises among the Bank's economists, *'the model helps us reach consensus on issues without leaving a lot of blood on the floor,'* in the words of one department chief (Chief 2). A staff economist explains how QPM serves as a medium for channeling individuals' disparate notions about the Canadian economy into productive debates:

Everybody has their own pet views, and these get brought into discussions, and often with a great deal of vigour. But QPM provides us with a common point of reference. Now of course, people will sometimes argue about the structure of the model itself, and say 'Well, this coefficient in this equation is a little too low, or this one's a little too high.' However, at least the paradigm is clear: you may argue a little about something like coefficients, but you know what it is you agree and disagree on. Discussion is only helpful if you've got a common base and can narrow down what you want to argue about. (Staff Economist 2)

In a similar way, he says, QPM offers individual researchers an avenue for integrating leading-edge work into the achieved consensus of the organizational paradigm of the economy, something its predecessor, RDXF, did not do:

RDXF used old-fashioned economic theory. So if you did research based on new ideas, the latest things that were happening in the profession, you'd end up handcuffed; because you'd say, 'OK, now how do I plug this into the broader paradigm? How do I put this to work for the Bank?' And you'd run up against RDXF and you just couldn't do it, because it didn't have the theoretical capability. So from a researcher's perspective, it was very frustrating. But now, with QPM, we've got a model based on theory that's very current, in terms of the profession's thinking. So QPM gives us a way to link new research to the day-to-day work of the Bank.

Another staff economist had a similar comment, pointing to the relationship between writing and modelling:

When people do research that's on the frontier, they want the paper that comes out of it to have some legs – they want the research to have an impact. And this can be a problem: in a policy institution, if you're out on the frontier, people tend to be wary; they don't want to be captive to fashion, and so they usually wait until an idea is trusted and true before they adopt it. And so papers on that kind of research can get ignored. But with QPM, because it's theoretically advanced, you're able to incorporate output from innovative work into papers in a way people will pay attention to. (Staff Economist 9)

Within the context of the Projection Exercise, QPM exerts a perspective-broadening influence on social interactions among the sector specialists. According to one specialist:

Without QPM, our views would be more narrow. We wouldn't need to understand the interactions and dynamics of how our judgment impacts on other people's sectors, or at least not to the same degree. (Staff Economist 10)

Another specialist elaborates on this notion, beginning by explaining how QPM integrates the individual 'stories' produced by the specialists:

The sector specialists look at different sectors in the economy. Each of us has in-depth knowledge of what's happening in our sector – what the historical relationships are, how we think things will play out in the future, and so on. During the Projection Exercise, our stories about the individual sectors are put into QPM and allowed to interact with each other. The model pulls it all together, allowing each story to influence and be influenced by the others, simultaneously. (Staff Economist 8)

He goes on to describe the implications of this for the specialists, contrasting the QPM era with that of RDXF:

In the old days with RDXF, the specialists could impose their different views on the model without having it complain too much. If two specialists had views that were inconsistent, and each insisted on imposing their view on the model, then you could just sever the links between the sectors and live with the results. Now, with QPM, you can't do that: it's much more interactive and simultaneous than RDXF was; you can't cut a piece of QPM out and have it work the same way it did before – if you cut a piece out, the model stops functioning. For the specialists, that means we need to think more collaboratively about our inputs now. The model forces us to work more closely together; it's much more a question of give-and-take than it used to be.

Another contribution of QPM to intersubjectivity within the Bank's community-of-practice relates to the model's role in textual interactions. As a common point of reference, QPM provides writer and readers with a shared mental schema that promotes mutual comprehensibility.[9] One executive describes how the model comes into play as he and his colleagues read 'analytic notes' produced by the staff economists:

A decision-maker needs to have in his mind a working model of the economy. 'Analytic notes' tend to be on topics such as wages, wage-setting behaviour, or the CPI (Consumer Price Index), or the impact of a move in the exchange rate on interest rates. So if someone mentions in a note that the price of oil has gone up, you can say, 'OK, that's going to affect exports for Canada, and it may also affect domestic prices.' (Executive 6)

(For a discussion of QPM as an important contextual influence on readers in the Bank, see Smart, 1993, and Paré & Smart, 1994.)

Another way that QPM fosters intersubjectivity among the Bank's economists relates to the socialization of newcomers, as they gradually learn to understand the organization's economic ideology, as another department chief explains:

QPM provides a common base of understanding, particularly for new people coming into the Bank. They can look at how the model behaves, and it kind of summarizes how we think about the economy. A lot of them have never thought about things like steady-state constraints on the stock of wealth or the level of saving, because the models they deal with in school are more the kind of ad hoc back-of-the- envelope thing you create to demonstrate a specific point. (Chief 3)

As well as contributing to intersubjectivity within the Bank, QPM acts as a bridge to academic economists outside the organization. A staff economist describes the importance of this function for the Bank's monetary-policy mandate:

One of the elements of a successful monetary policy is to build a constituency for the policy with the public. One part of this is for the Governor and deputy governors give lots of speeches; another is for our research here to cut into important issues and then to have people go to conferences where these things are discussed and make contributions, to build our reputation in the academic community. (Staff Economist 2)

As he explains, QPM plays an important bridging role at academic conferences:

QPM is a model we can be proud of; I'm proud to do research with it and then stand up at a conference and discuss the results in a paper. And QPM has definitely had an impact in the academic community. It's a huge undertaking to build a model like this – a lot of people and other resources; and therefore academics tend to have much smaller models. That means that we have a differentiated product from theirs. While QPM has a theoretical core that's common to many academic models, it also has a lot

> *of other richness built in that we think reflects the real world, empirically,*
> *as well as our expertise in monetary policy. So while there's enough*
> *common ground to communicate, at the same time we have an angle that*
> *the academics don't have.*

Finally, he goes on to mention the part that QPM plays in communicating with academic economists through Bank publications:

> *The Working Papers and Technical Reports we publish have a constituency-*
> *building aspect to them too. But they're also there so that we can get our*
> *model-related work out to people and receive useful feedback on what we're*
> *doing. We don't pretend to know all the answers, or the best way of doing*
> *things, and these sorts of exchanges are important for the Bank.*

QPM's influence on written and spoken discourse

I have mentioned the view of activity theorists that a professional organization's intelligence-bearing analytic tools both enable and shape its knowledge-building. The Quarterly Projection Model is an excellent example of this: as a 'tool of reasoning' and a 'tool of intersubjectivity' central to a particular type of knowledge-building in the Bank – the activity of converting statistical data into policy-relevant 'stories' about present and expected future developments in the Canadian economy – QPM has a pervasive influence on economists' thinking, writing, and speaking. In this section, I examine QPM's influence on the Bank's written and spoken discourse in some detail, again featuring the economists' own commentary. After briefly considering the notion of a *'QPM vernacular'* (to quote a staff economist), I explore the meaning of a term frequently mentioned by Bank economists – 'logical rigour' – and then look at the structure and content of the *White Book*. In this description we will see further instances of written and oral discourse, on the one hand, and economic modelling, on the other, operating together as intermeshed analytic practices.

The QPM vernacular

As with any professional group, Bank of Canada economists have, over time, developed a particular conceptual language to support their collaboration. In part, this language derives from the larger discipline of economics, and in part it is specific to the Bank. As an organization-specific influence on language use, one effect of QPM can be seen in the way that technical terms associated with the model have entered the economists' working vocabulary. While originally these terms were tightly linked to the use of the model, over time they have taken on a broader currency and are used in a more general way to describe economic phenomena. A staff economist explains:

> *QPM has definitely influenced the way I speak and write in my work. For example, I talk about 'running off shocks' and the 'speed of adjustment' and things like that. As sector specialists, we tend to use a sort of 'vernacular' associated with QPM for talking about what we see occurring in the economy during the quarter and how this compares with what had been predicted. But this QPM vernacular has spread around the Bank and become more widely used.* (Staff Economist 10)

In addition to the presence of new technical terminology, QPM has had other, more subtle influences on the discourse of Bank economists. I examine some of these influences below.

Logical rigour

In describing the influence of QPM on their discourse, the Bank's economists frequently invoke the importance of 'logical rigour.' By this, they appear to mean that the model performs a number of particular discursive functions: constraining the tendency to hedge on issues; providing a communal standard of logic; tying reasoning to consensual macroeconomic theory and, more specifically, to a 'general equilibrium' view of the economy; encouraging the precision of mathematics and model-specific referencing; and making reasoning more explicit and visible.

Constraining the tendency to hedge

According to one department chief, the use of a model such as QPM encourages economists to take a definite stance when discussing issues. He begins by pointing to hedging as an occupational habit among economists:

> *You know, in a way, economics isn't really all that scientific. If you put ten economists in a room to discuss something, you'll get at least eleven views, because some of us will always give two. There are always people who'll say, 'Well, I'm worried about this and this on the one hand, but I think possibly this and this on the other hand; and so I can't decide.' And you come away thinking, 'I don't know where that person stands, ever.'* (Chief 3)

He goes on to describe how QPM tempers this tendency:

> *One thing a model like QPM does is put constraints on oral and written discussion – both logical and empirical constraints. Someone using a model*

as an analytic framework, who's done some empirical work with it, will tend to take a position and say, 'Well, given the circumstances, this is what's going on.' So that's something QPM does: it imposes a rigour and forces people to ante up. It puts some bounds on people's hedging, so they can't get away with just expressing reservations.

Providing a communal standard of logic

In debates among the Bank's staff economists, the Quarterly Projection Model also serves as a communal standard of logic that mediates individual judgments. The department chief quoted above explains:

In conversation and meetings, when we're arguing about people's different judgments, QPM is always there in the background, as a common way of reasoning. And you just can't go too far away from it; otherwise there'd be no point in having it.

He goes on to say, more specifically, that in the context of the Projection Exercise and the production of the *White Book*, the model – as an analytic framework embodying organizational wisdom derived from lessons of the past – mitigates against the danger that 'strong personalities' with well-developed persuasive skills will impose narrow, misleading judgments:

QPM provides a rigour we didn't have before. The Projection Exercise used to be somewhat arbitrary sometimes, with the strongest personality tending to get their way, just by being more persuasive than others. They'd say something like, 'Well, based on my judgment, I see a GDP growth of 3%,' and then they'd argue for it 'til they won. So we'd end up putting that particular colouring on the analysis and on our policy advice in the White Book. But what we've got with QPM is a framework that's incorporated the experience that the Bank's had over the years; so we can hedge our bets more, in the sense of guarding against the excessive influence of strong individual judgments. Now, QPM does a lot of the talking for us; it's the mathematics of the model that frames the debate. And that means that no one person can impose their own particular view, simply by being more persuasive.

This interview excerpt could be interpreted as a claim by the department chief that QPM allows the Bank's economists Archimedean access to some larger, absolute truth beyond rhetoric. Taken this way, the excerpt would exemplify the notion, described by Philip Davis and Reuben Hersh (1987), that 'Mathematization means formalization, casting the field of study into the axiomatic mode and thereby, it is supposed, purging it of the taint of rhetoric, of the lawyerly tricks used by those unable to let the facts and logic speak for themselves' (pp. 53–54). However, it would be unfair to leave readers with a sense of the department chief quoted above as an epistemological naïf, given the way he went on to qualify his earlier comment:

> *So there's substantially more rigour in the Projection Exercise with QPM, and less of a reliance on individual judgment and people's powers of persuasion. Nevertheless, there's still an element of this of course, because there's inevitably a fair amount of judgment and debate that goes into working with a model.*

Tying reasoning to consensual macroeconomic theory

Another way that QPM is seen to encourage 'logical rigour' among Bank economists is by making their reasoning accountable to the particular theoretical view of the economy that is built into the model. As a staff economist puts it, '*QPM is sort of a touchstone and a discipline; without its formal theoretical structure, it'd be all too easy to talk glibly about things*' (Staff Economist 8). For example, given the 'general equilibrium' structure of QPM, economists' spoken and written analyses of causal relationships among economic variables tend to reflect the complex, multi-dimensional dynamics of the economy in a way they otherwise might not. A department chief provides an illustration:

> *Let's say you were discussing a question like, 'What would happen if the Government of Ontario decided to stop worrying about the deficit?' Someone might say, 'It would be bad for the economy: it would cause a downgrade of the credit rating and interest rates would go up.' But if you were using QPM to analyze the issue, you'd could put a little more rigour into the analysis: 'It would mean a higher level of indebtedness; and one implication would be that we'd have to borrow more from foreigners. So then we'd need more of a trade surplus to generate the dollars, or yen or whatever, that we'd need to pay them back. So, it would affect the net foreign asset position, and the equilibrium current account and the equilibrium exchange rate. And then there would be these particular implications for prices and therefore for monetary policy.' With QPM, you tend to work the inter-relationships through on a more sophisticated level.* (Chief 3)

A staff economist contrasts this model-influenced reasoning with arguments in the popular press:

> *Without a model like QPM, you can get into loose thinking. You see it all the time in how monetary policy is discussed in the newspapers. Things like: 'To solve the national debt problem, all you need to do is lower interest*

rates.' And the person does this simple calculation and says, 'Well, if we could lower interest rates to 1%, we'd save this much in interest on the debt, and we'd all be better off.' And as far as the simple arithmetic goes, it's perfectly correct. But it's a great example of a partial analysis. They're saying, 'Well, lower this and it will lower that,' as if everything else in the economy will remain unchanged. If you use QPM to think about the issue in a general equilibrium context, you'd see something very different: when you lower interest rates, you get large amounts of aggregate spending, which leads to greater inflation, which in turn leads to higher interest rates as investors demand more of a return. (Staff Economist 2)

Encouraging precision

Another way that QPM influences the discourse of the Bank's economists is by encouraging 'precision.' One aspect of this influence involves the use of mathematics. According to a staff economist:

You often hear the idea that mathematics is a kind of language, and that a model is a more precise substitute for long chunks of writing. In that sense, modelling is an unambiguous way of expressing things that you might otherwise write in words. A model allows you to express a line of logic in a way that normal language can't; and it makes the structure of that logic very clear, in a way that writing doesn't. Literary writers tend to like the ambiguities and fluidity of language, but for an economist, this can sometimes get in the way. A model gives us the kind of precision we like. (Staff Economist 9)

One could argue that this is an example of what sociologist David Maines (1993, quoted in Blyler, 1995) calls 'the ideology of rationalism' (p. 19). From the rationalist perspective, says Maines, 'precision [is seen to be achieved] through enumeration and mathematical representation,' an assumption that promotes the 'legitimation of quantification' and 'decreas[es] legitimation of the human utterance,' resulting in a 'distrust of ordinary language [which is] viewed as imprecise, ambiguous, evocative, and metaphorical.' However, I think this perspective implies a binary between mathematics and 'ordinary language' that the Bank's economists would see as overly simplistic.

Another aspect of the precision associated with QPM relates to model-specific referencing, as the staff economist quoted above explains:

It's interesting to contrast a discussion where you have someone talking about an idea they've been modelling with a discussion where someone's talking about something that hasn't been modeled. When you talk about a concept you're modelling, you can make a one-to-one connection between the model and the concept. When you talk about, say, 'general equilibrium' – it evokes a model, or a set of models, or a structure within a model; so it means something very precise and tells the person listening exactly what you mean. For example, I just went to the Canadian Economics Association meetings. I'd say to someone, 'I'm working on this model, in this way,' and the jargon I'd use would point to a fairly narrowly- defined segment of the modelling literature.

Making reasoning explicit and visible

Finally, QPM contributes to 'logical rigour' in another way: when economists use the model as a frame of reference when communicating their analyses, the reasoning underlying their conclusions is more explicit and visible to other people than it would otherwise be. (This recalls the comment of the Brookings Institution economist quoted earlier.) A deputy governor explains:

Generally, when someone's describing analytic work, they may be able to tell you a little about their logic, but they're probably going to forget to mention all the assumptions they're making. So a major benefit of having QPM is that, because its logical structure is defined explicitly, when people use the model as a framework for analyzing issues, you can follow their logic and see where they're coming from. With the explicit logic of the model, you can be certain of the rigour of the story. What the model does is give you greater visibility of people's thinking processes. (Executive 2)

The White Book

According to one of the staff economists who developed the Quarterly Projection Model, '*you build a model to tell stories about the economy*' (Staff Economist 9). This being the case, it comes as no surprise to hear an executive claim that '*QPM has fundamentally changed the way we talk and write about the economy here in the Bank*' (Executive 2). In this section, we will look further at this change, focusing specifically on how the innovations in QPM's structure have influenced the content and organization of the *White Book*.

First, with QPM, the Bank's inflation-control targets and monetary-policy actions are 'endogenous,' or intrinsic, to the model, rather than 'exogenous,' or outside it, as was the case with its predecessor, RDXF; and this has led to a significant change in the general orientation of the *White Book*. A deputy governor explains:

With QPM used in the Projection Exercise, the story you get from the White Book is very much anchored in a monetary-policy perspective: The focus is on how the components of demand add up, relative to the supply capacity of the economy, and, through that key relationship, on the inflation process and the inflation-control targets and possible policy actions. (Executive 3)

On the same theme, another deputy governor adds,

The story comes out of QPM much more clearly now, and so the White Book is more streamlined. It focuses squarely on what's important for monetary policy: What you get is, 'This is our policy recommendation and here's the logic that led us to it.' (Executive 2)

Second, to quote the same executive, '*QPM's forward-looking properties have altered the White Book.*' He elaborates:

To the extent that people's expectations are depicted as forward-looking in the model, it changes the way we talk about the inflationary process and about policy. So the White Book is less concerned than it used to be with the specifics of what the staff see happening in the near term and much more concerned with the long-run implications of developments.

And according to another deputy governor,

With this increased concern for the longer-run implications of things developing in the economy, we get a more complete macro-economic perspective, a much fuller view of the world. (Executive 2)

Third, QPM is a 'top-down, general equilibrium model' – that is, the economy is represented by a relatively small number of highly-aggregated major variables linked in a complex pattern of simultaneous relationships. A deputy governor describes the effect of this:

If you look at the White Book today and compare it to what it was like before QPM, you'll find that now there's much less detailed description of the economy, less detail about all the minor, disaggregated variables. This reflects the fact that there's a greater degree of aggregation in the structure of QPM, with a focus on a core of major variables. As well, due to the general equilibrium properties of the model, the White Book provides more explanation now on the dynamics among variables that underlie developments. (Executive 2)

He goes on talk about another related feature of the model:

And QPM also has stock-flow dynamics in it, which has to do with the question of debt accumulation. So now the White Book says something about the debt-to-GDP ratio, in a way it couldn't before. And we know that this aspect of the economy is well-modeled, so we have confidence in what the White Book has to say about it.

Finally, according to another deputy governor, QPM's ability to support sophis-ticated 'risk analysis' has also had an impact:

> *Since QPM is much more rigorous in dealing with the question of risk analysis than RDXF was, the alternative scenarios that the staff produce are taken a lot more seriously now, and so they're given greater prominence in the White Book than they were before.* (Executive 4)

Methodological reflections: engagement and detachment

As I hope is demonstrated by the study presented here, interpretive ethnog-raphy, as a methodology for studying the discourse practices that a social group employs in constructing its particular, indigenous life-world, offers an effective way of examining discourse and intellectual collaboration within a professional organization. Having said this, though, I need to acknowledge an important caveat: a researcher using interpretive ethnography to study the discourse practices of a professional organization must maintain a balance of *engagement with* and *detachment from* the informants' conceptual reality. Put another way, the researcher must be able to explore and describe the ideology of the organization without over-identifying with that ideology and losing sight of its status as a cultural construction.

In addressing this issue, we need, first, to consider the ethnographic researcher's engagement with the professional organization under study. Earlier I quoted Clifford Geertz's assertion of the need to 'swim in the stream of the subjects' experience' in order to 'gain some access to their conceptual world.' To accomplish this, the researcher needs to interact with members of the organi-zation over an extended period of time, usually focusing on a particular group of informants. In part, what the researcher is seeking are converging perspec-tives – commonalities across informants' first-order constructs – that point to significant areas of intersubjectivity, domains of shared focus, perception, and understanding. Ultimately, the researcher's aim is to connect observed areas of intersubjectivity into a larger pattern, so as to map out significant features of the organization's 'ideology.'

As I mention in an endnote in Chapter One, in using the term 'ideology' here I am not implying the Marxist notion of false consciousness nor the wilful distortion of reality for political or economic gain. Rather, in speaking of an organization's ideology I mean a shared world-view, in the sense suggested by Robert Heilbroner. Quoted in Chapter One, Heilbroner (1990) defines ideology as the 'frameworks of perception by which all societies organize and interpret their experience' (p. 103) and as the 'conceptual frameworks by which order is imposed on, and moral legitimacy accorded to, the raw stuff out of which social understanding must be forged' (p. 102). I think what Heilbroner is talking about here, in Geertz's terms, is the system of symbolic forms – the discourse – that members of an organization 'perceive with or by means of or through' (p. 102) and the particular conceptual world constituted through this discourse.

Viewed from this angle, the primary task of a researcher intent on studying the work-world of a professional organization is to map out its ideology through extended social engagement with informants. However, this involves two potential dangers. One is that the researcher may end up presenting a monolithic portrait of the organization that ignores individual differences in perspective, differences to be found in those 'private spaces of cognition' referred to by Charles Bazerman (1994b). Here the risk is to ignore what Mikhail Bakhtin (1981) calls 'heteroglossia,' the multiplicity of contending perspectives and voices from which human discourse and knowledge emerge. A second danger is that after working intensively over a period of time to develop an understanding of the organization's ideology, the researcher may come to identify with this ideology too closely, unable to see outside it, as is necessary if one is to situate the ideology in the broader currents of social life. To head off these dangers, the researcher's engagement with the organization under study must be balanced with a degree of detachment. In this vein, Bruno Latour and Steve Woolgar (1986) point to the importance of 'maintaining analytic distance upon explanations of activity prevalent within the culture being observed' (p. 278). Similarly, Martyn Hammersley and Paul Atkinson (1995, p. 102), counsel researchers to avoid 'total commitment,' 'surrender,' or 'becoming' – so that some part of the researcher's attention and awareness is held back, some degree of critical distance retained.

The researcher, however, faces the dilemma of how to preserve adequate critical distance from the ideology of the professional organization as he or she works intensively to develop an account of the organizational culture. Here I will return to my Bank of Canada study to explain how I attempted to balance engagement and detachment in my research. In my view, the centre-piece of the Bank's economic ideology is its shared 'paradigm' of the Canadian economy, a paradigm represented in the mathematical structure of the Quarterly Projection Model. In order to achieve a quasi-insider's sense of the nature and functions of this representation of the economy, and to explore its relationship to the Bank's knowledge-building and policy-making, during my study I interviewed 30 Bank economists, taking care to include people in different roles and at different levels in the organizational hierarchy.

As mentioned in Chapter Two, one of my research strategies was to look for convergences among the perspectives of the 30 Bank economists I interviewed, as indicators of the organization's economic ideology – a key part of the intersubjectivity necessary for accomplishing the collaborative intellectual work required in the monetary-policy process. An example of one such convergence is the similarity in how different economists characterized the Quarterly Projection Model – in terms of what it is and what it does. Earlier in this chapter we saw evidence of this shared understanding of QPM: the economists who were quoted displayed strikingly similar perceptions of the model as a representation of consensual knowledge about the Canadian economy and as an analytical tool.

So when I looked for convergences pointing to aspects of the Bank's economic ideology, I certainly found them. On the other hand, though, when I listened carefully enough to what the economists had to say, I also heard evidence of divergence. Here's an economist (quoted earlier), questioning the degree to which the Quarterly Projection Model really represents a consensual view of the Canadian economy:

> *Does QPM reflect the ideas about the economy that people around the Bank have in their minds? To a degree, I suppose. But it really depends on what views of the economy you subscribe to. There are lots of different economic theories out there in the literature, with their own strengths and limitations. And every economist evaluates those theories and decides which ones best describe the dynamics of the economy. Now what QPM does is bring together a particular set of ideas into an explicit working model. But the question is how much the model represents or influences the views people have in their minds, given that these views can be quite strong.* (Staff Economist 8)

I want to provide a further example of the duality of convergence and divergence within the conceptual world of the Bank's economists, in a case involving the economic theory encoded in the Quarterly Projection Model's mathematical structure. First we will hear a staff economist and a deputy governor (again in interview excerpts quoted earlier) talking about the primary theoretical assumptions inherent in QPM in ways that converge and point to intersubjectivity. The comments concern the model's Neo-Classical orientation and its preoccupation with the need to control inflation:

> *QPM reflects a view of the world that's broadly shared in the Bank, and it's largely a market-driven view. We see the economy as made up of different markets: labour, financial, agricultural, commodity markets. And we see structural relationships at play within these markets. For example, we believe that prices are determined by supply and demand relationships; and that excess demand leads to inflation, which hurts the economy.* (Executive 2)

> *Certain Neo-Classical ideas about relationships among prices and output and inflation and monetary policy are, in a sense, built right into the*

> *mathematics of the model through what's called the Phillips Curve. And*
> *this is linked to a key assumption of Bank policy: that there are large costs*
> *involved in having inflation run at high levels, and so therefore it needs to*
> *be controlled.* (Staff Economist 8)

Again, however, when I listened attentively to the 'private spaces of cognition' among the economists, I encountered other, divergent ways of seeing the world. For example, here is what another economist, known around the Bank as somewhat of a contrarian, has to say about the underlying theoretical basis of the Quarterly Projection Model:

> *What you have to understand about all this, in terms of where the Bank's*
> *coming from, is that central banks exist to preserve the savings of the rich.*
> (Staff Economist 9)

While my sense at the time of the interview was that this economist was playing the *provocateur* (and indeed he has a reputation of being something of a contrarian), the comment nevertheless provides a striking counterpoint to the other two quotations.

In my study, then, while I focused primarily on convergences of perspective in an effort to identify areas of intersubjectivity within the community (viewing this an essential aspect of the economists' intellectual collaboration), I also attended to signs of divergence. I assumed that this would allow me to map out key features of the economists' work-world, but, at the same time, to maintain a critical distance from the economic ideology at play in that world. I also employed another strategy in this vein. In an effort to situate the Bank's economic ideology in a larger professional landscape, I interviewed ten economists outside the institution, in university as well as public-sector and private-sector settings (seven in Ottawa, one in Montreal, and two in Washington, D.C.). Included in this group were two prominent critics of the Bank and its approach to monetary policy, a number of economists whom I suspected would be on the other side of the ideological divide from the Bank, and several others whose ideological positions were unknown to me. These interviews turned out to be extremely useful, both in helping me recognize further aspects of the Bank's economic ideology and in increasing my understanding of how that ideology, as a cultural construction, is both contested and supported within the profession of economics. (We saw an example of fairly strong criticism of the Bank's economic ideology from an outside economist quoted earlier in this chapter.) I have also, as a researcher, attempted to develop a more detached perspective on the Bank's reality by continuing to collect and analyze data from the organization in the years since I left the organization as an employee in 1996.

At the end of Chapter Five, we will take up the issues of validity, reliability, and generalizability as they relate to the study presented in the book.

Chapter Five

Genres of external communications

In earlier chapters, we have seen how the Bank of Canada's economists employ a discursive infrastructure of intertextually linked written and oral genres together with the technology of computer-run economic modelling to accomplish the collaborative work of generating, negotiating, and circulating knowledge about present and expected future developments in the Canadian economy – knowledge that is used by the Governor and his colleagues on the Bank's Governing Council in directing the nation's monetary policy. In this chapter we look at another discursive infrastructure of written and oral genres, again closely connected intertextually, together with another set of technologies to see how the two are used in combination by the Bank's economists to orchestrate the organization's external communications with other social groups in Canada's public-policy realm – the general public, government, the financial markets, the business sector, organized labour, and academia – a function viewed in the Bank as an essential part of the activity of the monetary-policy process (see Diagram 4). In addition to the highly intertextual character of the technology-mediated discourse described in the chapter, we will also encounter instances of interdiscursivity (Fairclough, 1992; Chouliaraki & Fairclough, 1999; Candlin & Maley, 1999), the occurrence within a text of language and conventions reflecting other genres, discourses, and styles; and multimodality (Kress, 2003; Kress & van Leeuwen, 2001; New London Group, 1996), the semiotic merging of language, image, and sound seen in much contemporary technology-mediated discourse.

Within the Bank, the activity of orchestrating the organization's communicative interactions with other social groups in the country's public-policy realm is known as the 'Communications Strategy.' With the Communications Strategy as its focus, the chapter examines the part played by an infrastructure of 34 technology-mediated discourse genres during a period of significant organizational change for the Bank. We will first consider two key features of these discourse genres: the rhetorical and other knowledge displayed by their users and the genres' relationship to processes of organizational change. Next we will look at the genres' role in the activity of the Communications Strategy, highlighting three primary functions: coordinating the intellectual work of numerous individuals occupying a range of professional roles; producing and communicating the 'public information' that conveys the Bank's official public position on its monetary policy; and acting as a site for individual and organizational learning.

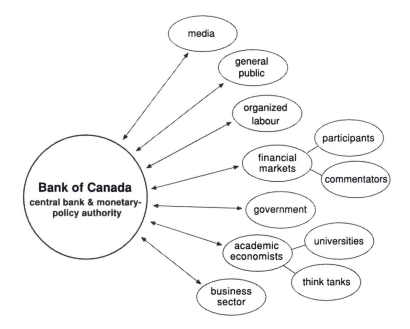

Diagram 4: Bank economists' view of the external public-policy world

As conceptual underpinning for the chapter, to complement the theoretical perspectives on genre, activity, distributed cognition, and situated learning outlined in Chapter One, I have drawn on theories – or 'experience-distant concepts' in the Geertzian idiom – regarding discourse; change in professional organizations; social aspects of the production and use of information; the fusing of texts and digital technologies; and organizational learning. Once again, I will attempt to bring these theories into 'illuminating connection' (Geertz, 1983) with 'experience-near concepts' embedded in commentary from informants, this time from a number of senior executives and several non-economist Bank employees.

Wanda Orlikowski (2001) presents three models of organizational change. She first identifies two models prevalent in the literature: 'planned change', in which managers respond to perceived shifts in the internal or external environment by rationally planning and implementing changes they believe will improve an organization's performance, and 'technological imperative', where a newly-introduced technology drives change in and of itself. After pointing to limitations in these two theories, Orlikowski then proposes a third model, 'situated change', where change occurs as individuals perceive and react, in an ad hoc way, to unfolding events in their work-world: 'organizational transformation is grounded in the ongoing practices of organizational actors and emerges out of their tacit (and not so tacit) accommodations to and experiments with the everyday contingencies, breakdowns, exceptions, opportunities, and unintended consequences that they encounter' (p. 226). Jean Lave (1996) describes the continuous and inseparable relationship between such situated change and collective learning:

> [L]earning is ubiquitous in ongoing activity, though often unrecognized as such. Situated activity always involves changes in knowledge and action [and] 'changes in knowledge and action' are central to what we mean by 'learning.' … People in activity are skillful at, and are more often than not engaged in, helping each other to participate in changing ways in a changing world. So in describing and analyzing people's involvement in practical action in the world [we] are in effect analyzing people's engagement in *learning.* (p. 5)

> Similarly, Etienne Wenger (1998) reminds us that: Learning in this sense is not a separate activity. It is not something we do when we do nothing else or stop doing when we do something else. … [L]earning is an integral part of our everyday lives. It is part of our participation in our communities and organizations. (p. 8)

The chapter also employs theory regarding the production and use of information. Charles Bazerman (2001) writes about the socio-rhetorical character of information as a 'human creation for human purposes' (p. 261). In describing the construction of 'public information' regarding the consequences of nuclear testing during the 1950s, Bazerman points to 'the intentional design of particular forms of information in particular historical circumstances [for the purpose of] influence[ing] individual and group action' (2001, p. 261). (On this theme, see also Bazerman, Little, & Chavkin, 2003.) In addition, the chapter draws on scholarship regarding the merging of texts with new digital technologies (Engeström & Middleton, 1998; Geisler, 2001, 2004; Geisler et al., 2001; Haas, 1996; Henderson, 1999; Luff, Hindmarsh, & Heath, 2000). Geisler et al. (2001) coin the term 'IText' to refer to the fusing and reciprocal mediation of texts and technologies and introduce the IText into theorizing of organizational genres and knowledge-building (pp. 291, 293–294). Barbara Carlson (2001) discusses the growing impact of a particular type of IText, the discourse presented through an Intranet, an internal web-based system for sharing information within an organization.[1] As we shall see, these Itexts have a decidedly multimodal character (Kress, 2003; Kress & van Leeuwen,

2001; New London Group, 1996), with their semiotic merging of language, image, sound.

The Communications Strategy

The Communications Strategy is a complex, technology-mediated collaborative activity through which the Bank orchestrates its discursive interactions with the outside groups mentioned earlier – the media, the general public, government, the financial markets, the business sector, organized labour, and academia. To see the significance of the Communications Strategy in the Bank's history as an organization, we need understand that the Bank's approach to communicating with outside groups has shifted dramatically over the last decade. The Bank of Canada, like other central banks around the world, has moved from being an institution that veiled its decision-making processes in secrecy and that maintained a reactive (some might say defensive) posture of monitoring and cautiously (some might say elliptically) responding to outside commentaries about its monetary policy, to being an institution that is committed to the principle of 'transparency' (of which more later) regarding its views on the Canadian economy and its own monetary-policy goals and actions. And this fundamental shift in approach has been accompanied by significant changes in the uses of discourse and technology within the activity of the Bank's work. While the discursive, intellectual work-world of any professional organization evolves continuously, dramatic change such as that experienced by the Bank of Canada during this period makes the dynamic interplay of activity, discourse, and technology more visible to a researcher.

I first learned of this change when I arrived at the Bank of Canada in June 2000 to continue my research for this book. When I heard about the new Communications Strategy in my first interview that day, I realized that since I had left the organization as a full-time employee in 1996, a sea-change had taken place in the Bank's approach to communicating with outside groups. Consequently, I decided to reorient my research to focus on the activity and discourse of the new Communications Strategy. As the two days I spent at the Bank interviewing informants and gathering other data progressed, and as I began to get a fuller sense of the change that had occurred, I explored the different facets of this activity.

In examining the activity of the Bank's Communications Strategy, this section of the chapter first presents a group of 34 discourse genres associated with this activity as well as various digital technologies and built environments that mediate the use of these genres. I then go on to suggest that this internal group of genres can be viewed as part of a larger inter-organizational genre system that also includes an array of external written and oral genres monitored by members of the Bank's staff for the purpose of gleaning information and perspectives from outside groups relevant to the Bank. Next, the genres and the built environments and digital technologies associated with them are conceptualized as integral parts of the activity of the monetary-policy process. I then discuss two significant features of the group of genres as a whole as well as the role the genres play in the activity of the Communications Strategy.

We will begin by looking at the various written and oral genres that come into play within the Communications Strategy. The symbol *** following a genre indicates either that the genre is relatively new, having emerged with the Communications Strategy over the last decade, or that it preceded the Communications Strategy but has changed significantly in form and function. The letters 'www.T' beside a written genre indicate that texts in the genre were, at the time of the writing of this book, currently available on the Bank's website; and for oral genres, 'www.A' indicates the availability on the website of an audio file of the communication event, and 'www.T' indicates the availability on the website of the written text on which the spoken performance was based. We see here instances of the multimodality that characterizes the discourse of the Communications Strategy.

First we will look at 15 published written genres (with the symbol Δ indicating the ten genres that Bank insiders refer to as the main 'communication vehicles' for the Communications Strategy, that is, the genres regularly used to convey the Bank's 'key messages'), as well as at ten oral genres that also play a part in the 'Communications Strategy' – oral genres that involve outsiders and so are visible to public view.

Written genres – published

- *Monetary Policy Report*, with 4-page summary (Δ,***, www.T)
- *Update to Monetary Policy Report* (Δ,***, www.T)
- *Bank of Canada Annual Report* (Δ,***, www.T)
- scheduled policy interest rate announcements (Δ, ***, www.T)
- Governor's presentations to Parliament (two each year to House of Commons, one to Senate) (Δ, ***, www.T, www.A)
- minutes from meetings of Board of Directors, featuring summary of Governor's presentation to Board (Δ, ***, www.T)
- lectures by Governor, to university audiences (Δ, www.T, www.A)
- speeches by Governor, usually to industry, business, and labour groups (Δ, www.T, www.A); and similar speeches by other senior members of Bank staff (www.T)
- formal presentations (usually) by deputy governors at major economics and public-policy conferences (Δ, www.T)

- information/consultation papers (***, www.T)
- press releases on issues related to monetary policy (www.T)
- *Business Outlook Survey* (***, www.T)
- letters from Governor in response to letters, phone calls, and e-mail messages sent to Bank by members of public
- *Technical Reports* describing finished research by Bank staff economists (www.T)
- *Working Papers* describing research-in-progress by Bank staff economists (www.T)

Oral genres – involving participants outside the Bank

- press conferences by Governor following scheduled policy interest rate announcements and following official release of *Monetary Policy Report*, *Update to Monetary Policy Report*, and *The Bank of Canada Review* (***, www.T, www.A)
- briefings by deputy governor to journalists in 'lock-up facility' immediately preceding official release of *Monetary Policy Report*, *Update to Monetary Policy Report*, and *The Bank of Canada Review* ***
- briefings by deputy governors to journalists and financial analysts following release of *Monetary Policy Report* and *Update to Monetary Policy Report* ***
- lunch meetings at Bank of Canada between senior Bank officials and people in government, business, financial markets, organized labour, media, and academia ***
- meetings between Governor and other senior Bank executives with editorial boards of newspapers and news magazines
- meetings of Governor, other senior Bank policy-makers, and staff economists with officials in various levels of federal and provincial governments
- informal presentations by senior Bank policy-makers, staff economists, and regional representatives to university audiences and to various industry and business groups ***
- meetings during visits by regional representatives to industries and businesses ***
- interactions between Bank economists and outside economists at conferences hosted by Bank on monetary policy and related economic issues ***
- regular telephone conversations between (a) Bank economists and market analysts, traders, and portfolio managers in Canadian financial institutions, and (b) senior Bank staff and journalists

In addition to the 25 written and oral genres listed above, we will look at 11 other internal written and oral genres that also play an integral role in the Communications Strategy – these are behind-the-scenes genres that, while an essential part of the Communications Strategy, are not visible to outsiders. (The word 'Intranet' after a genre indicates that texts in the genre are accessible to senior Bank staff on the organization's internal Intranet.)

Written and oral genres – behind the scenes

Written

- *Q & A's* (prepared questions-and-answers material) (***, Intranet)
- analyses by Communications Department of commentaries appearing in print and broadcast media following *Monetary Policy Report, Updates to MPR, The Bank of Canada Review, Bank of Canada Annual Report*, and lectures and speeches by Governor (***, Intranet)
- yearly report by Communications Department analyzing effectiveness of Communications Strategy (***, Intranet)
- yearly report by Financial Markets Department analyzing reactions of financial markets to Bank's monetary policy actions (***, Intranet)
- weekly analyses by Research Department of information provided by regional representatives regarding actions and views of business people and politicians ***
- reports by Communications Department on surveys of audiences for different types of Bank communications ***
- on-going analyses of financial markets' reactions to Bank's monetary policy actions
- daily 'clippings' package – compendium of articles from print media mentioning Bank of Canada or dealing with topics relevant to monetary policy

Oral

- meetings involving writers and editors during production processes for genres such as *Monetary Policy Report, Bank of Canada Annual Report, The Bank of Canada Review*, and Governor's speeches ***
- meetings between members of Communications Department and senior Bank staff to discuss aims and effectiveness of Communications Strategy ***
- weekly conference calls involving regional representatives and staff economists in Research Department ***

These 34 genres can be seen to function together as a single whole – what we might view as a sub-set of genres within the larger genre set of the monetary-policy process – in complex sequences of discursive events and rhetori-cal/epistemic acts (as I will discuss in some detail later in the chapter).[2] At the same time, the use of this genre sub-set is mediated by a variety of built environments and digital technologies such as those noted below (an *** beside a built environment or digital technology indicates that it is relatively new to the Bank):

- 'lock-up facility' for journalists, with its various digital information/ communication technologies ***
- press conference facility, where Governor and senior officials meet with journalists ***
- Bank's Intranet ***
- Bank's website ***
- digital management information systems ***
- telecommunication system linking Ottawa head office with regional offices ***
- e-mail links via Internet to contacts outside Bank ***
- Governing Council's dining room, site for lunches with visitors
- networked computers used in document production that are linked to computer-run economic models and to electronic document archives and data bases
- digital links to wire services, press agencies, etc.
- digital connections to financial markets in Canada, U.S., and abroad
- telephone, conference-call technology, fax

When we look at the sub-set of genres associated with the Communications Strategy, we see that one of its striking characteristics is the interconnectness of written and oral discourse, a feature we saw illustrated earlier, in Chapter Three, in the functional relationship between the written texts and spoken lan-guage employed in the Projection Exercise. One aspect of the intertextual links connecting written and oral genres within the activity of the Communications Strategy involves chains of genres closely linked in their use – such as the Bank's *Monetary Policy Report*, the *Q & A's* material produced for use by the Governor in preparing for the face-to-face press conference that immediately follows the official release of the *MPR*, and the press conference itself. Here we also see the way in which texts and digital technologies merge in the form of ITexts (Geisler, 2004; Geisler et al., 2001): electronic copies of both the *MPR* and the *Q & A's* are placed on the Bank's internal Intranet for viewing by Bank staff several days before the official release of the *MPR*; and then following the release of the *MPR*, the Governor's press conference – held in a specially-equipped built environment – is digitally recorded, with the spoken performance placed on the Bank's website as an audio file along with an electronic copy of the *MPR*.

If we examine the 34 genres and the various digital technologies and built environments noted earlier in the chapter, we will see other similar chains of written and oral genres, often with digital technologies and specially-constructed physical environments in play, and with ITexts as the frequent communicative outcome. As soon becomes clear in looking at the sub-set of genres embedded in the Communications Strategy, the genres comprise a highly multimodal discursive system of temporally- and functionally-linked written texts and spoken performances – all mediated by a complex network of technologies and built environments.

A related issue here is the blurring between written and oral discourse within certain individual genres. How, for example, would we categorize the Governor's speeches? In these spoken performances, the Governor reads, verbatim and in front of a live audience, a written text that has been carefully crafted through intensive collaboration and 'document cycling' (Paradis, Dobrin, & Miller, 1985; Paré & Smart, 1994; Smart, 1993) – the organizational process of reviewing and revising a series of drafts – involving a number of people and occurring over a period of days or weeks. Following the speech, the written text and an audio file of its spoken performance by the Governor will appear as complementary ITexts on the Bank's website. Should we classify the speech as an oral genre, or as a written genre? If one applies Bakhtin's (1986) distinction between 'primary speech genres,' which are informal and conversational, and 'secondary speech genres,' which are more formal, rhetorically complex instances of written discourse, a speech by the Governor would appear to be one of the latter.

In addition to the internal sub-set of genres embedded within the activity of the Communications Strategy, we can also identify genres produced outside the Bank that members of its staff watch closely in order to glean relevant information and perspectives from outside groups – for example, commentaries in the print or broadcast media on the Bank's monetary policy, published reports by economists working in the financial markets, articles in academic journals and other publications on economic and public-policy topics, published exchanges occurring in the House of Commons' daily question period (reported in *Hansard*, the daily record of debate in the Canadian Parliament), and the texts of federal and provincial annual budgets. The internal genre sub-set associated with the Communications Strategy and the array of external genres monitored by Bank staff can be seen to function together in a single complex and interactive network of discourse. Together, the internal genre sub-set and the assortment of related external genres resemble what Charles Bazerman (1994b) refers to as a 'genre system' – a network of genres that extends beyond a single organization to encompass the discourse used by two or more social groups to interact with one another in accomplishing mutually significant work (although I should note here that the discussion in this chapter does not cover in any specific detail the genres employed by the various outside groups with which the Bank interacts communicatively).

To move ahead with the argument here, I want to suggest that the members of the Bank's staff who participate in the activity of the Communications Strategy and in the other aspects of the monetary-policy process can be viewed as a community-of-practice affiliated with two sub-systems of activity – one sub-system associated with the Bank's work of economic knowledge-building and policy-making and the other with its Communications Strategy. Diagram 5 provides a sense of what these relationships look like when mapped out this way.

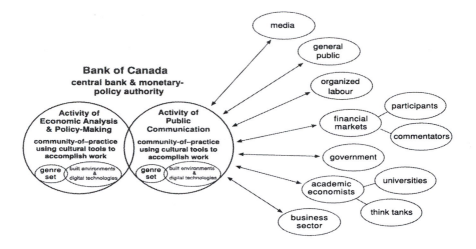

Diagram 5: A theorized depiction of the Bank economists' view of the internal and external dimensions of the monetary-policy process

Characterizing the Bank and its Communications Strategy in this manner is useful analytically in that it yields insights about the part that discourse genres, mediated in their use by digital technologies and built environments, play in the Bank's intellectual collaboration.

So then, what does this depiction of the Communications Strategy as a sub-system of activity employed within a community-of-practice allow us to notice that we might not otherwise? As we shall see, the characterization can help us recognize some of the various ways in which discourse genres function, mediated by digital technologies and built environments, to prompt, shape, coordinate, and apply the processes of collective thinking, socio-rhetorical action, and ongoing learning that enable an organization to perform complex intellectual work. At the same time, looking at the Communications Strategy in this way provides a window onto a professional organization's use of discourse genres in communicating with the array of outside groups with which it interacts in carrying out its mandate.

As a prelude to a later section of the chapter, where I examine the role of the sub-set of 34 genres outlined earlier in the activity of the Communications Strategy, we will look now at two particular features of the genre sub-set: the rhetorical knowledge displayed within the community-of-practice associated with the Communications Strategy; and the genre sub-set's relationship to processes of organizational change. In describing the role of the genre sub-set, I will again enlist the voices of a number of Bank senior executives whom I interviewed as well as the voices of several other Bank employees.

Two key features of the genre sub-set

Practitioners' genre knowledge

The distributed cognition that is, to use activity theorist Jean Lave's (1988) phrase, 'stretched over' the members of the Bank staff who comprise the community-of-practice engaged in the activity of the Communications Strategy includes a complex web of intersubjectivities – domains of shared focus, perception, and understanding that connect individuals intellectually within the community-of-practice – with particular intersubjectivities populated according to individuals' respective organizational roles. A central area of intersubjectivity is the shared rhetorical awareness of the ways in which the Communications Strategy's genres function. Below we will examine four types of such genre knowledge.

The executives involved in making monetary-policy decisions appear to share a common understanding of the two broad, closely-linked goals of the activity of the Communications Strategy and its genres: first, to persuade external audiences of the soundness of the Bank's monetary policy, and second, to contribute to the effectiveness of monetary policy by reducing public uncertainly about the Bank's thinking, goals, and intentions. According to the Governor:

> *At times central banks have to do difficult things, and it's much better if people outside the Bank of Canada understand monetary policy. It's particularly important that the financial markets be aware, but in the long run it's also important that governments and the public understand monetary policy as well. But it's not only a question of support for monetary policy; it's also a question of the effectiveness of policy.*

One of the deputy governors echoes this view of the dual goals of the Communications Strategy:

With monetary policy, there's the issue of persuasion, in that part of our communication is to try to get people to understand, and hopefully not just understand, but support our policy. In a democracy, your ability to pursue a policy is related to the public support it generates; otherwise, when things get tough, it's much harder to carry on with the policy. And for that support to be there, public understanding of the policy is essential. But the other thing, of course, is that monetary policy works better when people understand it and align their expectations and decisions accordingly. For example, if the public is convinced that we really are committed to keeping inflation under control, if they really do believe that inflation is going to be at 2%, then when it comes to wage negotiations across the country, people won't be asking for 10% increases on the assumption that there's going to be 8% inflation, and employers aren't going to give 10%. So it's a question of the efficacy of policy as well as political support. (Executive 3)

Another deputy governor, jokingly referred to by a colleague as the Bank's 'Communications Czar' because of his key role in co-coordinating the Communications Strategy, expands on this shared perspective:

The place I start thinking about the Communications Strategy conceptually, is – what do communications do for us? And you can cut into that several different ways. As a public-policy organization, there's one angle that says you need to be accountable, particularly in our case because, as a central bank, we've got a fair degree of independence from government. And then how do you achieve accountability? Well, you achieve it in part through transparency. And how do you become transparent? – through effective communications. The other angle in this is one of policy outcomes. And that gets into the whole issue of trying to minimize public uncertainty, in terms of what the Bank is up to with monetary policy and why – trying to influence public expectations of where we intend to go with monetary policy, whether it be [the expectations of] households, business, or financial markets, so that these expectations are in line with our goals for monetary policy. And again, you achieve that kind of policy outcome through transparency and effective communications. So communications is important to the Bank both in terms of generating support and in terms of the efficacy of monetary policy itself. (Executive 4)

(See Appendix J for the text of a speech by this executive on the topic of the Bank's Communications Strategy. The speech was delivered in September

2004 to a group of Canadian and U.S. financial-market professionals and later reprinted in the *Bank of Canada Review.*)

The particular aspect of the intersubjectivity and genre knowledge we see reflected in these instances of insider discourse – a shared cognizance of the goals of the Communications Strategy – can be viewed, in the context of activity theory, as distributed cognition in the form of a collective awareness of the larger aims of the activity system. One might speculate here that in any organizational activity system, at least some of the participants will have this kind of explicit 'discursive consciousness' (Giddens, 1984) of its aims, an important communal resource that complements the presumably much larger measure of 'practical consciousness' (Giddens, 1984) or 'tacit knowledge' (Polanyi, 1966) within the community-of-practice.

A second type of genre knowledge displayed by members of the community-of-practice participating in the activity of the Bank's Communications Strategy is an understanding of the division of discursive and intellectual labour involved. This type of shared knowledge includes an awareness of who is responsible for doing what, and when, in the collective accomplishment of two key tasks: first, monitoring texts in written and spoken genres produced by groups outside the Bank that either comment directly on the Bank's monetary policy or address other concerns relevant to the organization's work, such as economic research and theory, current financial developments, and broader public-policy issues; and second, composing written texts in different internal genres in order to respond to commentaries on Bank policy by outside groups. This genre knowledge is generally tacit, rather than inscribed in and communicated through formal written procedures. As a deputy governor responded, when asked about this: *'The Communications Strategy, the approach, isn't documented anywhere, so I'm not really sure how it gets communicated to Bank staff, though it certainly gets communicated somehow'* (Executive 3). This theme will be taken up later in the chapter in a discussion of how the sub-set of genres embedded within the Communications Strategy functions as a site for organizational learning.

Below, a deputy governor conveys his sense of how different members of the Bank staff, operating in a variety of professional roles, monitor texts in written and spoken genres produced by certain of the outside groups with which the Bank interacts – a collective, but differentiated-according-to-role, work effort that allows the organization to remain attuned to external discourses pertinent to its mandate for directing monetary policy:

For watching the media, we have people in the Library who read the newspapers and wire services – and they're very good at picking up items that specifically mention monetary policy or are related to the economy more generally. And they send us a daily clippings package with the items they've selected. As for what the [financial] markets are saying, our staff in [the] Financial Markets [Department] keep up with that, in a systematic way – they talk to people in the markets on a regular basis, getting their views, and also monitor the financial and business press. And for things of interest in the academic literature, the Library circulates a daily list of relevant items that have appeared recently, and the staff in the economics departments [Research; Monetary and Financial Analysis; Financial Markets; and International] get these pieces through the Library and read them. And then sometimes there's a news report in the press about a recent academic study or report, and we'll make sure we get a copy of it through the Library. Or one of our economists comes back from a conference and says, 'So and so gave a paper on such and such,' and they circulate the paper. So all in all, we're very much aware of what's being said in different venues outside the Bank. Our staff are continually picking up on these things and filtering it and sending it along to us [i.e., to the Bank's senior decision-makers]. (Executive 4)

Another deputy governor offers a similar perspective on the division of intellectual labour involved in this aspect of the Communications Strategy:

There are people out there, outside the Bank, who issue daily, weekly, monthly, quarterly, and annual commentaries on the economy – for example, the staff economists at major banks produce these, and private-sector firms as well. And then there are the [economic] forecasts produced by other people, such as the C.D. Howe Institute. And the Bank looks at all of this, with different people here having different responsibilities, different areas to watch. But we need to be aware of all this. (Executive 3)

He goes on to display his understanding of the multiplicity of regular one-to-one interactions between members of the Bank staff and individuals in outside groups:

And there's also the informal contacts between people in the Bank and people outside. There's a lot of this in the economics departments. For example on the academic side – in terms of research and theory – our people talk to academics doing similar kinds of research or who are doing forecasting, and they'll often exchange drafts of work-in progress as well. And there's also the continuous contact with people on the financial side [i.e., with analysts and participants in the financial markets].

Another facet of the shared genre knowledge regarding the division of intellectual labour inherent in the activity of the Communications Strategy concerns situations in which the Bank decides to respond to outside commentaries on its monetary-policy decisions and actions using one of several genres in the sub-set. In cases of what are perceived to be significant errors of fact in the news media, the chief of the Communications Department will typically, within a day or two, make a phone call to the particular journalist or reporter in question. According to a deputy governor, the phone call will go something like this:

> *Well, you know, you got the facts somewhat wrong in that recent piece of yours. This is actually how we're operating now…* (Executive 4).

He continues, pointing to another motive for this particular type of interaction:

> *it's also a question of educating the media, which is an ongoing effort, given the turnover of people in the media.*

When the Bank feels the need to respond to an interpretive critique of its monetary policy by an outside group (as opposed to perceived errors of fact in outside commentary), the Bank may decide to respond through written discourse in one of a range of genres. The same deputy governor quoted above explains:

> *It depends on the nature of the criticism – sometimes the media people are critical and it's not unreasonable, because reasonable people can differ on things. But at other times, we may think it's not quite as reasonable. And then, depending on whether we think it's important to get our message out and in what venue, we'll decide on a way to respond. On the other hand, if it's something significant that appears in an academic forum, we'll respond in an academic forum. For example, I just got an invitation to do a piece in a book that's coming out on what's happened with the economy over the 90's, a piece on monetary policy. And at first I was thinking I'm pretty over-committed with this kind of writing at the moment. But when I saw that the book will also have a piece by [a university economist who is a well-known and professionally-respected critic of the Bank's monetary policy] discussing our inflation-control targets, I thought, 'Well, I don't know if I will do it myself, but it will get done by someone around the place' – because I don't think having this kind of message out there, that we think is misleading, is helpful. [The critic's] view is very far from our view, so we need to respond.*

The speaker goes on to reveal more of his understanding of the Bank's nuanced approach to, and motives for, responding to external critiques of its monetary policy:

> *When the criticism out there is about our position on things, they can take*

that or not as they like – it's their interpretation. But we may choose to
debate their interpretation if we think it's wrong or misleading. We want
people to have a clear understanding of what we're thinking about and
how we're approaching a particular situation. And if we feel that they're
completely misinterpreting what we're trying to do, then that may call for a
speech or some other way of communicating our views.

He elaborates on the reasoning underlying the decision of whether the Bank
will choose to respond, and if so, in what particular genre:

We take different opportunities to deal with particular kinds of issues. For
example, I'll be giving a 45-minute presentation at the Western Economics
Association Meetings next month, quite a long paper. I thought it would be
a good opportunity to get some of our messages out, our views on certain
issues that have come up recently; and it's also about rejoining the debate
with [the critic of the Bank mentioned above] on the range of the inflation-
control targets. Another example: the issue of whether the foreign exchange
rate should be fixed or flexible – something that's been showing up in
the press lately. The Governor chose to give a speech on that the other
day, putting out the Bank's views. In fact, each time he gives a speech, he
ponders whether it should be the regular type of speech dealing with current
conditions in the economy, or whether there's some particular issue he
wants to focus on. So we're always very much aware of what's being said
out there, but whether we feel the need to respond, and when and how,
depends on the nature of the comment, who said it, how directly it relates
to the Bank's business, where it was said, whether it's likely to be taken
seriously, how important it is to get our side of the issue out, and so on.

This particular aspect of genre knowledge – the sense of what constitutes an
appropriate discursive response to a particular instance of external commentary
on the Bank's monetary policy – reminds one of Anne Freadman's (1994)
notion of 'uptake,' where a text in a particular genre, produced by one player,
will tend, in the natural course of socio-rhetorical events, to elicit a response
through a text produced in a second genre by another player. In this case, we
see a text produced by another organization, in a genre within the larger genre
system, evoking a discursive response from the Bank through one of the genres
associated with the Communications Strategy.

When the Bank does decide to respond to an interpretive critique of its
policy from an outside group – as picked up by the Bank's 'communicative
radar' in an external text in the genre system – by employing a particular Bank
genre, the composing of the text can be highly collaborative and iterative,
an instance of distributed cognition that serves several functions: it elicits

ideas from various individuals, enabling a collective mode of thinking, and it contributes to organizational learning (a topic that will be taken up in some detail later in the chapter). A deputy governor provides his perspective on this form of collaboration:

> *When you give a presentation, or a speech, there's always a paper to give out to the press. And when I'm preparing a presentation that has policy implications of any kind, I'll always run the paper by the Governor, the other deputy governors, the [senior] advisors, and sometimes certain other people as well. And I look very carefully at all their comments and I use them. So it's quite collegial in that sense. The MPR [Monetary Policy Report], the Update to the MPR, the Annual Report, the Governor's speeches – we all look at drafts of these, all the Governing Council, and other people too. It's always a collective effort, and you learn from doing it.*
> (Executive 4)

This comment reflects another type of genre knowledge that is important for writers within a professional organization: who should be included in the document cycling process for texts in any given genre. (Later in the chapter we will see a description of the collaborative draft-review-revise cycle in an account of the preparation of the Bank's *Monetary Policy Report.*)

A third type of the genre knowledge linked to the Bank's Communications Strategy is the vernacular of shared terms employed by staff members in talking about its activity and sub-set of genres. As mentioned earlier, Clifford Geertz (1983) points to the importance – for the ethnographic researcher attempting to illuminate the local, self-constructed reality of a particular social group – of looking carefully at 'key terms that seem, when their meaning is unpacked, to light up a whole way of going at the world' (p. 157). In interviews with my informants at the Bank regarding the Communications Strategy, a number of such terms came up repeatedly, including, for example, the dichotomy of 'Old Bank' versus 'New Bank' and the terms 'transparency,' 'primary communication vehicles,' and 'key messages.' This form of genre knowledge – the shared use of conceptually rich terms – would appear to be essential for the inter-personal communication required of genre users within a community-of-practice.

A closer look at the terms mentioned above will provide us with a sense of their communicative function in relation to the sub-set of genres we have been looking at in this chapter. The '*Old Bank*,' according to a deputy governor, was one where the organization believed that:

> *to be effective, monetary policy had to involve a lot of secrecy, to be surrounded by mystique, and that central bankers had to be very careful in*

*their communications. As an observer, you could take the Bank's words in
different ways, and you had to look at the entrails, as it were. The view was
that monetary policy was effective only if it surprised the markets, and so you
couldn't give out any clues about what you were going to do.* (Executive 4)

In contrast, as the 'New Bank,' equipped with its Communications Strategy,
the organization takes a very different view:

> *But now, we've really moved in the other direction, as have most of the
> world's other central banks, and we've moved towards much greater
> openness. Having inflation-control targets has helped a lot in this, because
> once the objective is clearly defined, and there's no quibble about the
> objective, then central bankers feel a lot freer about explaining what
> they're doing and why they're doing it. A large part of the fear in the past
> was always a fear of having a monetary policy that's too expansionary. So
> central bankers have become a lot more open, more transparent.*

This brings us to another term in the vernacular employed by members of the
community-of-practice using the genre sub-set – 'transparency.' The over-use
of this term in contemporary political and corporate discourse has made it
somewhat suspect. But what exactly does the term 'transparency' appear to
mean within the Bank of Canada? According the deputy governor quoted
above:

> *Transparency means something particular: it's not just about giving out
> all the information you have; just giving out more information is not
> necessarily being transparent. There's a distinction between giving out
> everything you have versus giving out only the information that's relevant.
> The second approach is informative, and helps people understand what
> you're trying to do, while the other isn't necessarily informative at all, since
> what's important can easily get lost in a maze of detail.*

The chief of the Communications Department offers a qualification to this
description of transparency:

> *There's a difference between appropriate openness and inappropriate
> openness on the part of the Bank. It's the difference between, on the one
> hand, trying to help people to understand how we look at world, what
> we think inflation is going to do, and what our longer-term goals for the
> economy are, and on the other hand, revealing what the Bank is going to
> do in the short term with interest rates, which way we're leaning – the Bank
> can do the former, but not the latter.*

The Bank's executives and department chiefs share the view that an important factor in achieving the goals of the Communications Strategy is allowing outside groups to understand something of how the organization looks at the world, and more specifically, of how it analyzes information about the Canadian economy.[3] Providing an example of this particular facet of transparency, the chief of the Communications Department talks about the Bank's communicative interactions with the 'Bank-watchers,' as Bank staff refer to members of two professional groups: analysts in Canadian financial markets who make a living by closely following the central bank and its monetary policy and advising clients on their investments accordingly, and financial journalists who write about the Bank's monetary policy in their news stories and columns:

> *The approach the Bank takes in its Communications Strategy – through the Monetary Policy Report, through the Governor's speeches, and so forth – is to help the people who watch us closely understand how we think. For example, with the 'Bank-watchers,' it's a case of, 'Look, you too can evaluate the same range of information, economic indicators, that we evaluate – the [Consumer Price Index] just went up, or didn't go up, whatever – and you can learn how we look at it.' And the good commentators, who are paid to say, 'Well, the Bank is going to move [i.e., adjust Canadian interest rates] or not going to move,' they – if they're doing it right – they're learning how the Bank sees the world. We're constantly trying to help people to understand how the Bank looks at the numbers, to understand all this, through our communications. It's almost like providing an ongoing do-it-yourself central banking course for people who are really interested.*

Parenthetically, in this quotation we also gain a sense of how people who work at the Bank, in characterizing it as a sentient, thinking entity, appear to possess an intuitive sense of the distributed cognition operating within the organization. In interviews, the informants repeatedly expressed similar perceptions. For example, a deputy governor referred to the regional representatives across the county as the Bank's '*ears and mouth in the regions*' and to the senior Bank officials in Toronto and Montreal as '*the Bank's eyes and ears in the [financial] market*' (Executive 3). Such metaphorically-expressed intuitions might be seen to reflect the informants' tacit awareness of the phenomenon of distributed cognition, adding a certain support to the theory-influenced observations and interpretations of a researcher.

Two further terms to mention here in connection to the genre knowledge displayed by participants in the activity of the Communications Strategy are 'primary communication vehicles' and 'key messages.' When members of the Bank staff use the first term, they are referring to a number of high-profile genres in the genre sub-set, including the *Monetary Policy Report*, the *Update to Monetary Policy Report*, speeches and lectures by the Governor, the *Annual Report of the Bank of Canada*, *The Bank of Canada Review*, and the Governor's presentations in the Canadian Parliament (two presentations each year in the House of Commons and one in the Senate). The term 'key messages' refers to the most salient points included in any particular text, such as the *Monetary Policy Report*, as when a deputy governor mentions the primary concerns of the Communications Department when analyzing commentaries in the media following the release of the *MPR*:

> *Were the key messages in the report picked up? Were we effective in*
> *conveying our key messages?* (Executive 5)

Later in the chapter we will see how the key messages in the *Monetary Policy Report* are highlighted in a summary text attached to the *MPR*.

Shared terms such as those discussed above constitute a linguistic and conceptual shorthand, imbued with historically-accrued shared meanings, that functions as an essential tool for genre users within a community-of-practice. And for researchers, focusing on such terms is an important way of gaining insight into the world-view of a community-of-practice, for as Clifford Geertz (1983) suggests in a quotation cited earlier, 'the vocabularies in which [practitioners within an intellectual community converse offer] a way of gaining access to the sorts of mentalities at work in [it]' (p. 157).

A final type of genre knowledge associated with the activity of the Communications Strategy that we will consider here, and one that is essential to the rhetorical effectiveness of its genres, involves the discursive construction of the public-policy world outside the Bank through the differentiation and characterization of a constellation of outside groups. The people in the Bank that I interviewed in my study repeatedly spoke about the seven social groups I have mentioned – the media, the general public, government, the financial markets, the business sector, organized labour, and academia, the latter taken to include both university economists and those working in private-sector 'think-tanks.' Further, those people I interviewed shared a number of very specific notions about the nature of each of these external groups as a distinctive audience for the Bank's communications. And frequently, this characterization of particular audiences was accompanied by tactical notions on how best to communicate with them.

Here, for example, a deputy governor talks about the Bank's 'strategic' approach to communications:

> *We've been trying to focus our communication vehicles to ensure that we*

know how we're using them – Who are the different audiences we want to get at? How frequently should we try to get at them? What arguments are relevant to them? And what kind of language do we want to use for each audience – the general public versus elite business groups, organized labor versus people in the financial markets? And then we have different ways of communicating with politicians as one audience, the analysts in the [financial] markets as another, and so on. We now have a Communications Department that helps with all this. So what we're doing these days is trying to be much more strategic: how to use communications, how to be effective. (Executive 4)

Another deputy governor echoes this rhetorical concern, again pointing to the role of the Communications Department:

If you want to communicate with someone, you have to know where they're coming from, what they're looking for, what's important for them? What are our common interests and how can we maximize the value of the relationship for both sides? And our Communications Department helps us with this. (Executive 3)

According to the chief of the Communications Department, with the advent of the Communications Strategy:

There's now generally a better sense [in the Bank] of relating to the specific audience, recognizing that there is one, indeed that there are many of them. And a sense of recognizing that to be accountable, you have to be able to explain what you're doing in a way that makes sense to a lot of different groups, and so you need different kinds of arguments and language, to approach different audiences in different ways.

This type of genre knowledge also extends to a shared sense of specific rhetorical tactics for communicating with a given audience. The Governor's senior assistant, an economist who works with the Governor to develop speeches and other texts, provides an illustration of this rhetorical approach:

We're trying to tailor our messages better to our different audiences. For instance, one audience may lend itself to more technical issues than another audience. For example, the Governor recently gave a talk at the Fraser Institute [a conservative economic think-tank] in Vancouver, and we thought it would be a good time to talk about productivity issues in the economy. Or with a speech in one of the regions, say: depending on the location, we always try to have something on the regional economy, and try to mention what most matters to them at present. (Staff Economist 8)

She adds an interesting side-note on the complexities that the use of new communication technologies can entail in this effort to produce audience-specific discourse:

> *Of course, it's tricky with these speeches, though. Regardless of the audience, we try to use simple language, because you can't get away from the fact that you're preparing the speech not only for that particular audience – speeches get broader distribution and coverage than they used to, now that we put them on our website as well. So you have to have a product that most people can understand.*

Another such rhetorical tactic involves monitoring media sources that a particular audience can be expected to follow, in order to anticipate views about monetary policy that this audience might pick up through the media. For example, as the chief of the Communications Department explains:

> *We follow the news on the Report on Business cable channel, which has more extensive coverage of the Bank. One part of trying to learn what particular audiences think of the state of economy, and monetary policy, and so on, is to monitor sources of information they're exposed to.*

The Governor describes a similar tactic:

> *My colleagues on the Governing Council and I feel the need to read everything we can find that's written about the Bank in the press, because that's where the public picks up a lot of its ideas. For example, whenever I go out to give speech, there's always a press conference afterwards, and I know that the questions I'm going to get often come up because of what people have been reading in the newspapers about the Bank. So to be prepared, I need to know what's being said in newspapers.*

The four types of genre knowledge described above are clearly essential to the functioning of the Communication Strategy's sub-set of genres. This is not to say, however, that *all* the members of the community-of-practice possess *all* this genre knowledge; rather, it is distributed in a differentiated pattern within the community-of-practice according to the organizational roles and experience of individual members. And as well, while a certain amount of the genre knowledge is explicit, it would appear that much more of it operates on a tacit level.

The relationship to organizational change

As sages through history have repeatedly told us, the world – in both its material and socially-constructed dimensions – is constantly changing. This truth – and this does seem to be the appropriate word in this instance – points to another significant feature of the genres associated with the activity of the Communications Strategy: their relationship with processes of organizational change. As we can see in the shift in the Bank of Canada's external communications practices over the decade since the initial implementation of the Communications Strategy, changes in work activity, discourse genres, and technology appear to occur dialectically, in complex patterns of causality. One way of thinking about this causality is to call on the three theoretical models of organizational change described earlier: *planned change, technological imperative*, and *situated change* (Orlikowski, 2001).

In the evolution of the Communications Strategy' sub-set of genres, we can see certain evidence for the causal influences of planned change and technological determinism. For example, as an instance of planned change, Gordon Thiessen, Governor of the Bank from 1994 to 2001, appears to have been the prime mover in a rationally conceived and implemented change in the way the Bank communicates with other social groups in Canada's public-policy realm. According to one of the deputy governors:

> *Gordon Thiessen was really the driving force behind all of this – from his very first speech as Governor in 1994, when he emphasized communication and accountability. And there were other speeches as well, and two of the Governor's lectures – for example the Gibson Lecture that the Governor gave in 1998 has a long section on transparency and accountability, and how this improves the efficacy of monetary policy. He's been really determined about it over his time as Governor. Indeed, during Gordon's tenure innovations have been taken every year practically, in one way or another, to try to strength and improve our effectiveness on the communications side.* (Executive 4)

But this gives rise to the question of why the Governor, immediately upon first taking office in 1994, decided on this dramatically innovative line of action. The deputy governor quoted above provides one answer: '*If we put things in an historical context, you've had a growing trend within society for more information and for wanting public institutions to be accountable.*' And consequently, as another deputy governor says, '*There's been a convergence among central banks around the world towards greater clarity, transparency, openness*' (Executive 4). However, having myself been an employee at the Bank during the transition in 1994 from the tenure of the former Governor to that of Gordon Thiessen, I would add another detail to this historical perspective. The preceding Governor had received much public criticism for the Bank's high-interest rate policy of the early 1990s, a situation not at all mitigated by the perception of the media and some members of the Canadian Parliament that he could at times be somewhat brusque in his interactions with journalists and Parliamentarians. Further, this criticism of the Bank's policies and the public perceptions of the former Governor's communicative style were accompanied by calls from some quarters to radically restructure the Bank to better represent the different regions of the county and break down the central-Canada, Ottawa-centric world-view seen by many in the country as insulating the Bank from the local economic concerns of the different regions of the county. In any event, while we appear to have reasonably good evidence for the existence of planned change on the part of Governor Thiessen, his agency in regard to the activity and genres of the Communications Strategy was clearly a response to a number of historical trends and events, both national and global, in the political and economic environment in which the Bank operates.

At the same time, though, other vectors of change also appear to have been at play during the period since the initial implementation of the Communications Strategy. On one level, it would appear that the emergence of new digital information/communication technologies such as the Internet and the Intranet has prompted important changes in the Bank's discourse genres. And while it is difficult to gauge the degree to which these changes are indeed a manifestation of technological determinism, in the sense of technology, as a broad and inevitable social force, superseding human agency, it remains that there has been a clear correlation between the availability of new technologies and the evolution of the Bank's genres. (Parenthetically, though, we must remember that the correlation of events and causality between them are not the same thing. As a deputy governor puts it:

> *You know, if you think about it, you always see fireman at fires. And generally, the bigger the fire is, the more firemen you'll see there. So there's a definite correlation between fires and fireman. But does that mean you can say that the fireman themselves are setting the fires, that they are the cause of the fires?* (Executive 5)

One of the Bank's English-language editors tells an interesting counter-story, however, about technological determinism:

> *As you know, the [members of the Governing Council] and others throughout the Bank rely on the daily clippings package prepared in the Library. Well, last year the Library tried to eliminate the service. They said, 'Well with the Internet, people can go on it themselves and find the*

material.' And there was a huge reaction; in fact, all hell broke loose. You had everyone from [the Governing Council] down saying, 'Yes, you could find the stories yourself, if you had eight hours a day to do it.' But nobody has time to go on the Internet looking for that stuff. And so that proposal died very quickly.

Another counter-example of technological determinism concerns the continued wide circulation in the Bank of hard-copy drafts of work-in-progress, annotated with reviewers' handwritten notes and comments, and the hardcopy versions of internal and external reports that Bank staff expect to receive and continue to read. Why is the intensive document cycling that goes on in the Bank generally not done electronically rather than on paper? And why do Bank staff not employ laptop computers or electronic readers for reading reports, rather than continuing to rely on hard copies. One could cite tradition and inertia as a reason, but a much more important factor, I think, is ease of portability – people in the Bank carry their work with them, on the bus, on the train, on the plane, everywhere they go, and in such locations a paper text is more practical to work with than an electronic text on a laptop computer or an electronic reader, particularly if the reader wishes to annotate the text. (Brown & Duguid, 2000, and Sellen & Harper, 2002, both provide compelling arguments to account for the continued, and indeed expanding, use of paper documents in a digital world.)

Finally, the concept of *situated change* appears to account for a great deal in the evolution of the activity of the Communications Strategy and its genre sub-set. The chief of the Communications Department provides an example of this causal factor:

With the development of the Bank's website, there wasn't any bureaucratic control structure to get it going. If that had been the case, we'd probably still be debating what should be on the site. It just kind of happened. Some people who were interested in it looked around and saw what other people out there in other organizations were doing, talked to people in the Bank who had material that could go up on the Web, and it's evolved from there.

This quotation reflects a subtle but important variation on Orlikowski's (2001) notion that change occurs as individuals respond, in ad hoc ways, to new developments in their work-world. While she sees organizational change as 'grounded in the ongoing practices of [individual] organizational actors' (p. 226), the data I gathered in the Bank suggest a more communal version of situated change, one in which the community-of-practitioners acts collectively to improve the rhetorical effectiveness of the genres associated with the Communications Strategy. A deputy governor provides a sense of this collective effort:

We try to keep abreast of outside commentaries on monetary policy – from the media, from other economists, and so on. It's a question of gauging whether our messages are getting through. Are we explaining things properly? It's about getting feedback – we're trying to communicate, and communication is always a two-way street. And when you send out a message, was it understood the way you meant it to be, or was it understood differently? And if it's not understood the way you intended, then you have to gauge why this was. Is it because people have different opinions about the state of the economy? Or is it because we missed something in our communication – that our message simply didn't register with people or that we were too opaque? You want to get a sense of this and adjust accordingly. The Communications Department has a group that tries to help us see whether we've been effective in conveying our messages and how we can improve. (Executive 3)

As the deputy governor suggests, the Bank's Communications Department is responsible for guiding the ongoing communal effort to increase the effectiveness of the genres used to communicate with outside groups. The senior assistant to the Governor, who is a member of the Communications Department, explains:

One of the things that the Department does is try to think about how the Bank can better orchestrate its external communications in order to accomplish what it wants to do with all its messages on monetary policy. We look at strategies for how we can get better at conveying our messages more clearly in the future. We're always asking, 'For the various means of communications, and our different audiences, what are the most appropriate ways of delivering those messages?' And then this also involves passing on suggestions to the Governing Council about the Bank's communications, including how to best match the messages to their audiences. (Staff Economist 8)

The discussion here touches on the concept of organizational learning, a theme that will be developed further later in the chapter.

Having examined two key features of the sub-set of genres embedded in the Communications Strategy – the genre knowledge displayed by genre users and the genres' relationship to processes of organizational change – in the next section of the chapter I turn to the role that the genres play in the activity of the Communications Strategy. In this account I again include numerous excerpts from interviews in order to produce a 'thick description' that conveys a sense of how the participants themselves experience and construct theories about their work-world.

The role of genres in the Communications Strategy

Functioning as a culturally-constructed tool in a local sphere of goal-directed professional activity, the sub-set of genres associated with the Bank of Canada's Communications Strategy is a multi-faceted, socio-rhetorical medium for accomplishing complex intellectual work within an organizational community-of-practice – a discursive infrastructure, as I have referred to it earlier. The role that the genres play in the Communications Strategy's comprises three primary functions. First, operating through an organizationally-defined division of cognitive labour, the genres serve as a site for co-coordinating the intellectual and discursive efforts of a large number of individuals (just as we saw occurring in the Projection Exercise in Chapter Three). Second, the genres generate, shape, and communicate a particular organizational brand of 'public information' (Bazerman, 2001) – the 'official' discourse, written and spoken, that constitutes the Bank of Canada's public position on its monetary policy. And finally, the genres act as a locus for organizational learning – specifically, two kinds of learning: first, learning that occurs by attending to the views of outside groups regarding issues essential to the Bank's mandate of directing monetary policy – most notably the issues of how the Canadian economy functions and how monetary policy interacts with the economy; and second, the development of rhetorical knowledge about the effective use of the genres themselves.

Coordinating intellectual work

Linked to the organizationally-defined division of intellectual labour inherent in the activity of the Communication Strategy, the genres serve to co-coordinate the efforts of numerous individuals performing a range of professional roles. Senior executives, staff economists, regional representatives, corporate communications specialists, editors, a speech-facilitator, library personnel, and others collaborate as members of a community-of-practice and genre users to accomplish the work of orchestrating the Bank's communicative interactions with other players in Canada's public-policy arena.

To gain a sense of how the genres associated with the Communications Strategy perform this function, we will look at the sequence of discursive events involved in the production, public release, and promotion of the Bank's *Monetary Policy Report*, its '*highest-profile communications vehicle*' (to quote a deputy governor). A graphic representation of this sequence of discursive events is provided in Diagram 6.

I will describe the sequence of discursive events associated with the *MPR* in a degree of detail that will provide a context for the accounts of two other primary functions of the genres that follow in this section. In this description, we will see a complex pattern of collaborative intellectual and rhetorical work, configured according to the participants' organizational roles, with all of this effort oriented towards accomplishing the two larger goals of the Communications Strategy discussed earlier: establishing public understanding of and support for the Bank's monetary policy and contributing to the effectiveness of the policy by reducing public uncertainly about the Bank's thinking, goals, and intentions. We will also see how oral and written genres are used interactively and, at the same time, how these genres are mediated by a range of digital technologies and built environments. While temporally sequenced, the sequence of discursive events linked to the *MPR* is also cyclical and frequently recursive; however, in order to represent it in narrative form, as I wish to do here, we need to cut into the cycle at some specific point, and so we will begin with the preparation of the *Monetary Policy Report*, a twice-yearly occurrence.

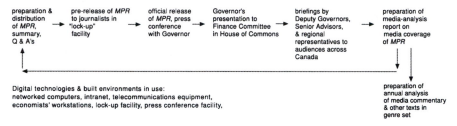

Diagram 6: The sequence of discursive events associated with the genre of the Monetary Policy Report

Within the Bank, the *MPR* is considered the Communications Strategy's most important genre – the organization's foremost discursive vehicle for communication, transparency, and accountability. The *MPR* reminds readers of the Bank's longer-term monetary-policy strategy of guiding the Canadian economy over time towards specific inflation-control targets, outlines the Bank's view of current conditions in the economy, describes the organization's recent monetary policy actions and their impact, looks ahead to what the Bank believes the future holds for the economy, and sometimes hints at the future course of monetary policy. (Readers may wish to refer back to excerpts from the April 2004 *Monetary Policy Report* included in Chapter Three, or to the *Summary of the April 2005 Monetary Policy Report* in Appendix I.) A deputy governor describes the organization of the text:

> *The MPR has three parts to it. One part looks back over what the economy has done over the last six months. Then there's a second part on financial markets, where we also talk about why we've adjusted interest rates, if we indeed have adjusted them. Those two parts are what I think of as our statement of accountability – what's happened to inflation relative to our inflation-control targets, and what we've done to achieve those targets. Then there's a third part which is the outlook – where we see things going,*

looking ahead over the next six to twelve months or so. (Executive 4)

For the Bank, the *MPR* functions as a stable rhetorical medium for enacting the organization's commitment to transparency and accountability, a commitment it views as central to the Communications Strategy.

The production of the *Monetary Policy Report* occurs at the intersection of two sub-systems of activity: one sub-system associated with the work of economic analysis and policy-making and the other with the Communications Strategy. The Bank staff involved in preparing the *MPR* draw on locally-constructed knowledge produced through the activity of data-gathering, economic analysis, and policy-making and transform this knowledge into a unified, consistent discourse of 'public information' (Bazerman, 2001) intended for outside audiences within the different social groups mentioned earlier. The movement from dynamic disciplinary knowledge to comparatively static public information will be described in some detail later in this section.

The preparation of the *MPR* is highly collaborative, involving more than a score of Bank personnel: staff economists in three different departments, the members of the Governing Council, English- and French-language editors, translators (who translate English text into French), as well as graphics and production specialists. As the collaborative production of the *MPR* proceeds, it exhibits a highly-conventionalized pattern of professional roles, work practices, and social interactions. Viewed through the lens of activity theory, the *MPR* is a culturally-constructed tool used to distribute cognition and organize intellectual work according to an organizationally-defined division of labour. The following description of the collaborative process underlying the production of the *MPR* provides a sense of its intricate complexity.

Here is how a deputy governor describes the production of the *Monetary Policy Report*, as he experiences it:

The Research Department and [the Department of] Monetary and Financial Analysis take the lead in preparing the first draft, with input from [the] International [Department] – with all this work being coordinated by the chief of [the] Research [Department]. Before the drafting even starts, though, we [i.e., the speaker and two other deputy governors] sit down with the writers from the departments to identify broad themes. Then they do a first draft and send it on to me and [the two other deputy governors]. We then meet with the authors to talk about our response at a very high level – we give them our take on the broad messages and the way things fit together. And then they generally go back and produce a revised draft. From there, we have a week-by-week schedule that lasts about four weeks, with each new draft going to the full Governing Council. Each time, the Governing Council will have a discussion of the draft, and people's comments [annotated by hand on individual copies] are collected and sent

back to the authors. So it's all very much an iterative process. And then it
gets to the point where someone in the Governing Council – it's been me
in the past – takes it over and works on the sensitive parts towards the end
of the report where we talk about conclusions and how to characterize the
policy thinking behind the analysis. And then the [English-language] editors
in [the] Communications [Department] get drawn into the process, at a
stage about three weeks from publication, and we work together on drafts
that we cycle through the Governing Council for comments. At the same
time as we're working together on this, the editors are also working with
the people in production and layout, getting it all ready for the printers.
And then of course there's also the translation process [to produce a French
version of the text] and the editing in French. (Executive 4)

As the deputy governor explains, towards the end of the production of the
Monetary Policy Report, a separate summary of the report is also prepared
through its own document-cycling process:

At the same time as the report itself is being written, the editors are also
working with people in the Communications Department along with me
and [a Senior Advisor] on creating a separate summary of the MPR, four
pages or so. And there will usually be several iterations between us before
the summary goes to the Governing Council for review. This summary is a
relatively new initiative for us.

One of the two English-language editors, in another interview, picks up the narrative here at the point when the editors typically get involved in the production
process, which she describes as '*a team effort, to say the least!*':

Well it's angst, heavy-duty angst. Once the report comes to us, it's [a deputy
governor acting for the Governing Council] and us and the Governing
Council. We set up a very stringent schedule, a three-week schedule: we get
the draft from [the deputy governor] we have a day to edit; we return it to
him, it gets revised, goes to the Governing Council; they have two days to
look at it, it comes back to him; he does those revisions, gets it back to us;
we have a day, they have three days – it goes like this, over a three-week
cycle. We have a three-week cycle of practically editing in the bathtub, and
it is heavy, heavy, heavy.

The editor goes on to describe the nature of the editors' particular organizational
role in working on the various iterations of the report:

Our main job is to try to make the report approachable, understandable,
readable, as much as is humanly possible. We do a lot of rewriting. The
first couple of drafts, I'd say we virtually rewrite it 75%. Sometimes it's
restructuring, sometimes it's rewording. The whole idea is to make it

understandable to people outside the Bank: 'Why are we doing what we're
doing? – What's happened in the economy? What did that tell us? Why are
we doing what we've done? And what's the outlook from here?' *The average
business person out there, certainly, has to be able to understand it.*

As this account reveals, the production of the *Monetary Policy Report* is highly
conventionalized, with the benefit to the organization of reliability and effi-
ciency. As one of the English-language editors comments, '*The whole thing
has become a pretty structured, cohesive process, twice a year. Now they know
what to expect, and we know what to expect, and it works very well.*' However,
this was not always the case. According to the editor, when the *MPR* was first
produced in 1995, the composing process was much more *ad hoc*, and it took
several years for the current structured process to emerge and stabilize.

At the same time as the *Monetary Policy Report* and its summary are being
prepared, a matching set of questions-and-answers material (*Q & A's*, in the
Bank vernacular) is also being produced. These *Q & A's* are intended for the
use of Bank staff who will be responding to questions from members of the
media and other audiences about the *MPR*, including, typically, the Governor,
the deputy governors, one or two senior staff economists, and the regional
representatives. The chief of the Communications Department describes the
collaborative process of constructing the *Q & A's*, an account that once again,
when viewed through the lens of activity theory, illustrates the distributed
cognition and complex division of labour involved:

*The Communications Department coordinates the preparation of the Q &
A's package. Typically in coming up with the questions, we have a number
of sources. One involves monitoring the media for recent commentaries on
monetary policy, because we know this commentary is likely to show up in
the questions the journalists ask. As well, we pick up on questions in letters
sent to the Governor or in e-mail messages sent to the Bank through our
Website. And we also usually get some questions from the staff economists.
But we (i.e., staff in the Communications Department) also put on our
pretend media hats and try to think of slightly off-center questions that
journalists could pose, questions that the economists might not think of. And
then when we have the list of questions defined, there will be some questions
where we wouldn't worry about developing an answer; it's more by way of,
'You could get this question coming at you from this angle.' But then there
are other questions where we do develop answers. Most of these questions
would have the answers prepared by the staff economists, though some [of
the answers] could come directly from a deputy governor – you know, the
members of the Governing Council have talked about them; or the Governor
himself may decide there are a couple of questions in particular where he
wants to develop his own answers and share them with his colleagues and*

get some feedback on them, and then send them to us.

As the chief explains, the *Q & A's* are used to a varying degree, and in different ways, by the Bank staff responsible for responding to questions from journalists and others about the Bank's monetary policy as represented in the *MPR* following its official release: '*People draw on them as they will, or not, depending on how experienced and comfortable they are in dealing with the media and other audiences.*'

While individual *Q & A's* packages are created for specific communication events, such as the release of the *Monetary Policy Report, The Bank of Canada Review,* or a speech by the Governor, they are cumulatively integrated over time into a broad, comprehensive set of *Q & A's*. This text, organized by topic and constantly updated and revised, is available on the Bank's Intranet as an IText (Geisler, 2004; Geisler et al., 2001) for shared use within the organization by those preparing for communicative exchanges with external audiences. As collaboratively-produced texts serving as an important rhetorical resource for a variety of different people in the Bank, the *Q & A's* – both the individual packages and larger text – are an excellent example of distributed cognition in action (or in activity, perhaps we should say).

When the final versions of the *Monetary Policy Report*, the summary, and the *Q & A's* have been completed – usually several days prior to the official release of the *MPR* – they are all posted to the Bank's Intranet so that senior members of the organization in Ottawa as well as the regional representatives across the county can have easy access to them. The material on the Intranet is also accessible to senior members of the Bank staff travelling on business outside the county, as the chief of the Communications Department explains:

> *Say a deputy governor is off in the U.S. on business, and is going to face questions from the media about the MPR – they can dial in and remind themselves of the questions we're anticipating, and the answers to them.*

As a deputy governor puts it, regarding the Intranet, '*With this kind of access, everyone is wired*' (Executive 2).

Next in the sequence of discursive events is the pre-release of the *Monetary Policy Report* to the media in what is known as the 'lock-up facility' (see Photograph 3). Two hours prior to its official public release at a press conference, copies of the document, with an attached summary that opens with a one-page statement of the 'highlights,' is given to journalists from the wire-service agencies and newspapers who are assembled in a specially-equipped room at the Bank. One of the Bank's deputy governors describes the event:

> *With the MPR, we now do a 'lock-up.' We have a facility where the journalists come in a couple of hours before the release of the report, and*

it's all equipped for them to prepare their stories. Then they're given the report. And they also have the attached summary, which begins with the highlights page – boom, boom, boom, boom, boom – these are the five key messages. And part way through, several of the deputy governors come into the lock-up to make a 5- or 10-minute presentation on the key messages, and are then available for not-for-attribution discussion. And it's usually a pretty good exchange (see photograph 4). And then finally, at the official release time, we pull a switch and all the stories go out at the same time, so it's a level playing field for the different news people. (Executive 4)

Photograph 3: Journalists at work in the 'lock-up facility' (Photo: Gord Carter / Bank of Canada

Photograph 4: Deputy governors meeting with journalists in the 'lock-up facility' (Photo: Gord Carter / Bank of Canada)

A particularly interesting aspect of the 'lock-up' as an innovation for the Bank is its staff's perception of the event as a temporal and architectural solution to a serious rhetorical problem. Previously, journalists would not see the *MPR* until its official release, at a press conference with the Governor. From the Bank's perspective, this situation tended to impose a pattern of hasty and distorted reading and subsequent flawed reporting by the journalists – a pattern the Bank felt did not serve its purposes for the *MPR*. The deputy governor quoted above describes what this scene used to look like:

> '*Literally, in the past, when the MPR was released, you'd see [the journalists] reading the report and writing their stories at the same time, because the competition is so intense that the timeliness of getting those headlines out there quickly was crucial to them.*'

The Governor of the Bank explains how this affected the journalists' reading of the *MPR* and their subsequent production of news stories about it:

> *We found ourselves in a situation where the fierce competition among the wire-services and newspapers to get their headlines out first meant that we often had somewhat garbled and sometimes even wrong messages coming out because they didn't have enough time to really read the report.*

According to the Governor, the implementation of the 'lock-up facility,' an innovation for the Bank proposed by the chief of the Communications Department, '*has improved things dramatically*; [*the journalists*] *have got all the time in the world to read the report, absorb the information, and write their stories.*' The deputy governor adds:

> *You don't want the journalists' stories to misrepresent what it is we're trying to get across in the MPR. With the 'lock-up,' the journalists are given time to digest the information and understand what's there before they write their stories on it. The summary, with the key-messages page, is very important here as well, in that it focuses people on the essential points.*

And on a more general note, he comments, '*You're always trying to manage the communications process effectively, trying to minimize misinterpretation by the media. And there's a lot of infrastructure that goes with that.*' Here we see an illustration of the mediating influence on genre users of a built environment and its digital technologies, in this case a mediating influence that has been intentionally designed to have a preconceived effect on readers. The Bank has used the 'lock-up facility' as well as a particular genre feature, the summary and 'key-messages' page attached to the *MPR*, in an attempt – and a successful attempt from its perspective – to influence how a key audience approaches and reads the document, builds an understanding of its contents, and produces a subsequent written commentary. In a sense, borrowing (and slightly stretching) a term from Bakhtin (1981), one might say that in the 'lock-up' event, with its temporal and spatial 'infrastructure,' the Bank has created a chronotope intended to shape the journalists' behaviour as readers and writers, forcing a moment (or in this case, two hours) of kairos upon them.

Immediately after the 'lock-up' comes the official release of the *Monetary Policy Report* at a press conference in another area of the Bank where the Governor meets with journalists, the event being recorded for television and radio. At the same time, the *MPR*, along with the summary, is posted to the Bank's official website. Later that same day, the Governor visits the House of Commons in the Canadian Parliament – a ten-minute walk from the Bank – to make a presentation before the Finance Committee on the *MPR*. According to a deputy governor, '*When the Governor goes to the House [of Commons], he's trying to get across the key messages we're trying to communicate, so as to avoid misinterpretation*' (Executive 3). Similarly, in the days that follow the release of the *MPR*, other senior people – usually three of the deputy governors – go to Toronto and Montreal to brief different 'Bank-watchers': analysts in the financial markets who are paid to follow the central bank and its monetary policy closely and advise their clients accordingly and financial journalists who write about monetary policy. In addition, several senior Bank economists travel to meetings of economists' associations in major centers across Canada to give presentations on the *MPR*, while the regional representatives meet with journalists and others in their respective parts of the country. (For all these communicative interactions with outside audiences, the *Q & A's* material is available, as an IText on the Bank's Intranet, to serve as a communal rhetorical resource.) As a deputy governor comments, with all this follow-up activity to the *MPR*, '*there's a rather concerted effort to be pro-active and get out to meet with people to try to give them a clear sense of what our current thinking is and the analysis behind the MPR*' (Executive 4).

In the weeks following the release of the *Monetary Policy Report*, the Bank's Communications Department produces a document known as the 'media-analysis report' on the coverage that the *MPR* receives in the Canadian media. According to the Governor,

> *In monitoring the media after an MPR, to see how well monetary policy is being understood, there are three things we're interested in: 'Are the messages being picked up out there, in the various commentaries? Is what's being picked up understood? And what's the reaction?'*

This is how the chief of the Communications Department describes the process of preparing the media-analysis report:

*Within about two weeks of an important communications event, we produce
a report of four or five pages. It includes a summary of the media coverage
on the MPR, and some analysis of it – how much coverage there was, in
which news-services and newspapers, how much prominence they gave it,
whether or not our key messages were adequately represented, what the
criticisms were, and any other kinds of significant comments journalists
might have brought to it. That's for the print media and stories pulled off the
Internet from news sites. And then we also have a communications firm that
monitors the broadcast media for us, TV and radio, following the release
of the MPR. They monitor the hundreds of news items that appear on radio
stations and TV stations, and prepare short summaries for us; and then,
for any particularly interesting items, we can also order the full transcripts
from them. And we include a summary and analysis of this material in our
own final report as well. When it's done, the final report is shared with quite
a large number of senior people through our internal website (i.e., Intranet).*

As we can see, the collaborative effort that occurs during the production, release,
and promotion of the *Monetary Policy Report* is extremely complex, and the
cluster of genres involved provides an important measure of achieved stability
to the work. Similar sequences of discursive events can be viewed in the production, release, and promotion of other 'primary communication vehicles' in the
genre sub-set associated with the Communications Strategy, such as speeches
by the Governor, the *Update to the Monetary Policy Report*, the *Bank of Canada
Annual Report*, and *The Bank of Canada Review*, each with its own complex
pattern of distributed cognitive and rhetorical action, configured according to
the participants' organizationally-defined professional roles.

Producing and communicating public information

A second primary function of the sub-set of genres associated with the
Communications Strategy is to generate, shape, and communicate a distinctive
organizational brand of 'public information' – the 'official' discourse, in both
written and spoken forms, that represents the Bank of Canada's public position on the economy and monetary policy. This discourse conveys the Bank's
views on the present and expected future state of the Canadian economy and,
consequently, the appropriate monetary policy for the country, while at the
same time reflecting the organization's awareness of outside commentaries on
its monetary-policy actions and mounting responses to these commentaries.

When we look at the Bank's economic knowledge-building and policy-
making, on the one hand, and its Communication Strategy, on the other, as
overlapping sub-spheres of activity, we see that their respective genre sub-sets

are motivated by very different aims. The activity of economic knowledge-building and policy-making – gathering and analyzing statistical data and other information and then using the resulting analysis in making decisions on monetary policy – is intended, through its sub-set of genres, to foster and manage disparate views and lively debate. Here, disciplinary knowledge in the form of economic analysis is generated, negotiated, debated, provisionally stabilized, and then used as a communal resource for policy-making and as an stimulus for further knowledge-building. In Chapter Two we saw a deputy governor referring to the Bank as an '*extremely disputatious place, a very tough shop, intellectually. People like to probe and critique ideas before they accept them*' (Executive 2). (Here, though, we need to acknowledge that a professional organization such as the Bank cannot encourage a fresh debate each and every day about its foundational goals or concepts or practices – such as the pivotal monetary-policy policy goal of inflation-control, the organizational paradigm of the Canadian economy, or the use of the Quarterly Projection Model. Some things have to be accepted as the truth-for-now or as best practices, or else the organization would never be able to accomplish its work of directing monetary policy.) The larger aim of this activity is to produce provisionally-stabilized knowledge – created through the process of sound analysis, rigorous debate, and negotiated consensus – to inform monetary-policy decisions and actions.

The activity and genres of the Communications Strategy, on the other hand, are designed for some something quite different. In contrast to the way in which the work of knowledge-building and policy-making relies on diverse perspectives and lively debate, with provisional disciplinary knowledge emerging as the outcome, the Communications Strategy is intended to build a consistent, unified public position on the state of the Canadian economy and the appropriate monetary policy for the country – a technocratically-produced and ideologically-inflected discursive commodity for external distribution. In the production of this public information, the genres associated with the Communications Strategy are intended to ensure the consistent presentation of the primary messages that the Bank wishes to get across in its communicative interactions with other social groups in Canada's public-policy realm. (It stands to reason that the Bank could not have the Governor making a statement about monetary policy in Montreal in the morning and a deputy governor saying something contradictory about policy in Vancouver in the afternoon – the financial markets would react frenetically and the Bank's credibility and effectiveness would be seriously impaired.) In its monovocality, the public information created and communicated by the Bank appears very much akin to Bakhtin's centripetal or 'official' discourse.

What we see here, then, is dynamic, ever-evolving disciplinary knowledge produced through one sub-system of activity with its sub-set of genres being transformed into another type of discourse through a different sub-system of activity and its genres. In contrast to the production of disciplinary knowledge occurring through the analysis of data and the thrust-and-parry of discursive exchanges among professional colleagues, we see a movement in another direction – the commodification of disciplinary knowledge into the monovocal and relatively inert discourse of public information.

A case in point is the *Q & A's* package – pre-prepared questions-and-answers material – that is created along with the *Monetary Policy Report* for use by Bank staff in responding to queries from journalists and other audiences about the Bank's monetary policy as articulated in the *MPR*. As a deputy governor puts it, '*The Q & A's are intended to provide the appropriate answers to certain lines of questioning*' (Executive 4). The intention is to make certain that the public messages communicated by different members of the organization are consistent on a range of concerns related to monetary policy. The distinction here, according to the deputy governor, is '*between issues that are still being explored and debated in the research*,' where diverse and often opposed perspectives are still in play within the activity of the Monetary-policy process, and '*the Bank's formal views on things, where you have to have a consistency of message*' – the 'official' discourse and unified public position produced through the activity and genres of the Communications Strategy.

While knowledge created through the activity of economic analysis and policy-making is continuously being transformed into public information through the activity of the Communications Strategy, at times information also moves in the opposite direction – from the activity of the Communications Strategy to that of economic analysis, where it is absorbed into processes of knowledge-building and policy-making. An example of this can be seen when information about the views of outside groups such as business associations, the financial markets, governments, and organized labour is fed back to the Bank's head office in Ottawa by regional representatives in different parts of the country, as part of the Projection Exercise. As described in Chapter Three, during this highly-collaborative month-long operation a team of staff economists uses the Quarterly Projection Model to consolidate and interpret information about different sectors of the Canadian and then inscribes the resulting economic analysis and monetary-policy recommendations in a document known as the *White Book*, addressed to the Bank's Governing Council. Below, a deputy governor describes how information on the views of outside groups is integrated into the Projection Exercise, referring to a document known in the Bank as the *Green Book*, one of the genres associated with the work of knowledge-building and policy-making:

> *The regional representatives do a lot of work meeting with various*
> *businesses, associations, government, universities – to interact and*

exchange views. The reps gather the views of people in the regions about their predictions of economic growth, inflation, and so on. And then they feed back this information to us in a formal way [as opposed to the more informal, ongoing flow of information communicated to the Bank's Research Department through weekly conference calls], four times a year, during the Projection Exercise. So that in addition to the staff's work in putting together the White Book, there's also a process where we bring in the reps from the regions to tell us what people out there appear to be thinking about, and the reps work with the Research Department to quantify this information – they quantify what they call 'the balance of opinion' on different issues – for example, on what people think sales volumes are going to be over the next twelve months, or the trend in inflation, say. The reps will give us [i.e., the Governor and his senior colleagues] a presentation on this, and they'll also produce a document we call the Green Book. The reps' job in all of this is to tell us what they think business people and others out there across the county are thinking, and it's very useful information. (Executive 3)

(Beginning in 2004, a version of this text has been published outside the Bank as the *Business Outlook Survey.*)

This duality of discourse types employed within the Bank – the discourse of knowledge-building and policy-making on the one hand, and that of media-oriented 'public information' and external communications on the other – can be viewed as a particular kind of interdiscursivity (Fairclough, 1992; Chouliaraki & Fairclough, 1999; Candlin & Maley, 1999), the occurrence within a text of language and conventions reflecting different genres, discourses, and styles. In this case, we see two distinctly different kinds of discourse and knowledge continuously feeding into and reflecting one another within the activity of the monetary-policy process.

Acting as a site for organizational learning

A third primary function of the genre sub-set associated with the Communications Strategy is to act as a locus for organizational learning. In the following pages we will examine two kinds of organizational learning: first, the acquisition of economic knowledge relevant to the Bank's mandate for directing monetary policy – most notably, knowledge of how the Canadian economy functions and how monetary policy interacts with the economy; and second, the development of genre knowledge – specifically, rhetorical knowledge about the nature of the different audiences for the genres associated with the Communications Strategy and about audience-specific tactics for using these genres effectively. We will be looking at what these two types of learning entail and, in the case of genre knowledge, at how the learning occurs.

In its ongoing effort to learn more about how the Canadian economy functions and how monetary policy acts upon the economy, the Bank is constantly monitoring published research produced by university economists and economists in private-sector financial institutions and 'think-tanks' for relevant empirical findings, theories, economic models, and forecasting methods. A deputy governor talks of this relationship:

> *With the academic literature, it's not just a question of arguing with it; it's important to us in that it provides a window onto the world, an economic window. We have our own research, of course, and research from other central banks, but the academic window is very important too. It's a shared enterprise, learning more about the economy.* (Executive 4)

He goes on to discuss the specific example of 'inflation targeting,' that is, central banks' use of specific inflation-control targets as the basis for directing monetary policy:

> *When the Bank started [using inflation-control targets as the centerpiece of monetary policy] in the early '90s we had nothing to go on except the New Zealand experience. It was only when the academic literature came out three or four years later that we understood much better – it gave us a perspective – that what we did intuitively was absolutely the right thing to do. Now there's been an explosion of literature on this, and it's been very helpful to us in understanding why what we did in 1991 was absolutely the right thing to do.*

The deputy governor elaborates on the Bank's relationship with academic economists, first describing a conference the organization had recently hosted and then mentioning a strategy for encouraging academic research on topics of particular concern to the central bank:

> *We just had another conference, leading up to the next decision-point [on setting out, in collaboration with the Federal Government, a five-year path of inflation-control targets]. Two issues on our minds as we try to reach a decision are downward nominal wage rigidity and the zero interest-rate bounds. And we had a number of papers on both these issues, some by our own people and others were invited papers from academics. One of the advantages of commissioning outside research by academics, two advantages really, is that it gets some interesting work done for us, and more broadly, it may also encourage Canadian academics to do research in areas we're interested in, areas relevant to monetary policy.*

Similarly, the Bank is continuously engaged in trying to learn from its exchanges with people working in the financial markets about the 'transmission mechanism' for monetary policy – the process through which monetary policy acts upon the economy through the financial markets. As the chief of the Communications Departments explains:

> *On the transmission side [i.e., the implementation of monetary policy],*
> *the Bank is always willing to be persuaded that some of our operational*
> *assumptions could perhaps be improved by more information from the*
> *markets – in terms of the 'real-world' risks that accompany one course*
> *of action versus another. For the Bank, monetary policy acts through*
> *the markets, and so anticipating how the markets will respond to a given*
> *monetary policy action, or lack of action, is very much at the heart of*
> *day-to-day policy management. The Bank is always trying to learn more*
> *about how the financial markets react, and there are people working in the*
> *markets who are knowledgeable about this.*

Another deputy governor elaborates on the Bank's organizational commitment to this particular object of learning:

> *And a good deal of our monetary-policy work is about learning more about*
> *how the [Canadian] economy works and how monetary policy is transmitted*
> *to the economy. Each of the links in the transmission mechanism – short-*
> *term interest rates, long-term rates, spending, consumption, wage increases,*
> *and so on – is very uncertain. Now we certainly do have a view here in the*
> *Bank, based on our own research and experience and also the research of*
> *others, but we can't really say that there's a lot of strong empirical evidence*
> *for each element in the chain. And so we're always looking to the views of*
> *people in the [financial] markets to see what we can learn.* (Executive 4).

He goes on, summing up, '*If you see that others have views on the economy that you don't, then you want to learn about that too – they just might be right about things. You definitely can't risk ignoring them.*' What we see articulated here is the conscious intention on the part of an organizational community-of-practice to learn from its communicative interactions with outside groups.

With regard to the second type of organizational learning related to the Communications Strategy's sub-set of genres – the development of rhetorical knowledge about the functioning of the genres themselves – the community-of-practice is continually attempting to learn more about the different audiences for various genres and to devise effective rhetorical tactics for communicating effectively with these audiences. For example, the frequent lunch meetings at which senior members of the Bank host guests from different outside groups are viewed as an opportunity for this kind of learning. Below, the chief of the Communications Department provides us with a sense of this:

There's quite a lunch program for journalists, business people, and other groups – labor, government officials, and so on – who are invited in. It's usually with the Governor, the members of the Governing Council. They're very informal lunches; basically they're just chats – a chance for the Bank to get across some general perspectives on the economy, but especially to listen to what their guests have on their minds. It's quite a good opportunity to hear what people are saying directly. Basically, it's trying to get to know the whole constituency out there a little better.

Another example of the ongoing effort by the community-of-practice to develop rhetorical knowledge about the genre sub-set associated with the activity of the Communications Strategy is the attempt to learn, rhetorically, from the experience of communicating with the media and the financial markets. The chief of the Communications Department provides an illustration of this, describing the production of two yearly internal reports:

At the end of the year we [i.e., the staff in the Communications Department] produce a roll-up report that evaluates our success in actually getting our messages through to the media over the year, identifying the main occasions when we were trying to communicate key messages – and did they actually show up in the media coverage? And there's a parallel effort in [the] Financial Markets [Department] to evaluate the same events from the point of view of the reactions in the markets, a lot of which doesn't appear in the media, but rather in the behavior of the markets, or things that market participants might tell our analysts. The Bank has systematized all this now, and we're doing it on an annual basis as a means of gauging our success in communicating. We put a lot of effort into our communications and we need to know how we're doing with it and learn to do it better.

A deputy governor describes the organizational role of the Communications Department in facilitating this kind of learning, giving the example of the rhetorical knowledge needed to communicate effectively with one particular outside group, the media:

The Communications Department keeps a watch on the media: 'Do our messages get through clearly? What kind of feedback did we get?' And they also advise us on how to send our messages; they advise us on this, and they help us manage the relationship with the media. If you want to communicate with someone, you have to know where they're coming from, what they're looking for, what's important for them, what our common interests are and how we can maximize the value of the relationship for both sides. And certainly, our Communications Department helps with this – they advise us on this, with the media. (Executive 4)

For individual staff economists who aspire to advance to senior levels in the organization, learning to participate competently in the activity of the Communications Strategy is extremely important. As a deputy governor puts it, *'If economists want to get ahead in the Bank, they better be prepared to communicate with the outside world as well as inside'* (Executive 3). Developing this ability means acquiring the rhetorical knowledge needed to participate in a new sub-set of genres. Typically, economists who are at the point in their careers where they are ready to advance in this way have already developed considerable expertise in using the genres embedded in the activity of economic knowledge-building, but now need to learn to function effectively in the activity of the Communications Strategy, with its very different genres. The chief of the Communications Department describes this transition as a process of moving beyond expertise in *'vacuum-packed research and analysis'* to develop competence with a more politically-nuanced discourse. He offers an illustration of what this transition might involve:

> *Let's say a staff economist is out giving a public presentation and gets a question about the Bank's view on the current level of unemployment. The economist could give a technically correct answer and say that unemployment isn't explicitly represented in the Bank's models of the economy at all, and so they can't address that question. Or they could say – and this would be a more intuitive, a more communicative approach – 'Well, yes, of course unemployment is extremely important, but as you know, employment is a natural outgrowth of a successful economy, and price stability [i.e., inflation-control] is essential for that.' It's the instinct to provide an answer that's – small 'p' – more politically acceptable rather than a technically correct one, which could almost be like throwing a grenade into a crowded room because it's not the right approach for that particular audience. It's that transition from the world of vacuum-packed research and analysis to the real world of dialogue and winning respect for the organization, showing competency, increasing credibility.*

This brings us to the question of how this type of rhetorical knowledge is attained. To what degree do individuals acquire the rhetorical knowledge needed to operate in a new sub-set of genres explicitly, through formal instruction or coaching, and to what degree do they acquire it implicitly, through day-to-day participation in professional practice? In addressing a similar question, Jean Lave and Etienne Wenger (1991) point to the significance of the 'situated learning' that occurs continuously, though for the most part tacitly, in communities-of-practice – and that involves all members, veterans as well as newcomers, through their ongoing involvement in organizational activity. Lave and Wenger attribute such learning to two factors: first, the 'situated negotiation and renegotiation of meaning' (p. 51) associated with ordinary everyday social interaction; and second, the dynamic character of organizations themselves, which are constantly reinventing themselves in response to changes in 'activity and the participation of individuals involved in it, their knowledge, and their perspectives' (p. 117).

With Lave and Wenger's claim for the prevalence and force of situated learning as context, we will now look at some homegrown theory posited by the chief of the Communications Department, with regard to the question of whether staff economists being trained for an external communications role acquire their rhetorical knowledge of the relevant genres through formal, explicit training or through more tacit forms of experience. First, he explains the imperative for the Bank's staff economists to develop the rhetorical knowledge required to participate competently in the activity and discourse genres of the Communications Strategy:

> *We're expecting everyone to become better at communicating. Among other things, it's a willingness to listen, to put a human face on what before might have been, in the 'Old Bank,' a more centralized, big-brother-knows-best approach. And this is built right into the performance appraisal system. If people want to rise in the ranks, beyond the point of being a good technician, then they need to see how communications works, and what it is that allows someone to move up the ladder.*

One the one hand, the chief explains, the Bank has taken a formal approach to promoting this kind of genre knowledge:

> *The Bank has had a leadership development program now for a number of years. It's an attempt to become a little more systematic at developing the qualities that will provide the Bank with a good supply of future leaders, and communication is a key part of this. The Communications Department helps in communications training, media training – arranging courses for people in the Bank who are going to be called on to give speeches, presentations.*

A sense of what this type of formal training might involve is provided by a staff economist, the Special Assistant to the Governor, as she describes a course she is planning to take outside the Bank:

> *It's a three-day course. Apparently they'll be talking about media relations, how to deal with Parliamentarians, promoting greater understanding in the public, Internet technology, and how to manage change. And they also have a 'special' at the end: 'transparency versus creative ambiguity' [she laughs] – I'm very intrigued by that; I think we're getting into philosophical questions here.* (Staff Economist 8)

At the same time, though, the chief of the Communications Department has his doubts about the sufficiency of such formal training, as he explains: '*It's impossible to send every new person who might go out and meet the public outside for training. Maybe training can help somewhat, but I think it's really more of an internal communication issue.*' In elaborating on the last point, the chief goes on to convey a personal theory of his that is similar to the conceptualization of situated learning discussed earlier:

> *I think the change here in the Bank has happened through a combination of new organizational procedures and culturally-assimilated values. Yes, there have been formal efforts to provide media training, to teach the tricks of the trade. But there's still another kind of change required. And I think it's something that people have to pick up, through their work, more by osmosis than through a training course that will suddenly turn a person into someone who can go out and communicate effectively to the public. You're not going to do a miracle transformation with someone a year before they get to be a deputy governor. It's got to be building all along. To see that there's your professional inside work and that this is different from what you do when you're communicating outside – I think it's a cultural thing, something that has to be learned implicitly around the Bank, in people's work experiences.*

As the chief points out, however, regardless of how the development of rhetorical knowledge related to the genres of the Communications Strategy occurs, the organization holds definite expectations regarding people's success in achieving this particular kind of learning, with career rewards and other consequences at stake:

> *We're expecting everyone to become better at communicating, in the sense of listening and responding. It's about a willingness to listen to people, putting a human face on what before might have been, in the Old Bank, a more centralized, big-brother-knows-best approach. And all of this is now built right into the performance appraisal system.*

In a final observation, the chief touches on another aspect of situated learning within a community-of-practice, what Jean Lave and Etienne Wenger (1991) refer to as the growth of a 'knowledgeably skilled identity':

> *Where it's really hit home is with people who want to move up in the organization, to become a chief, a senior ddvisor, a deputy governor – they're seeing what's necessary to do that, through watching others and gradually getting involved themselves and taking on the role.*

From this perspective, learning to be effective in using the genres of the Communications Strategy demands that an economist develop a new aspect of his or her social and professional identity, so that *learning to do or act* and *learning to be* are inseparable. (See Smart, 2000, for a discussion of this dimension of situated learning as a factor in developing the ability to participate in a new genre.)

And how would the chief evaluate the Bank's overall success in fostering the kind of rhetorical knowledge that members of the community-of-practice need in order to participate effectively in the activity and genres of the Communications Strategy?

> *I think that now, among the staff generally, there's a better sense of relating to the audience, recognizing that there is one, indeed that there are many of them. And a sense of recognizing that for a public-policy organization to be accountable, you have to be able to explain what you're doing in a way that makes sense to a lot of different groups of people.*

Methodological reflections: issues of validity, reliability, and generalizability

Like all scholarly research, interpretive ethnography faces questions about its validity, reliability, and generalizability. A researcher presenting an ethnographic account needs to address these concerns in ways that are logically persuasive but also consistent with his or her assumptions about the social world and the nature of knowledge (Merriam, 1988, 1998). With regard to validity – that is, the degree to which a study demonstrates what the researcher claims it does – Martyn Hammersley (1992) contends that ethnography should be judged according to its own logic and standards. He claims that conventional 'realist' or 'correspondence' notions of validity are inappropriate for ethnography, since readers cannot evaluate the 'truth' of an ethnographic account, given that, as social actors themselves, they have no independent, objective access to social reality to compare against the account. Instead, Hammersley suggests that readers should assess the validity of an ethnographic account on the basis of two factors: its 'plausibility,' or its consistency with the readers' prior assumptions about the world; and its 'credibility,' as inferred from the circumstances in which the research was conducted and the evidence marshaled in support of the account.

Leaving to my readers' own judgment the issue of how plausible my account of the professional work-world of the Bank's economists appears, I would argue for its credibility on several grounds. First, I would point to the 13 years I spent in the organization working as an in-house writing consultant and trainer, a professional role that gave me access to informants at all levels in the Bank's hierarchy. As John Van Maanen (1988) observes, sound ethnography requires that a researcher develop a context-specific interpretive ability derived from prolonged experience in the setting under study. I would contend that my long-term experience in the Bank as a participant-observer, unusual for a researcher, allowed me to develop a quasi-insider's perspective on the economists' professional world and that this enhances the authenticity of my account. (In Chapter Four we considered the ethnographer's need to balance familiarity and engagement with the work-world of his or her inform-ants with a pronounced degree of critical detachment, and I described my own attempts to achieve such a balance.) As further support for the credibility of the account presented here, I would cite the amount and variety of spoken and documentary data gathered and analyzed in the study (Denzin, 1997; Mishler, 1986), as well as the situated nature of my interpretive process and my regular discussions of emerging concepts and themes with informants (Agar, 1980). In a similar vein, I would point out that the account features the extensive use of quotations from informants, a characteristic seen as strengthening ethnographic texts (Cintron, 1993; LeCompte & Goetz, 1982; Van Maanen, 1988).

Reliability, or the extent to which a study and its findings can be replicated by other researchers, is simply not a relevant issue for interpretive ethnography, given its reliance on the extended personal involvement and situated interpretive process of an individual researcher in an ever-changing social environment (Sanjek, 1990, cited in Beaufort, 1999). The researcher should, however, ensure that his or her role in the site and the theoretical orientation taken are both acknowledged, and that the data-gathering and interpretive procedures are well-described. In the account presented in this book, I have tried to remain accountable on this score.

With regard to the generalizability of the study, we need to consider whether we can, with any certainty and usefulness, generalize aspects of this account of the Bank economists' discourse practices and intellectual collaboration to other professional organizations. Clearly, one must be cautious here: a researcher cannot legitimately move from presenting an account derived from a study of a single professional organization to asserting with authority that the 'grounded' theory produced from it will apply to other organizations. On the other hand, I would certainly contend that my account of the Bank's monetary-policy process can serve as a heuristic resource for researchers wishing to examine the discourse and intellectual collaboration of professionals in other organizations. Elliot Eisner (2001) argues persuasively for such heuristic use of theory derived from qualitative studies in particular local settings:

> [Theory] distills particulars in ways that foster generalizability. Although theory loses some local color when particulars are left behind, theory makes distinctions and packages thematic relationships so that they will travel well; when we distill, we come away from a research site with ideas that can sensitize us to situations and events like the ones from which the theory was derived. ... The generalizations derived from qualitative case studies are essentially heuristic devices intended to sharpen perception so that our patterns of seeking and seeing are more acute. We don't use the generalizations drawn from the specific case to draw conclusions about other situations, but rather we use them to search those situations more efficiently. (p. 141)

And indeed I would go further than simply making a claim for the heuristic value of my study for other researchers, to argue that, unless the Bank is highly idiosyncratic, which I think unlikely given its central place in the contemporary socio-economic culture and its interactions with other Canadian and international organizations, certain aspects of the account presented in this book very likely do apply to other organizations. To support this assertion, I would cite three factors: First, in many ways the account accords with published research by other scholars who have examined the discourse practices of professionals in various organizational sites. For example, Dorothy Winsor (U.S. engineers), Charles Bazerman (British scientists and a U.S. inventor/ entrepreneur), Catherine Schryer (Canadian physicians and veterinarians), Britt-Louise Gunnarsson (Swedish, German, and English bankers), Richard Harper (staff at the International Monetary Fund), Anthony Paré (Canadian social workers), Beverly Sauer (U.S., British, and South African mine-safety experts), and A.D. Van Nostrand (government and industry players in the U.S. defense procurement system) have all produced extended accounts of professional discourse that resonate with the findings of my study. Second, as a writing consultant I have worked with engineers, scientists, business managers, and bureaucrats in a number of professional organizations, and I have seen many significant parallels in these sites to what I have observed in the Bank of Canada.

And third, as methodologists have argued, ethnographers need not refrain from discussing a study's significance for theory in their disciplines. On the contrary, as Martyn Hammersley and Paul Atkinson (1995) suggest, the development of theory – specifically, 'grounded theory' (Glaser & Strauss, 1967) derived inductively from qualitative data – can be a prime contribution of ethnography: 'An important feature of ethnography is that it allows us to feed the process of theory generation with new material. ... In this way the fertility of the theoretic imagination can be enhanced' (pp. 177–8). According to Judith

Goetz and Margaret LeCompte (1984), such theorizing 'enables [ethnographic] researchers to ... integrate [their] results into the overall corpus of knowledge that constitutes their particular disciplines' (p. 207).

I believe it is reasonable to suggest, then, that aspects of the account derived from my study are likely to be applicable to other professional organizations, although perhaps in a descending scale of probability: Bank of Canada ➔ other central banks ➔ other economic policy organizations ➔ other public-policy organizations ➔ other professional organizations. Having said this, though, the question of just how applicable the findings of this study of the discourse practices of the Bank's economists are to any other particular professional organization can only be settled with any certainty through on-site research in that organization.

Chapter Six

Conclusion: addressing the 'So what?' question

The implications of [an ethnographic] study indicate how the research is useful beyond an intriguing analysis of a unique case. ... It is difficult to respond to the question, 'So what?' However, any study is weakened if the researcher cannot answer that question. (Goetz & LeCompte, 1984, pp. 195, 197).

In this final chapter I address the question invoked above by Judith Goetz and Margaret LeCompte. The first part of the chapter presents a summary of the ethnographic account presented in the book. The summary begins with a wide-angle description of the Bank of Canada's monetary-policy process and then focuses in on the discourse genres that mediate this activity. The second part of the chapter considers the study's various implications – for discourse theory, for research in organizational discourse, and for the teaching of organizational writing.

A summary of the account

The Bank's monetary-policy process

Derived from an extended (1984–2005) ethnographic study of the discourse practices of economists at the Bank of Canada, a study oriented by a socio-epistemic view of organizational discourse, the account presented in this book has described the economists' intellectual collaboration as they go about their work – a broad writing-intensive activity known within the Bank as the 'monetary-policy process.' We have seen how the Bank's cohort of approximately 175 economists (along with a number of other employees) uses written and spoken discourse together with various technologies and built environments to accomplish the three primary functions of the monetary-policy process: knowledge-building, policy-making, and external communications. We have also seen that the knowledge-building function can be viewed as comprising two sub-functions: conducting theoretical and empirical research that informs the Bank's evolving 'paradigm' of the Canadian economy (to employ the economists' own term), represented mathematically in the Quarterly Projection Model; and using the computer-run QPM to aid in 'current analysis,' the work of analyzing statistical data and other, more qualitative information to produce narrative arguments, or 'stories,' about current and expected future economic developments in Canada.

We have noted as well how key elements of the Bank's monetary-policy process are socially constructed. This was seen, at the broadest level, in the activity of knowledge-building – or 'inscription,' to use Latour and Woolgar's (1986) term – in which large amounts of statistical data and other information are continuously transformed, collaboratively and through several stages, into specialized written knowledge about the Canadian economy. We have also observed the socially-constructed nature of other elements in the monetary-policy process: the Bank's over-arching policy goal of price stability; the organization's paradigm of the Canadian economy and its mathematical representation in the Quarterly Projection Model; the conventionalized social interactions in the meetings occurring during the Projection Exercise; the narrative arguments or 'stories' produced by the economists; and even the statistical data received from Statistics Canada in the quarterly National Accounts. Similarly, the Bank's 'Communications Strategy' reflects a communal construction of the perceived social world outside the organization as comprising a particular constellation of groups and audiences with which the Bank interacts communicatively.

We have also seen that the monetary-policy process is highly rhetorical, with acts of persuasion playing a pervasive part in knowledge-building. We have heard the Bank described as an '*extremely disputatious place … a very tough shop, intellectually*' and have observed the staff economists' ongoing efforts to convince the Bank's senior decision-makers of the soundness of their '*views, judgments, and ideas*' (quoted earlier). More specifically, we have observed the occurrence of debate, persuasion, and provisionally-achieved consensus during the in-house construction of the Quarterly Projection Model and in the series of negotiations that take place during the Projection Exercise. We saw a further instance of the rhetorical character of the monetary-policy process in the Bank's ongoing efforts to explain and justify its policy actions to the general public as well as in its external communications with academic economists, journalists, politicians, labour advocates, professionals in the financial markets, and members of the business community.

The study's exploration of the monetary-policy process also revealed a tension between the 'normalizing' conformity of activity and discourse that organizations tend to foster among their members and the countervailing presence of individual agency and creativity, divergent views, and self-reflexivity. Thus we saw, on the one hand, convergences of focus, perspective, and understanding among the Bank's economists that are necessary for productive intellectual collaboration. On the other hand, though, we observed instances of purposeful variations on the conventions of established written genres as well as forums for debate, mechanisms for regularly evaluating and adjusting the Bank's analytical practices, and a considerable degree of self-reflexivity among the economists regarding the limitations of their analytical tools and the partial and provisional nature of the economic knowledge they produce.

A genre-mediated activity system

Seen through the prism of an activity-based theory of genre, the Bank's monetary-policy process is an 'activity system' – one in which the organization's economists and certain other employees, collaborating as a community-of-practice, employ an array of culturally-constructed tools to accomplish the particular configuration of intellectual work needed to produce specialized knowledge about the Canadian economy, to apply this knowledge in directing the country's monetary policy, and to communicate with external audiences regarding policy. Variously symbolic, social, and physical in nature, these cultural tools facilitate the distribution of cognition – that is, thinking, knowing, and learning – across the activity of the monetary-policy process, its participants, and their work practices. This distributed cognition includes a complex web of intersubjectivities – domains of shared focus, perception, and understanding that connect individuals intellectually within a community-of-practice – with particular intersubjectivities populated according to individuals' respective organizational roles.

Viewing the monetary-policy process as an organizational activity system that joins knowledge production with knowledge use, we examined in some detail two sub-spheres of activity associated the Projection Exercise and the Communications Strategy, focusing on the production of two major documents, the *White Book* and the *Monetary Policy Report*, respectively; and in the case of the Communications Strategy, we identified a sequence of discursive events running through the activity. We also observed that the activity system is mediated by a number of key cultural tools: a set of multiple written and oral genres (with the oral genres frequently taking the form of regularly-scheduled, document-focused meetings with conventionalized roles and social interactions); technologies such as computer-run mathematical models, an Intranet, and ITexts (i.e., the fusing of texts and digital technologies, seen for example, in the audio webcasts of the Governor's speeches and press conferences accessible on the Bank's website); and specially-designed built environments, such as the staff economists' networked workstations and the Bank's 'lock-up facility' for financial journalists. In all of this, we saw that the activity of the monetary-policy process is enabled by a discourse that is highly intertextual, interdiscursive, and multimodal in character.

As an organizational activity system, the monetary-policy process has a history dating from 1935, when the Bank of Canada was founded. Over this period, the repertoire of cultural tools, including the set of discourse genres, employed by the Bank's economists to accomplish their work has continually evolved, with old tools being retired or undergoing enhancements and new tools being introduced. Of particular interest in the present study was the evolving use of computer technology in the Bank to run successive generations of mathematically-based economic models. Against this historical backdrop, we traced the construction of one such tool – the computer-run Quarterly Projection Model. We saw how three staff economists collaborated in building the model, a project that lasted four years, and we read their account of how they worked hard to negotiate with, and at times fend off, skeptical and professionally-threatened colleagues in order to replace an older model, RDXF, with QPM. (To be fair, we also heard a senior executive suggest that these model-builders '*tended to over-dramatize things a little, depicting themselves as martyrs ... [and that] at times they also tended to rub people the wrong way, unnecessarily*'). This conflict over the development and implementation of QPM is an instance of the tension between the conservative, 'normalizing' influence of the Bank on its economists' discourse and work practices and the clear presence of individual agency, differing interpretations of economic events and issues, and animated negotiation of competing ideas.

In depicting the development, use, and ongoing enhancement of the Quarterly Projection Model as a mathematical representation incorporating state-of-the-art economic theory, an innovative methodology, and empirically-derived understandings of how the Canadian economy functions, the study also shows a professional organization advancing in its work by building achieved knowledge into its technological tools, which are then in turn used to engender new knowledge. Further, in describing the use of the computer-run QPM in the activity of the Projection Exercise, the study shows us how the built-in 'intelligence' of the technology is merged with the cognition, insight, and intuition of the human mind as manifest in the economists' 'professional judgment.'

We also saw the Quarterly Projection Model serving a dual socio-epistemic role in the economists' knowledge-building, functioning both as an 'organizational device' for coordinating collaborative work and as a 'tool of reasoning' for interpreting the significance of statistical data and other information. We observed that the joint, intermeshed use of written discourse and computer-assisted modelling gives rise to a distinctive pattern of social interaction and a style of collective thinking that allow the Bank's economists to produce specialized knowledge about the Canadian economy and apply this knowledge to policy-making.

From knowledge-building to policy-making and external communications

Taking a broad organizational view of the monetary-policy process – as a writing-intensive, genre-mediated activity comprising knowledge-building, policy-making, and external communications – we saw a continuously-operating, loosely-staged cycle in the Bank economists' intellectual collaboration, a cycle that constitutes a process of inscription (Latour & Woolgar, 1986). Various written, spoken, and mathematical outputs produced by junior staff economists responsible for monitoring and analyzing different sectors of the Canadian economy are communicated to more senior and experienced staff economists, who develop these outputs into a document known as the *White Book*, presenting a comprehensive and forward-looking view of the economy and a set of related policy recommendations, a document that is in turn presented to the members of the Bank's Governing Council, who use this view of the economy and the related recommendations in making strategic (broad, long-term) and tactical (specific, immediate) decisions about the country's monetary policy and in communicating with external audiences about policy.

At the same time, in observing this loosely-staged cycle in the Bank economists' intellectual collaboration, we saw how the discourse of narrative argument is employed to generate, embody, and communicate economic knowledge. 'Stories' produced by the economists to identify and explain developments in the Canadian economy function both as conceptual devices for generating analyses of statistical data and other information and as discursive vehicles for communicating the results of such analyses to more senior colleagues. In examining the collaborative production of the 'monetary-policy story' – the Bank economists' fullest characterization of the state of the Canadian economy – we observed how narrative discourse functions as an evolving knowledge-bearing representation that 'moves,' cumulatively and chronologically, across a number of different genres, both distributing cognition among and synthesizing intellectual contributions from staff economists working in different organizational sites and time frames. Integrating the role-defined individual contributions of a large number of staff economists into a single, unified narrative about the Canadian economy, the 'monetary-policy story' provides the organization's senior decision-makers with regular access to the staff's ongoing analyses of economic events, serving as a discursive resource both internally for informing monetary-policy decisions and externally for explaining and justifying the Bank's policy to the public.

A focus on discourse genres

In this section we will consider the discourse genres of the monetary-policy process in more detail.

Genre chains, genre set, and genre system

The study has highlighted the central role of discourse genres in the intellectual collaboration needed to accomplish the Bank's work. We saw two chains of interconnected genres, with one genre chain associated with the Projection Exercise and another with the Communications Strategy. In both cases, we observed written and oral genres functioning in a highly intertextual fashion, mediated by technologies such the Quarterly Projection Model and the Bank's Intranet and website and by specially-designed built environments, such as the staff economists' workstations and the 'lock-up facility' for journalists.

Carolyn Piazza (1987) has pointed out that in professional organizations, 'written and oral language [are] inextricably interwoven and mutually support-ive' (p. 125). We saw this very clearly in the two genre chains mentioned above, with the close relationship between written genres and the conventionalized spoken interactions that are an integral part of the creation and use of work documents – as for example, with the sequence of meetings occurring during the Projection Exercise as part of the production of the *White Book* as well as the series of weekly policy meetings during the quarter in which the previous *White Book* is employed as a benchmark for discussions, sometimes explicitly and at other times implicitly.

Also featured in the study were the phenomena of the 'genre set' and the 'genre system.' The genre set we examined – the range of written and oral genres enacted by the Bank's economists and other employees within the activity of the monetary-policy process – provides a discursive infrastructure for organizing complex collaborative intellectual work. We observed the Bank's economists employing the genre set to accomplish knowledge-building and produce 'stories' about the Canadian economy that are used in policy-making and in communicating externally regarding monetary policy. The genre set includes, for example, 'issue notes,' 'analytic notes,' 'research memoranda,' 'technical reports,' and key policy documents such as the *White Book* and the *Monetary Policy Report*, along with the spoken discourse of the various related meetings. As well, we saw that this genre set is part of a larger genre system that extends beyond the central bank to encompass written and spoken monetary-policy-related discourse produced by other players in the public-policy realm such as governments, academics, the media, the business sector, and organized labour.

Functions of the genre set

As mentioned above, the set of written and oral genres that mediates the activity of the monetary-policy process provides the Bank's economists with a discursive infrastructure for organizing complex collaborative work. In this role, the genre set serves four essential functions. First, acting through and also reinforcing an organizationally-defined division of intellectual labour, the genre set prompts and co-coordinates the diverse efforts of numerous individuals in a wide array of professional roles. Senior executives, staff economists, corporate communications specialists, editors, library personnel, and others – all are guided, through their participation in the genre set, in making the particular contributions that together allow the Bank to carry out its organizational mandate.

Second, the genre set serves an important socio-epistemic function: in distributing cognition and engendering areas of intersubjectivity, the genre set generates, shapes, provisionally stabilizes, and circulates specialized written knowledge about the Canadian economy that is used as a communal resource for policy-making and as a stimulus for further knowledge-building. At the same time, and this brings us to the third function, aspects of this dynamic, ever-evolving disciplinary knowledge are continuously being transformed, also through the genre set, into the monovocal, relatively inert discourse of 'public information' – the official discourse, written and spoken, that communicates the Bank of Canada's public position on its monetary policy.

Fourth, the genre set functions as a site for individual and organizational learning. As we saw with junior economists participating in the Bank's Projection Exercise and with more senior staff economists being groomed as spokespersons for the Bank in its external communications, individuals' growing experience with particular written and oral genres is a key part of learning to participate effectively in the activity of the monetary-policy process. As examples of organizational learning, we saw how the sub-set of genres associated with the Bank's Communications Strategy, operating as part of a larger inter-organizational genre system, provides the Bank with a discursive interface for assimilating new knowledge from outside sources regarding how the Canadian economy functions and how monetary policy influences the economy; and we also observed how the community-of-practice collectively seeks to find more accurate ways of characterizing the outside audiences for particular genres and to develop effective rhetorical strategies for communicating with these audiences.

Genre knowledge

The genre set that mediates the activity of the monetary-policy process both depends on and contributes to various intersubjectivities – domains of shared focus, perception, and understanding – that are essential to the intellectual collaboration of the Bank's economists. A fundamental area of intersubjectivity here is genre knowledge – a shared rhetorical awareness, within the community-of-practice, of how its various discourse genres function. For the Bank's economists, key aspects of genre knowledge relate to, for example, the organizational goals of different written and oral genres; the specific information needs of particular internal and external audiences; the ways in which certain written and oral genres function together in chains of technology-mediated discourse to organize activity and accomplish work; and the division of discursive and intellectual labour that underlies the production, circulation, and use of particular documents. While these and other aspects of genre knowledge are essential to the functioning of the genre set, it is of course not the case that *all* the members of the community-of-practice possess *all* this genre knowledge – rather, genre knowledge is distributed in a differentiated pattern within the community-of-practice according to the respective organizational roles and levels of experience of individual members. As well, it is important to note that while some of the genre knowledge associated with the monetary-policy process is explicit, it would appear that much of this knowledge is tacit.

Genres, analytical practices, and representations

In textual form, the discourse of the monetary-policy process is multi-faceted, encompassing not only written and spoken language, but also mathematical equations, statistics, numerical tables, and visuals such as graphs and charts. This poly-symbolic, interdiscursive discourse reflects the interactive functional relationship between the set of written and oral genres associated with the monetary-policy process and other elements in an organizational repertoire of symbol-based analytical practices and representations. As we have seen, for the purposes of knowledge-building a key complement to the genre set is the practice of economic modelling, in particular the use of the computer-run Quarterly Projection Model, which serves as the Bank economists' primary and most widely-shared analytic tool.

The genre set functions jointly with the Quarterly Projection Model to generate and embody a particular intersubjective reality – a 'paradigm' of the Canadian economy: a *'view of how the economy works; that is, how it's structured and what the linkages are'* (quoted earlier). This paradigm of the economy, which is created, maintained, and revised through the economists' discourse practices, lies at the centre of their work-world – infusing the economists' activity and discourse, the paradigm is represented in the mathematical equations of the Quarterly Projection Model as well as, more elliptically, in the economists' written and oral genres. The paradigm, while evolving over time, engenders and sustains a relatively well-defined and stable intersubjectivity among the economists, allowing them to articulate, reflect on, negotiate, and extend their shared understandings of the economy. (As explained in Appendix B, the Bank's paradigm is ideologically oriented towards a Neo-Classical understanding of the economy, while also having certain Keynesian aspects.) More operationally, QPM functions as an analytic tool that applies the economists' paradigm of the Canadian economy to the ongoing work of interpreting statistical data and other information.

In examining the interplay between the economists' writing and their use of the Quarterly Projection Model within the activity of the monetary-policy process, the study revealed reciprocal lines of influence between these two symbol-based analytic practices. We saw this dialectic in the development, 'selling,' implementation, and ongoing enhancement of QPM; in the Projection Exercise, the month-long collaboration to produce the *White Book*; and, more generally, in the effects of QPM on the economists' discourse (a QPM 'vernacular' and the various dimensions of 'logical rigor'). Given the degree of interaction between writing and economic modelling as two symbol-based, technology-assisted analytic practices central to the monetary-policy process, we might expect to see certain commonalities of function. Below, I identify aspects of such functional congruence, listing five observations that hold both for the written genres of the monetary-policy process and for QPM.

- The genres/QPM originate in a fundamental exigency: the Bank's need for a specific kind of knowledge about the Canadian economy to support its policy-making and external communications, with the objective of guiding the Canadian economy towards price stability and the larger goal of enhancing the economy's performance over time.

- The genres/QPM are sites for communal, distributed thinking. They enable complex processes of socially-negotiated reasoning that produce the specific knowledge about the economy needed by the Bank for carrying out its mandate. In this way, to borrow a phrase that Greg Myers (1990) uses to describe texts, the genres/QPM are 'structures both for thinking and for social interaction' (p. x).

- The genres/QPM operate as historically-achieved loci of shared meanings and understandings that are central to the organization's reality structure and system of knowledge. In this vein, the genres/QPM play a key role in establishing and sustaining the 'public spaces where inter-subjectivity is negotiated' (Bazerman, 1994b, p. 146). At the same time, the genres/QPM provide an interface between intersubjective reality and the 'private spaces' (Bazerman, ibid) of individual cognition as well as a site for negotiating competing views of economic events and issues.

- Through their respective symbol systems, the genres/QPM embody, in part or in whole, implicitly or explicitly, the organization's paradigm of the Canadian economy. At the same time, they operate as analytic cultural tools for applying this paradigm to the work of interpreting economic data and other information.

- The genres/QPM function to enable *both* stability *and* change. On one level, the genres/QPM allow for discursive continuity among colleagues and over space/time. On another level, in their linguistic or mathematical forms the genres/QPM are visible objects open to self-reflexive evalua-tion and adjustment by their users, and thus can serve as potential vehi-cles of change. Discourse genres and economic models such as QPM are invented, adjusted, or abandoned in response to internal factors (e.g., rethinking of the Bank's goals or organizational structure) or to external factors (e.g., in the case of genres, public demands for greater transpar-ency in the central bank's decision-making, or in the case of QPM, the need to stay current with theoretical and methodological trends in the academic discipline of Economics).

These commonalities of function shared by the written genres of the monetary-policy process and by QPM reflect the highly interactive relationships that exist between the two primary analytic practices employed by the Bank's economists – writing and economic modelling. Not surprisingly, these commonalities also find expression in the interdiscursive character of the various representations produced through these analytic practices.

Genres, change, and learning

We saw that the monetary-policy process, as a broad activity of knowledge-building, policy-making, and external communications, exists in a state of continual flux. For example: the specific objectives of monetary policy, the particular forms of knowledge needed for making policy decisions, the con-figuration of organizational roles and tasks, the analytic practices, the network of technologies, the set of discourse genres, as well as the pattern in which cognition is distributed across these various elements of the activity system – all of these evolve incessantly.

We also observed that certain changes in the activity of the monetary-policy process resulted from explicit, conscious decisions on the part of the Bank's economists – often involving organizational forums and procedures specifically intended to allow for evaluating and, where deemed necessary, modifying aspects of the activity. However, in addition to such *planned change* in the monetary-policy process (here I use Wanda Orlikowski's [2002] terms), we also saw instances of *situated change* occurring as individuals responded, in ad hoc ways, to unfolding developments in their work-world. We did not, however, see any clear instances of *technological imperative*, where a new technology appears to drive change in and of itself, superseding human agency.

The relationship between discourse genres and change was also apparent in the implementation of the Quarterly Projection Model, in the Projection Exercise, and in the Bank's Communications Strategy. For example, we saw an instance of *planned change* related to the Projection Exercise when the content and discourse structure of the *White Book* were redesigned by two senior staff economists in response to the demands of its executive readership. And we saw evidence for *situated change* in the evolution of the genres associated with the Communications Strategy, as, for instance, with the ad hoc development of the written and spoken material posted on the Bank's website.

With regard to the learning associated with the monetary-policy process, in certain cases this learning appeared to accompany specific identifiable changes in the activity system itself, as illustrated in the turn towards institutional transparency that came with the implementation of the Bank's Communications Strategy, with the new performance demands that this imposed on work groups and individuals. In other cases, we saw learning happening in a more general way as Bank economists engaged in everyday collaborative activity, with its ongoing negotiation of meanings and views, as during the Projection Exercise. Learning occurred for individuals as they developed their understanding and abilities, but could also be seen to be taking place on a collective, organizational level – with both kinds of learning contributing to the organization's effectiveness in accomplishing its work.

The duality of genre

As we have seen, the genre set associated with the monetary-policy process displays both a tendency towards normalization and convention and a potential for creativity and innovation, exhibiting the tension between stability and change that characterizes organizational activity and discourse. The provisional continuity of the genre set, particularly with written genres, allows for the reliable production of the specialized economic knowledge needed by the Bank to accomplish its mandate for directing monetary policy; simultaneously, however, the genre set remains sufficiently flexible to allow for individual inventiveness in particular instances of genre use (with the degree of flexibility varying from one genre to another) as well as for overall evolution in the organization's discourse.

We saw several situations in which writers produced atypical texts within the normally stable and conventionalized genres of the 'issue note' and the 'research memorandum,' in each case with the conscious intention of achieving a particular rhetorical effect by running against the grain of readers' habitual expectations. These situations illustrate the freedom of rhetorical action available to writers each time they produce a genre, while conversely, the fact that none of the innovations was taken up subsequently by other writers to become a permanent textual feature of the genre reflects the genres' relative inertia. We also saw the Bank's genre set adapt, in a significant yet measured way, to the political and technological demands that came with the organization's new Communications Strategy for managing its communicative interactions with external audiences.

Implications for discourse theory

In this section, I present a number of theoretical claims derived from the study presented in the book. These theoretical claims are the kind that, to quote Clifford Geertz (1973), 'hover over' the account produced from the study, and in this respect, are similar in nature to Anselm Strauss and Barney Glaser's 'grounded theory' (Glaser & Strauss, 1967; Strauss, 1987; Strauss & Corbin, 1998) – themes and concepts emerging directly from the analysis of a particular body of qualitative data.

As mentioned in Chapter Five, I think it reasonable to suggest that certain of the discourse practices featured in the ethnographic account produced through my Bank of Canada study are also likely to be found in other professional organizations, although perhaps in a descending scale of probability: Bank of Canada ⇒ other central banks ⇒ other economic policy organizations ⇒ other public-policy organizations ⇒ other professional organizations. Below, then, I discuss aspects of the account that support and add some texture to existing theory as well as other facets of the account that I believe extend theory beyond its current bounds. I begin with the study's implications for a socio-epistemic theory of organizational discourse and then consider the implications for an activity-based theory of genre.

A socio-epistemic theory of organizational discourse

First, and most generally, the study offers support for the socio-epistemic theoretical view that professional organizations produce, through their discourse practices, the particular kinds of knowledge they need for carrying out their work. Further, the study reinforces the notion that such knowledge is created rhetorically, through communicative exchanges and acts of persuasion among an organization's members, often regarding how empirical data are to be interpreted. At the same time, however, the study also shows that such knowledge-building may also involve communicative interactions with outsiders, as members of the organization seek external information and perspectives that are relevant to their work.

Additionally, the study supports the theoretical view that in professional organizations, written discourse is frequently used in combination with other analytic practices and symbol systems in complex collaborative acts of interpretation and reasoning. This leads to a key implication of the study: that in many organizations, symbol-based tools of analysis – such as computer-run mathematical models – may play such a significant part in the collaborative production and use of knowledge within the organization's work that one cannot fully comprehend the role of written discourse without considering how these tools, the analytic practices they enable, and the representations they produce intersect with texts, writers, and readers. Indeed, in such cases of knowledge-building, writing may be so thoroughly intermeshed with other technology-supported, symbol-based analytic practices that their respective epistemic contributions cannot be fully understood independently of one another.

A related implication concerns the paradigmatic 'economy' created through the discourse practices of the Bank's economists and represented in the Quarterly Projection Model as well as in the economists' written and oral genres. Here we see a parallel with Peter Medway's (1996) concept of the 'virtual building' evoked through alpha-numeric texts, drawings, and spoken language by architects, builders, and associates in related professions as a verbal/graphic construct for facilitating collaboration in the design and construction of a physical building. In both cases, a locally-produced and symbolically-represented conceptual reality – an abstract surrogate for some aspect of the physical or social world – serves as a focal point for establishing and sustaining intersubjectivity: domains of shared focus, perception, and understanding that connect the members of a community-of-practice cognitively and are essential for collaborative knowledge-building.

Computer-run mathematical models representing a particular aspect or dimension of the physical and/or social world would appear to be central to intellectual collaboration within professional organizations in many fields other than economics: physics, geology, climate science, oceanography, medicine, and demography are examples that immediately come to mind. In disciplinary knowledge-building, a computer-run model serves as a surrogate object of study, an analytic tool for applying theory to the interpretation of empirical data, and a focal point for co-ordinating collaboration and fostering intersubjectivity. Such a model, functioning jointly with written and spoken discourse, makes possible a pattern of social interaction and a style of collective thinking that allow the organization to accomplish its work in the world. The influence of a computer-run model on an organization's discourse may be explicit, as in documents containing model-generated numbers and graphics; as well, however, since a model's symbol-based representational reality may frame the 'professional gaze' of the organization's members and thus infuse their work, the influence of the model can extend far beyond explicit traces in documents. Indeed, such a model may be a central expression of the particular professional ideology orienting the organization's work-world.

Another implication for a socio-epistemic theory of organizational discourse is that in many professional organizations – particularly those responsible for directing some area of public policy, and where the organization's policy decisions are based largely on its own internal research and analysis – we are likely to see a continuously-operating, loosely-staged cycle within the organization's knowledge-building, policy-making, and external communications. In this cycle, technical experts produce analyses that are communicated to more experienced colleagues, who synthesize these analyses in texts conveying a more comprehensive view of that part of the world for which the organization is responsible and presenting related policy recommendations, with these texts in turn given to the organization's senior decision-makers, who draw on them in making policy decisions and in communicating with outside audiences regarding policy. At the same time, within this cycle, narrative argument may play a central role in enabling intellectual collaboration and in generating, embodying, and communicating specialized written 'knowledge-in-the-making' (to borrow a term from Bruno Latour, 1987).

A final implication here relates to theory on collaborative writing in professional organizations (as advanced most notably by Lisa Ede and Andrea Lunsford [1990], by a collection edited by Mary Lay and William Karis [1991], and by Geoffrey Cross [2001]). In the case of the Projection Exercise and the production of the *White Book*, for example, we have seen how intelligence, thinking, and knowledge are distributed among, or 'stretched over' to use Jean Lave's (1988) phrase, participating colleagues and their work practices and tools, so that in a very real sense we can speak of an act of organizational authorship. We have also seen how the intersubjectivity fostered through the Quarterly Projection Model (with its inherent paradigm of the economy), through a set of written and oral genres, and through the narrative known in the Bank as the 'monetary-policy story' provides an essential underpinning for the economists' textual collaboration. As well, we have observed how QPM serves as an 'organizational device' for coordinating the social interaction that enables the economists to 'think in partnership' (Pea, 1993) as they go about the work of creating the specialized written knowledge needed by the Bank for directing monetary policy. Indeed, this social interaction among the organization's economists can also be viewed as spanning time, in the sense that the textual regularities in a genre – regularities instituted by people in the past as solutions to particular rhetorical challenges – function as both prompts for and constraints on current writers, so that the economists' textual collaboration operates in a way that transcends the present moment.

An activity-based genre theory

An organizational activity system is a historically- and culturally-situated sphere of goal-directed collaborative activity. Within such an activity system, cognition – thinking, knowing, and learning – is distributed across a community-of-practice, its work routines, and its various cultural tools. These cultural tools, with their respective affordances, or functional capacities, exert a strong mediating influence on participants' discourse and intellectual collaboration. Such tools can include, for example, digital technologies, built environments, analytical practices, systems of classification and standards, and written and oral genres of discourse. A professional organization's legacy of inherited cultural tools, reflecting numerous decisions to stabilize and make available to the collective particular forms of tool-embedded knowledge, carries significant traces of the organization's intellectual history.

Within a professional organization, individual written genres, as cultural tools mediating activity, operate as typified, text-based forms of social action oriented to the creation of knowledge and its application in the accomplishment of work. More specifically, a written genre can be viewed as a communal rhetorical strategy encompassing texts, composing processes, reading practices, and social interactions, a strategy that allows a professional organization to regularize writer/reader transactions in ways that ensure (or at least encourage) the reliable, consistent production of specialized knowledge. Typically, individual oral genres – for example, regularly scheduled and conventionalized meetings – are also central to the construction and use of knowledge within an organization.

At the next level of aggregation is the 'genre chain,' a group of written and oral genres functioning together in a highly-intertextual fashion and mediated by various digital technologies and built environments. Such genre chains frequently exhibit a great deal of interactivity among written and oral genres, with the lines of demarcation separating written and spoken discourse sometimes becoming quite blurred, as for example in the case of a speech with a collaboratively-produced written text and a spoken performance. At a still higher level of aggregation is the 'genre set' – the full repertoire of genres, written and oral, employed by the members of a professional organization as they collaborate in performing the organization's work. In addition to its intertextual nature, an organization's genre set may also be characterized by a high degree of interdiscursivity, the occurrence within a text of language and conventions reflecting other genres, genres, and styles; and multimodality, the semiotic merging of language, image, and sound (as in the case of a speech which originates as a written text, is presented orally, and is also recorded and made available as an audio-file on a website). Finally, we have the 'genre system', which extends beyond the genre set of a single professional organization to also encompass genres produced by outside social groups with which the organization interacts, and which functions as a discursive forum for its ongoing 'conversations' with these external audiences.

Functions of a genre set

An always-present cultural tool within any sphere of literate organizational activity, a genre set operates as a discursive infrastructure that enables the members of a community-of-practice to accomplish complex collaborative intellectual work. A genre set will typically comprise a number of written and oral genres that – mediated by a range of technologies and built environments – function intertextually and interdiscursively to prompt and coordinate the collaboration that allows the organization to achieve its goals and carry out its mandate.

A genre set performs at least four key functions. First, operating through and also reinforcing an organizationally-defined division of intellectual labour, the genre set organizes the efforts of numerous individuals in a variety of professional roles. Second, a genre set has a socio-epistemic function: in distributing cognition and engendering areas of intersubjectivity, the genre set generates, shapes, provisionally stabilizes, circulates, and applies the specialized knowledge the organization needs for its work. Third, and following from the previous function, while one part of a genre set may – by fostering a multiplicity of views and promoting continuous internal debate – facilitate the creation of dynamic, evolving disciplinary knowledge, another (overlapping) part of the genre set may serve to transform this disciplinary knowledge into a body of unified and relatively inert 'public information' to be communicated to the world outside the organization.

And finally, a genre set functions as a site for individual and organizational learning. For individuals, gaining experience with written and oral genres is an essential part of learning to participate productively in the work of a professional organization. On a collective level, we can identify at least two types of organizational learning: first, with the organization's genre set operating as part of a larger inter-organizational genre system, there is the learning that accrues from assimilating relevant information and perspectives from outside groups; and second, there is the development of communally shared rhetorical knowledge about the effective use of the organization's genres themselves, including knowledge about different internal and external audiences and proven tactics for communicating with them.

Aspects of written genre knowledge

Within a sphere of organizational activity, written discourse genres both rely on and engender various intersubjectivities. One key form of intersubjectivity is genre knowledge – the shared rhetorical awareness of the ways in which the genre set mediating the activity functions. The study presented here suggests that some of this genre knowledge will be explicit (the 'discursive consciousness' of Giddens, 1984), while much of it will be tacit (Giddens's 'practical consciousness').

Within organizational activity, knowledge of written genres has at least four overlapping aspects. First, there is knowledge of the activity system within which the genres operate: an understanding of the activity system's larger goals, work routines, and use of various intertextually connected cultural tools. Second, there is an awareness of the division of intellectual labour that organizes the textual dimension of activity within the organization, including an awareness of which members of the community-of-practice are responsible for particular functions, such as those associated with document cycling, in the collaborative production and use of any given written genre. The third aspect is the discursive knowledge that enables individuals to participate actively in the production or interpretation of texts in particular genres. This kind of knowledge includes an understanding of how these texts, in their production and use, intermesh with other technology-supported analytical practices and representations. A particular example here is an understanding of how particular written genres are employed jointly with computer-run mathematical models to analyze statistical data and communicate these analyses. Indeed, certain aspects of written genre knowledge may be so thoroughly bound up with expertise in the use of technology-supported analytic practices and representations that the two are indistinguishable. And finally, there is knowledge of the ways in which the written genres in the organization's genre set interact with the written genres of other social groups in the larger genre system. This knowledge includes a sense of the organization's discursive construction of the outside world as a landscape of particular external audiences, an awareness of when the organization needs to respond to discourse produced by other groups, and an understanding of the rhetorical strategies employed for communicating with them.

Genres, change, and learning

An organizational activity system, while having a marked cultural-historical dimension, exists at any particular moment only through the agency, actions, and ongoing social negotiations of the people currently participating in it. Such a system evolves constantly, recreated continuously in response to internal tensions or initiatives, to the possibilities afforded by newly available tools, or to external pressures and influences. Thus the particular kind of specialized knowledge that an organizational community-of-practice needs for carrying out its mandate as well as the occupational roles and tasks, analytic practices, technologies, and discourse genres needed to produce and apply this knowledge are all continually changing. Certain changes in the activity system result from explicit, conscious decisions made by members of its community of practice – these are instances of *planned change*. At the same time, however, *situated change* occurs in instances where individuals respond, in ad hoc ways, to everyday events in their work-world.

Given the emergent, dynamic, and socially-interactive nature of an organizational activity system, all members of an organizational community-of-practice, old hands as well as novices, are always engaged in learning as an ongoing part of performing their work. Whether responding to planned systemic change in activity, negotiating meanings in everyday interactions with colleagues over work tasks, or bringing new interpretations to routine events, the participants in an activity system are continuously expanding their understanding and abilities.

To turn to discourse genres specifically, changes to written genres, whatever the nature of the change and whatever the cause, typically necessitate and prompt learning for individuals as well as learning on an organizational level. For an individual, such learning might involve, for example, adapting to an altered audience for a particular genre and developing new rhetorical strategies for communicating with this audience. Another type of learning, this time of an organizational kind, might involve the ongoing collective effort to access and integrate relevant information and knowledge from outsiders via the external genres within the genre system, with new approaches constantly required due to the evolution of these external genres.

Individuals learn to produce texts in genres that are new to them through a process that Jean Lave and Etienne Wenger (1991) call 'situated learning,' where a newcomer (whether new to an organization or new to a particular role), takes an active part in producing texts, but in an attenuated role and under the guidance of a more experienced person, and with limited responsibility for the outcome. For Lave and Wenger, such genre-related learning also involves 'the development of knowledgeably skilled identities' (p. 55), where a gradually increasing mastery of organization-specific tools and procedures is congruent with a growing sense of professional identity. Drawing on work by Yrjo Engeström (1992), we can add another dimension to this picture of situated learning by characterizing the development of expertise with written genres as an 'interactive accomplishment, constructed in encounters and exchanges between people and their artifacts' (p. i). Here we see such expertise emerging out of the individual's experience of collaborating with workplace colleagues in tool-mediated activity.

Implications for research in organizational discourse

The study reported in this book illustrates how the methodology of interpretive ethnography, as originated by Clifford Geertz and further developed by other researchers, can be fruitfully used to explore a professional organization's discourse and intellectual collaboration. More specifically, the study illustrates how the methodology can be employed to examine the activity of knowledge-building, policy-making, and/or external communications within an organization. As the study shows, interpretive ethnography, with its capacity for revealing how a social group uses a particular configuration of symbol systems to construct a distinctive conceptual world, can serve well for researchers wishing to study a professional organization's use of technology-supported, symbol-based analytic practices and representations in producing and applying specialized knowledge.

At the same time, the study underscores the importance, for researchers, of maintaining a balance of *engagement with* and *detachment from* the local reality of the professional organization under study. I have argued that such a balance is necessary if the researcher is to portray the organization in a way that encompasses both the intersubjectivity that enables intellectual collaboration and the differences in perspective that animate it, and that represents the organization's ideology while also acknowledging other perceptions and versions of reality. In the end, interpretive ethnography's value for studying a professional organization's work-world hinges on the researcher's ability to recognize and represent, in Bakhtin's (1981) terms, the dialogic interplay of 'centripetal' and 'centrifugal' forces that characterizes human discourse.

I will end this section with a comment on the length of time an ethnographic researcher needs to spend actively engaged as a participant-observer in an organizational site. While my study at the Bank of Canada has covered more than 20 years, this time period is obviously exceptional (and some might say obsessive). Based on my own experience and that of other researchers, I believe that a researcher employing the methodology of interpretive ethnography could conduct a full, in-depth study of the work-world of an organizational site by spending a year regularly observing the work of professionals in the site. While this is admittedly a fairly arbitrary rule of thumb, I think that a year should allow sufficient opportunity to gain access to the conceptual world created and inhabited by the organizational community-of-practice under study, using the methods for gathering and analyzing data described in this book.

Implications for teaching organizational writing

This book makes the claim that written discourse is typically deeply enmeshed, in locally specific ways, in the cultures, work activities, and socio-technical practices of professional organizations. In the production of the specialized knowledge that an organization needs to accomplish its work, writing is often combined with other technology-supported, symbol-based analytic practices and representational forms. For example, a computer-run mathematical model may play such a central part in the collaborative creation and use of knowledge that we cannot fully comprehend how writing functions within an organization without considering how the model, and the particular analytic practices and representations it enables, intersects with texts, with writers, and with readers. Indeed, certain aspects of the knowledge of written genres may be so thoroughly bound up with expertise in the use of technology-supported analytic practices and representations that the development of writing competency cannot achieved outside of this context.

As well, written discourse in organizations is invariably highly inter-textual, arising out of prior acts of reading, speaking, listening, and writing – all of which are similarly enmeshed in the contours of local organizational cultures and linked to particular work routines and social practices. Such dense patterns of intertextuality render the acquisition of written genre knowledge even more complex, as do the interdiscursive and multi-modal character of organizational discourse.

This picture is further complicated when we consider the socio-cognitive dimension of genre acquisition, with learning to produce a particular written genre viewed as, to borrow first from Yrjö Engeström (1992) and then from Jean Lave and Etienne Wenger (1991), an 'interactive accomplishment, constructed in encounters and exchanges between people and their artifacts'

(p. i) an accomplishment which, for individuals, involves the 'development of knowledgeably skilled identities' (p. 55). This conception of learning would imply that developing the ability to produce texts in a new genre of organizationally-situated written discourse is an extremely multi-dimensional and demanding accomplishment. Indeed, research has shown us that writing in school is radically different from writing in professional organizations, cautioning us against overly sanguine expectations for academic instruction in organizational writing (Dias, Freedman, Medway, & Paré, 1999; Freedman & Adam, 2000; Freedman, Adam, & Smart, 1994; Paré, 2000; Smart 2000).

Having acknowledged these caveats, I want nevertheless to offer several general observations about how I think schools might enhance their efforts to prepare students for writing in professional organizations. Such preparation should, I would argue, occur in discipline-specific programs and courses, such as those in Economics, Public Administration, Business Administration, and Finance, rather than in detached, more general writing courses. In this discipline-specific instruction, writing projects should be embedded in work activities in which specialized disciplinary knowledge is produced for and applied to clearly-defined ends. Further, such writing projects should require close collaboration among students, with individuals assigned particular roles and responsibilities. These projects should include experience with multiple interconnected genres, both written and oral, as well as with discipline-specific technologies, analytic practices, and representations. As a complement to such discipline-specific instruction, client projects (where students work with businesses, non-profit organizations, or community groups to accomplish writing-intensive tasks) and internships in professional organizations are highly desirable in my view. Client projects and internships both have the advantage of getting students out into particular organizational sites, where writing is rooted in local activity, motives, and practices.

A few words of conclusion

I began the book by pointing out that the economic policies of major financial institutions such as the European Union Central Bank, the U.S. Federal Reserve and central banks of other countries, the International Monetary Fund, and the World Bank have been receiving increasing attention in the news media. The study presented here has taken readers inside one such site, the Bank of Canada, to examine the discourse practices employed by the organization's economists and certain other employees as they collaborate in producing specialized knowledge about the Canadian economy and applying this knowledge in making monetary-policy decisions and orchestrating the Bank's external communications. If other researchers were to produce ethnographic studies of the discourse practices of professionals in similar financial institutions, we would then be able to compare findings across studies, with a view to identifying recurrent patterns that could allow us to make new and broader theoretical claims about the way that discourse functions in these institutions. I believe such research would have a twofold benefit: it would contribute to strengthening scholarship in organizational discourse, while at the same time opening up a public window onto the economic ideologies and policy-making of institutions that play such an important role in the global economy and so heavily influence the material conditions of our everyday lives.

APPENDIX A: Data used in the study

Data collected at the Bank of Canada

The study draws on the following data, collected over the period 1983–2005:

Interviews

- senior executives: 37 (24 tape-recorded)
- department chiefs: 20 (12 tape-recorded)
- staff economists: 28 (22 tape-recorded)
- other Bank employees: 6 (4 tape-recorded)

Reading protocols (all tape-recorded)

- senior executives: 8
- department chiefs: 3
- staff economists: 4

Presentations at in-house writing seminars

- senior executives: 8 (6 tape-recorded)
- department chief: 1 (tape-recorded)

Presentations at orientation sessions for new employees (none tape-recorded)

- senior executives: 4
- department chiefs: 3
- staff economists: 6

Meetings between a writer and a reviewer

- 3 (all tape-recorded)

Bank documents

- internal work documents: approximately 200
- published documents: approximately 60

Field-notes

- approximately 2300 pages

Data collected outside the Bank of Canada

In addition to the data collected at the Bank of Canada, I also interviewed ten economists outside the Bank: four academics, three private-sector economists, two former public-sector economists, and one economist employed in a public-policy research institute. Seven of the interviews were conducted in person and three over the telephone. As well, I collected scores of newspaper and magazine articles concerning the Bank.

APPENDIX B: Situating the Bank's economic ideology

As background to this study of the discourse practices employed by Bank of Canada economists in accomplishing collaborative intellectual work, I want to situate the organization's economic ideology within the larger disciplinary landscape of economics. To develop this overview, I have drawn on readings in the literature of economics, on newspaper and magazine articles concerning the Bank, and on interviews both with Bank economists and with ten professional economists who work outside the Bank. I begin by describing the currently prevailing 'New Classical' theory of how economies function, move on to a 'Neo-Keynesian' counter-view, and then mention criticisms mounted within the profession against both the Neo-Classical and Neo-Keynesian approaches. Finally, I consider where the Bank of Canada's paradigm of the Canadian economy fits into this overview of the discipline.

The Neo-Classical view

With the 1936 publication of *The General Theory of Employment, Interest and Money*, John Maynard Keynes revolutionized the thinking and practices of Western economists, introducing an innovative analytic framework of theoretical concepts, technical terminology, and methods of measurement. In the 1940s, the Keynesian approach, with its distrust of unfettered market forces and a faith in the ability of governments to promote economic growth and employment, established a hold on the discipline that continued for the next three decades. In the mid-1970s, however, the monetarist theory developed by University of Chicago economists began to displace the Keynesian perspective, and in the early 1980s a variation on monetarism known as the Neo-Classical economics took centre stage, where it has remained since.

The Neo-Classical school assumes that a national market economy is a fundamentally stable system: market forces and free competition allocate society's resources effectively, so that little or no government intervention is necessary. The central premises of this view are threefold: First, an economy naturally moves in the direction of expanding output and full employment; and because the system is self-adjusting, with markets tending to balance supply and demand, any deviation from this path will only be temporary. From this perspective, business cycles are seen as an inevitable response to a changing economic environment, with recessions and unemployment the unfortunate but unavoidable consequence of random factors and the fallible decision-making of individuals and business firms.

Second, since market forces, left unimpeded, will produce the best possible outcomes for the economy, governments should refrain from excessive involvement; indeed, interventionist government policies are more likely to contribute to a country's economic problems than solve them. In particular, fiscal policy (i.e., raising money though taxes and spending it on public initiatives) has little or no long-term positive impact on overall levels of economic activity or employment. For example, because an economy has a 'natural' rate of unemployment determined by 'structural' imperfections in the labour market, the level of unemployment is, over the long run, relatively impervious to government policies. In the end, artificial attempts by governments to stimulate consumer demand and business investment only result in a self-defeating rise in inflation. Further, the repeated deficits and accumulated debt associated with excessive government spending seriously hinder a country's economic performance. Conversely, reduced government involvement in the economy – through lower taxes and less social spending; privatization and a restricted public sector; and the deregulation of business, industry, and labour practices – increases capital investment and heightens incentives for workers and entrepreneurs, thereby enhancing productivity and creating jobs. Therefore, governments should limit themselves to modest initiatives in areas such as job training, research and development, and improvements in physical infrastructure.

Third, national governments, through the medium of monetary policy, should place the highest priority on reducing inflation, since inflation, while it may provide a temporary stimulus, eventually brings higher interest rates and has a debilitating effect on the economy. And given that inflation largely stems from immoderate government spending, fiscal constraint is essential for progress towards price stability. Finally, because there is no permanent trade-off between inflation and unemployment, achieving price stability does not, in the long run, mean more employment; in fact, in time, low inflation will contribute significantly to job creation.

The discourse of Neo-Classical economics relies heavily on advanced mathematical techniques, with a particular concern for 'precision and rigour' in the formulation of ideas and arguments (Klamer, 1984). The mathematical models devised by Neo-Classical economists are extremely complex in their embodiment of theoretical concepts such as 'market clearing' and 'rational expectations.'

The Neo-Keynesian critique

Neo-Keynesian economists continue to advocate many of the broad themes of Keynesian theory, albeit updated according to the experience of recent decades. The essence of Neo-Keynesian criticism of Neo-Classical economics is the counter-claim that a national market economy, left to its own devices, is subject to debilitating fluctuations, so that government intervention is required to maintain desirable levels of growth and employment. More specifically, for Neo-Keynesians the Neo-Classical view is flawed in several ways. First, the notion that market forces, left unencumbered, will naturally produce the best possible outcomes for the economy in terms of growth and employment is a fallacy. Constrained by factors such as monopoly, under-employment, and lack of investment, markets are basically unstable. Recessions, with their severe job losses, are the most obvious form of this instability, a consequence of insufficient spending on goods and services. Indeed, unacceptable levels of unemployment can persist over very long periods of time.

Second, for the Neo-Keynesians, the Neo-Classical stand against government intervention in the economy is seen as misguided. Governments can and should play a major role in directing and coordinating market forces in order to control fluctuations in the economy. In particular, governments should act to lessen the impact of recessions through fiscal and monetary policies – policies involving taxation, government spending, borrowing, and interest rates – that stimulate consumer demand and thereby reduce unemployment. Contrary to the claims of the New Classicists, such measures can produce positive effects, both immediate and long-term, on economic activity and employment without incurring significantly higher levels of inflation. The government deficits that may result are not a problem as long as they are kept in check over time.

Third, and this is a key consideration in relation to the role of central banks, the Neo-Keynesians view the Neo-Classical economics as excessively preoccupied with controlling inflation, at the expense of short-term economic growth and job creation. Monetary policy can be used to encourage acceptable levels of growth and employment, and central banks should strive to maintain a balance among inflation, economic output, and employment. Since harsh anti-inflation measures can lead to recessions and high unemployment, a moderate rate of inflation is an acceptable trade-off for increased job creation.

Neo-Keynesians also frequently assert that Neo-Classical economics harbours a conservative political bias that favours certain social groups over others. Here the claim is that a preoccupation with inflation rather than unemployment, the notion that redistributing wealth undermines people's incentives, and the perception of social equity as a realm apart from the 'hard' world of economics all reflect a lack of sympathy for the less privileged. Neo-Keynesians see this bias manifested in the Neo-Classicists' focus on the long-term benefits of economic policies for the economy as a whole and their apparent disregard for transitional costs – particularly unemployment – typically borne by particular social classes. Further, some Neo-Keynesians see Neo-Classical economists' reliance on the abstractions of formal mathematics as a further manifestation of conservative tendencies.

Criticisms of mainstream economics

Other critics within the discipline have pointed to limitations common to both the Neo-Classical and Neo-Keynesian approaches, seeing them as together constituting a 'mainstream economics' with shared epistemological, theoretical, and methodological foundations. Paul Ormerod (1994, 1998) argues against their mechanistic representation of reality: 'Conventional economists … see the economy as a machine and not as a living organism' (1998, pp. 91–92). Another limitation is the depiction of the human being as 'Rational Economic Man' – an isolated individual characterized by self-interested and hyper-rational behaviour. Ormerod suggests that mainstream economics is further constrained by an over-reliance on mathematics. One instance of this over-dependence on mathematics is the use of economic models for forecasting future trends in an economy. According to Ormerod, such models 'have made little or no progress in improving our ability to … predict the world' (p. 112). David Colander (1991) seconds Ormerod's criticism that orthodox economics is overly dependent on formal mathematical techniques. According to Colander, 'In mainstream economics the tools, specifically formal modelling and sophisticated econometric techniques, too often become ends; playing with the tools becomes a game [and] many mainstream economists lose sight of how to apply to reality the lessons learned from the game' (p. 157).

Another criticism of mainstream economics comes from feminist economists such as Marianne Ferber and Julie Nelson (1993). Denying the purported value-free orientation of economics, the authors see an 'androcentric bias' in the kinds of problems chosen for inquiry, the assumptions made, the methods of research, and the interpretation of findings, a situation they attribute to the traditional male domination of the profession. In orthodox economic theory, Ferber and Nelson see a world in which the experience of women and families is either absent or falsified, so that, for example, little economic value is accorded to child-rearing or housework and the connection between poverty and gender is largely ignored. More generally, they see humans depicted as atomistic, emotionally disconnected, rationally maximizing individuals obsessed with material consumption, a characterization they view as more reflective of 'masculine mythology' than reality. And, similar to Ormerod and Colander, Ferber and Nelson view the methodology of economics as constrained by an over-reliance on abstract mathematical formalism. Marilyn Waring (1999) extends Ferber and Nelson's critique to the international sphere. Waring argues that by focusing solely on economic activity in the marketplace, the United Nations 'system of national accounts' used by prominent agencies such as the World Bank and the International Monetary Fund renders invisible women's labour in the household, thereby institutionalizing the exploitation of women.

A final line of critique of mainstream economics comes from certain eminent figures within the discipline who take issue with the economic policies of the major financial institutions that anchor globalization – the International Monetary Fund, the World Bank, the World Trade Organization, and the world's central banks. 2001 Nobel laureate Joseph Stiglitz (2002), for example, contends that globalization can be a positive force, particularly for developing nations, but only if these financial institutions change the way they operate – reforming policies designed primarily to serve the interests of the industrialized nations and the financial markets and displaying a broader social and economic vision. This general argument has also been espoused by other prominent economists such as Jeffery Sachs (2005), Jagdish Bhagwati (2004), Paul Krugman (2000), and Lester Thurlow (1997).

The Bank of Canada's economic ideology

Following this broad characterization of economics as a discipline, we will turn now to the question of where to locate the Bank of Canada's paradigm of the Canadian economy. To begin with, the Bank's paradigm of the economy clearly resides in the realm of mainstream economics, that is to say, within the common territory shared by the Neo-Classical and Neo-Keynesian approaches. More specifically, we have good reason to associate the Bank's paradigm of the Canadian economy fairly closely with the Neo-Classical branch of the discipline, as reflected in excerpts from interviews with two Bank economists regarding the Quarterly Projection Model, the organization's primary analytic tool:[1] According to the first economist,

> *We see the world as made up of markets that function, not of markets that fail; and so QPM reflects what we call a Neo-Classical view, where policy intervention has a role and is necessary for some purposes, but isn't central to the functioning of the economy. Other people have very different views about that and see the world differently. But here at the Bank, we wouldn't build a model where government spending was necessary to keep the economy from collapsing. So QPM has natural self-equilibration mechanisms built into it, based on the theory of a functioning market system.* (Staff Economist 4)

The second economist remarks that:

> *Certain Neo-Classical ideas about relationships among prices and output and inflation and monetary policy are, in a sense, built right into the mathematics of QPM through what's called the Phillips Curve. And this is linked to a key assumption of Bank policy – that there are large costs*

involved in having inflation run at high levels, and so therefore it needs to be controlled. This relates to one of the big questions in the debate between the Neo-Classicists and the Keynesians: Is it acceptable to have high levels of inflation over the longer run? The Keynesian view is that the costs aren't as big as it might seem and there are definite benefits. Whereas the Neo-Classical view, the one we tend to believe in, is that there are significant costs and no benefits. (Staff Economist 8)

An observation by one of the Bank's deputy governors leaves a similar impression: *'Central banks around the world have converged towards the idea that the markets create an order, and you disrupt this order at your peril, so that too much government intervention in the economy doesn't work'* (Executive 2).

At the same time, however, we have grounds for seeing the Bank's paradigm of the economy as also embodying certain Neo-Keynesian assumptions. According to one of the economists involved in building the Quarterly Projection Model, its mathematical structure embodies both Neo-Classical and Neo-Keynesian perspectives:

QPM is Neo-Keynesian in the short run and Neo-Classical in the medium to long term. What that means is that markets don't clear on their own on the basis of price in the short run, but they do in the long run; there's an equilibrium achieved in the long run that's determined by tastes, preferences, technology, and so on. So you get short-run disequilibria that are resolved in the long run. (Staff Economist 9)

On the whole, then, it is probably most reasonable to see the Bank's paradigm of the Canadian economy as a Neo-Classical paradigm that is shaded with certain Neo-Keynesian assumptions. And to end by reiterating one of the main themes of this study, the Quarterly Projection Model, as the quotations from staff economists above suggest, is an essential mediating device for applying this paradigm of the economy to the activity of knowledge-building and policy-making within the Bank of Canada.

APPENDIX C: A sample of equations from the Quarterly Projection Model

A2.1   Household behaviour: consumption and wealth

$$(1 + \tau^c)\tilde{p}^c c - \Omega tw \tag{A1}$$

$$\Omega = 1 - \gamma \delta^{\sigma}(1 + r)^{\sigma - 1} \tag{A2}$$

$$tw = hw + fw \tag{A3}$$

$$hw = \frac{1 + r}{1 + r - \gamma(1 + \zeta)}(y^{lab} + risk - seign) \tag{A4}$$

$$fw = \frac{1 + r}{(1 + n)(1 + \zeta) - (1 + r)}(y^{lab} + risk - seign - (1 + \tau^c)\tilde{p}^c c) \tag{A5}$$

A2.8   Foreign trade

$$netx = \left(1 - \frac{1 + r + \varphi^{fb}}{(1 + n)(1 + \zeta)}\right)fb \tag{A18}$$

$$v^m m = p^{cm}c^{mshar}c + p^{im}i^{mshar}i + p^{gm}g^{mshar}g + p^{xm}x^{mshar}x \tag{A19}$$

$$m = c^{mshar}c + i^{mshar}i + g^{mshar}g + x^{mshar}x \tag{A20}$$

$$netx = x - m \tag{A21}$$

$$\tilde{p}^{netx}netx = \tilde{p}^x x - \tilde{p}^m m \tag{A22}$$

$$p^{netx}netx = p^x x - p^m m \tag{A23}$$

$$c^{mshar} = \frac{\tilde{c}^{mshar}}{pfx} \tag{A24}$$

APPENDIX D: Sample questions from an interview with a department chief

- Generally speaking, what do mathematical models allow economists to do that they couldn't do without them?

- What purposes do mathematical models serve in the Bank? More specifically, what's the purpose of a large macroeconomic model like the Quarterly Projection Model?

- Could you talk about how economists in your department use QPM in their work?

- Is there a particular body of economic theory underlying QPM?

- In what ways does QPM's use for monetary-policy analysis determine its structure (versus, for example, a model used by economists at the Department of Finance or one used by labour economists)?

- Do you think QPM has an influence on how Bank economists think about the economy and about policy issues?

- Can you talk a little about the history of QPM? How and why was it developed and how did it come to replace RDXF?

- I'm interested in looking at how economists use writing and modelling in combination in doing economic analysis. Do you have any ideas about this?

APPENDIX E: The schedule of a Projection Exercise

Research Department *Departement des Recherches*

Date: February 22, 1998

To/A: Projection participants

From/De: Projection Coordination Research Department

Subject/Objet:		Schedule for the March Projection
Thursday	February 22, 2 p.m.	Issues meeting, International Department conference room
Wednesday	February 28	National Accounts Evening
Thursday	February 29	Official Receipt of National Accounts.
Monday	March 4, 3:00 p.m.	Deadline for submission of monitoring files exogenous variables including ROW variables.
Wednesday	March 6, a.m.	No judgement round is completed and put into hypertext. Multivariatefilter is run potential output is set.
Thursday	March 7, a.m.	Deadline for submission of var_TUNE and var_SHK files, (see RN-95–060 for details on Var_SHK files.)
Friday	March 8, p.m.	Specialists' Round round in hypertext.
Monday	March 11, p.m.	Distribution of Individual Specialists' Rounds to each specialist and their supervisors.
Tuesday	March 12, 2:30 p.m.	Starting Point Meeting, Research Department conference room, 4West. (See RN-95–050 for details on the structure of the Starting Point Meeting.)
Wednesday	March 13,10:30 a.m.	Secretariat meeting.
Monday	March 18, noon	Final tunes.
Friday	March 22, p.m.	Circulation of Chiefs' round.
Tuesday	March 26	Approximate date for Chiefs' Meeting.
Thursday	April 11	Approximate date for circulation of White Book.
Tuesday	April 16	Approximate date for presentation to management.

APPENDIX F: The agenda for a Chiefs' Meeting

Canadian Projection Secretariat

Agenda for Chiefs' Meeting on March Staff Economic Projection

1. Overview
2. The projection
   - The outlook over the monitoring quarters.
   - Shocks from the rest of the world projection.
   - Fiscal Policy.
   - Monetary conditions, interest rates and the exchange rate.
   - The projection dynamics.
3. Risks

March 27, 1996

APPENDIX G: An unusual epigraph from an 'issue note'

January 31, 1991

file 275–9-5

SQUEEZE.CTM

The Big Squeeze: Overview of Revisions to the Foreign Trade Sector in RDXF

You can't always get what you want
But if you try sometimes
You just might find
You get what you need
The Rolling Stones

The purpose of this note is to introduce and motivate the proposed revisions to the foreign trade and foreign exchange sectors of RDXF to be incorporated in the MARCH 1991 version of the model.

In its current incarnation the trade sector of RDXF is much too detailed in light of what is effectively useful in Projection Exercises and given the cost involved in dedicating scarce personnel resources to the quarterly forecasts. Moreover, parameter estimates for many equations are deemed unsatisfactory and the error terms for a number of equations are fairly large creating some problem in the staff projections. In order to save on staff resources, improve the quality of the projections, facilitate the interpretation of the projection scenarios and – in spirit with the model development project currently underway in the Research Department – reduce the size of RDXF and improve its internal properties, a major project was undertaken to revise the foreign trade and foreign exchange sectors of RDXF.

The proposed revisions, which are documented in a series of papers1, include: (1) a substantial reduction in the level of disaggregation of traded goods, services, and international investment income flows; (2) a new exchange rate equation that is easy to understand and tracks well in dynamic simulations; (3) the abolition of capital flows variables; and (4) updated parameter estimates specifications for variables that are to be retained in RDXF.

The determination of the appropriate degree of model compression was based on (1) an evaluation of the nature of the information that is usually reported in the staff projection write-ups, (2) a realistic appraisal of our ability to forecast certain variables, and (3) an assessment of the main characteristics of Canada's external trade. By the first two criteria, all capital flows items were eliminated and services as well as international investment income flows components were reduced to a bare minimum.

APPENDIX H: The first page of an unconventional 'research memorandum'

RV91-O53

PAQM: Q & A

A play, of sorts, in one act, ideally suited for reading on the bus. 'By the way, any resemblance of characters to any persons living or dead is purely coincidental. Have fun.

Scene: the Bank of Canada cafeteria. 'Doug' gazes mournfully at his untouched plate of lunchtime offerings. Pushing his lunch tray away with a sigh he eyes the arrival of 'Mike' another economist. Mike asks if he conjoin Doug for lunch and Doug quickly agrees. The conversation, between bites, flows quickly and easily...

Mike: So I hear that you guys arc working on some pretty weird stuff for your model, rational expectations, stock-flow dynamics, steady-state equilibria and stability analysis... (*Mike shakes his head.*)

Doug: (*laughs*) Well I don't know how weird that is, it seems to us to be the only logical place to start, given the kinds of models we say we want to build at the Bank.

Mike: (*doubtful tone*) You won't see me defending RDXF, but it's hard for me to see why you need all this hi-tech stuff...

Doug: Not so hi-tech really, but whatever you call it, whether you need it or not depends on what you want your model to do. Nowadays, we look at questions of policy simulation ~ as opposed to pure forecasting – and that places special demands on how your model is constructed. The first thing I consider before working on a model is the kind of questions we want to the model to answer. The way you build it depends on what those questions are.

Mike: I think I understand the distinction between a policy simulation model and a pure forecasting model but I don't see how it feeds into all this.

Doug: Well Mike, you haven't been here as long as some people so let me give you the two-minute historical tour of forecasting-cum-projection at the Bank.

Mike: Sure. (*Eyes his 'famous pizza' suspiciously*)

Doug: When RDXF was invented in the 1970s, it was designed to do just one thing: forecasting. Essentially, it was constructed to undo a lot of what its predecessor, RDX2 had done by removing a lot of structure from that earlier model and replacing it with what you might call richer time-series properties. The beauty of RDXF, as it was perceived at the time, was that its control could be decentralized and the forecast process could be automated. Everyone got to play her

1. The model is the Policy Analysis Quarterly Model, or PAQM (paq-m) for short

Aiome/ret/moddcvA«^>»qmg«nd».aunl I Page 1 of 14

APPENDIX I: *Summary of the April 2005 Monetary Policy Report*

BANK OF CANADA

MONETARY POLICY REPORT

– April 2005 –

Summary

Overview

The global economy has been unfolding largely as expected, and prospects for continued robust growth are quite favourable, especially over the near term. Against this backdrop, the outlook for the Canadian economy through to the end of 2006 is essentially unchanged from that in the January *Monetary Policy Report Update*.

The Canadian economy continues to adjust to major global developments. These include the realignment of currencies in response to global imbalances, the higher prices of both energy and non-energy commodities, and growing competition from emerging-market economies.

The sectoral adjustments to these developments are becoming more evident. Many Canadian commodity-producing sectors are expanding. However, firms in a number of other sectors exposed to international trade are facing pressure from the appreciation of the Canadian dollar and from foreign competition. On balance, net exports have been a drag on the economy. But with robust domestic demand, some sectors—such as retail, wholesale, and housing—have been growing strongly. Canadian monetary policy continues to facilitate the adjustment process by aiming to keep inflation at the 2 per cent target and the economy operating near its production capacity. The Bank continues to judge that the economy is operating slightly below its full production capacity.

Highlights

- There is increasing evidence that the Canadian economy is adjusting to global developments, which include the realignment of currencies and higher commodity prices.

- The Bank's outlook for the Canadian economy is similar to that in the January *Update*, with growth projected to be about 2 1/2 per cent in 2005 and 3 1/4 per cent in 2006.

- With the economy moving back to its production capacity in the second half of 2006, core inflation should return to the 2 per cent target around the end of next year.

- In line with this outlook, a reduction of monetary stimulus will be required over time.

- There are both upside and downside risks to this outlook, which continue to relate largely to global developments and to the associated relative price changes.

This is a summary of the Monetary Policy Report *of the Governing Council of the Bank of Canada. The Report is based on information received up to the fixed announcement date on 12 April 2005.*

BANK OF CANADA MONETARY POLICY REPORT SUMMARY—APRIL 2005

After appreciating sharply in 2003 and 2004, the Canadian dollar has been fluctuating in a range of around 80 to 83 cents U.S. since the beginning of the year.

The Bank's base-case projection calls for annualized growth of about 2 1/2 per cent in the first half of 2005 and 3 per cent in the second half. Growth of about 3 1/2 per cent is expected over the four quarters of 2006, consistent with returning the economy to full production capacity in the second half of that year.

Expressed on an annual average basis, growth in 2005 is projected to be about 2 1/2 per cent, down slightly from the January *Update*, while the projection for 2006 is little changed at about 3 1/4 per cent.

We continue to expect core inflation to move back to the 2 per cent target around the end of 2006. Based on the scenario implied by oil-price futures, total CPI inflation is projected to remain slightly above 2 per cent this year and to move slightly below 2 per cent in the second half of 2006.

Growth in the Canadian economy this year and next is anticipated to come primarily from domestic demand, as net exports are expected to exert a drag on the economy. To continue to support aggregate demand, the Bank decided to leave the target for the overnight rate unchanged at 2.5 per cent on 1 March and 12 April. In line with the Bank's outlook, a reduction of monetary stimulus will be required over time.

The global and Canadian economic outlooks remain subject to both upside and downside risks and to uncertainties. These risks include the pace of expansion in Asia, and the prices of oil and non-energy commodities. A further risk relates to the resolution of current account imbalances, with the risk of a disorderly correction growing over time, should these imbalances persist.

Most of the uncertainties with respect to the Canadian outlook continue to relate to how the economy is adjusting

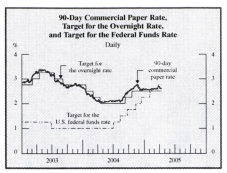

90-Day Commercial Paper Rate, Target for the Overnight Rate, and Target for the Federal Funds Rate

to the relative price changes associated with major global developments.

Recent Developments

After growing at an annualized rate of 2.9 per cent in the third quarter of 2004, the Canadian economy grew by only 1.7 per cent in the fourth quarter. This was weaker than the projections in both the October *Report* and the January *Update*.

The major factor behind this slower growth was a decline in exports in the second half of 2004. Although part of this drop represented a fall from unexpectedly high levels in the second quarter, it more fundamentally reflected the ongoing adjustment to the past appreciation of the Canadian dollar. In contrast, final domestic demand continued to grow robustly in 2004. Household spending increased, supported by monetary stimulus and ongoing gains in real incomes. The pace of business investment rose sharply towards the end of the year, and businesses accumulated inventories in the second half.

The weaker-than-projected growth in the fourth quarter was largely offset by upward revisions to GDP estimates for earlier quarters. The level of economic activity at the end of 2004 was therefore broadly in line with the

2

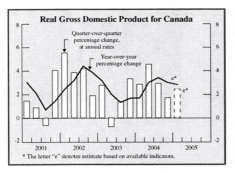

Real Gross Domestic Product for Canada

Quarter-over-quarter percentage change, at annual rates

Year-over-year percentage change

* The letter "e" denotes estimate based on available indicators.

including favourable financial conditions. As well, the continued strong economic performance of non-Japan Asia is expected to make a relatively larger contribution to global growth than previously expected.

The underlying momentum of the U.S. economy remains robust. Continued strength in business investment is expected, and exports should be helped by the past depreciation of the U.S. dollar. However, the impact of higher interest rates and higher oil prices will likely dampen household spending.

For Canada, despite strong external demand, especially from the United States and Asia, net exports are expected to continue to subtract from growth during 2005 and 2006. This reflects both the influence of the past appreciation of the Canadian dollar—which is restraining export growth and encouraging imports—as well as strong growth in investment, which has a high import content.

Economic growth this year and next is expected to be supported primarily by continued strength in domestic demand. We expect business capital spending to increase even more strongly than last year, because of high commodity prices, favourable financial conditions, high profits, and further declines in the prices for imported machinery and equipment. Consumer spending is also likely to continue to grow strongly owing to projected gains in real incomes, the effect of monetary stimulus, and high levels of consumer confidence. Housing investment is not projected to grow but should remain at a high level. Government spending should grow in line with revenues, since we expect that governments at all levels will continue to work to maintain fiscal balance.

Higher oil prices are still expected to have a modest adverse effect on aggregate demand in 2005. But an increase in investment and production in the energy sector should more than offset the negative effects by 2006.

Bank's expectations in the January *Update*, and slightly below the Bank's estimate of potential output. So it remains the Bank's judgment that the economy was operating with a small output gap at year-end. This view is broadly supported by the responses of firms to questions about pressures on production capacity in the Bank's spring *Business Outlook Survey*.

Core inflation has been broadly stable over the past year, fluctuating in a range of 1.5 to 1.8 per cent. Other measures of the trend of inflation have also remained below the Bank's 2 per cent target. The modest amount of slack in the economy and lower prices for import-intensive goods have worked to keep core inflation below 2 per cent, but higher energy prices have pushed total CPI inflation to an average of just over 2 per cent since last August.

Prospects for Growth and Inflation

Overall, the global economy has performed as anticipated, and growth is projected to remain relatively strong at around 4 per cent in both 2005 and 2006. While oil prices have moved sharply higher, other factors are helping to underpin the growth of the global economy in the near term,

BANK OF CANADA MONETARY POLICY REPORT SUMMARY—APRIL 2005

With the expected slowing of inventory accumulation, we project annualized growth to average about 2 1/2 per cent in the first half of 2005, about 3 per cent in the second half, and about 3 1/2 per cent through 2006. This scenario, which includes a reduction of monetary stimulus over the projection period, implies that the economy will return to potential in the second half of 2006.

One uncertainty around the outlook relates to the trend rate of growth of potential output. Over the past two years, growth in labour productivity has been close to zero, and increases in production capacity have been largely maintained by rapid growth in labour inputs. For the economy's production capacity to expand at our assumed growth rate of 3 per cent, labour productivity growth will need to return to a trend growth rate of around 1 3/4 per cent going forward. The likelihood of such growth is supported by the recent and projected increases in business investment in Canada and by continued rapid growth in labour productivity in the United States.

Core inflation should remain below 2 per cent through 2005 and most of 2006, owing to the continued small amount of excess supply in the economy, the effect of the stronger Canadian dollar, and the lower prices of some consumer goods from countries such as China. There is a risk of some passthrough of higher energy and other commodity prices to consumers, but the risk looks to be small, and the effect will likely be spread out over time.

All told, we expect core inflation to stay near 1.7 per cent through the end of this year. With the economy

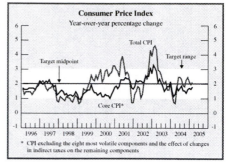

Consumer Price Index
Year-over-year percentage change

* CPI excluding the eight most volatile components and the effect of changes in indirect taxes on the remaining components

returning to potential in the second half of 2006 and with expectations well anchored, core inflation should rise gradually to 2 per cent around the end of 2006. Based on the scenario implied by oil-price futures, total CPI inflation is projected to stay above 2 per cent for some time, before moving below 2 per cent in the second half of 2006.

Projection for Core and Total CPI Inflation Year-over-year percentage change*						
	2005				2006	
	Q1	Q2	Q3	Q4	H1	H2
Core inflation	1.7	1.6	1.7	1.7	1.8	1.9
	(1.7)	(1.6)	(1.7)	(1.7)	(1.8)	(1.9)
Total CPI	2.1	2.1	2.3	2.3	2.2	1.8
	(2.4)	(2.0)	(1.5)	(1.5)	(1.7)	(1.8)
WTI (level)**	50	56	57	57	56	54
	(47)	(47)	(45)	(45)	(43)	(42)

* Figures in parentheses are from the January *Monetary Policy Report Update*.
** Assumption for the price of West Texas Intermediate crude oil (US\$ per barrel), based on an average of futures contracts over the two weeks ending 7 April 2005.

The Bank of Canada's *Monetary Policy Report* is published semi-annually in April and October. Regular *Updates* are published in July and January. Copies of the full *Report*, the *Summary*, and the *Update* may be obtained by contacting: Publications Distribution, Communications Department, Bank of Canada, Ottawa, Ontario, Canada K1A 0G9.
Telephone: (613) 782-8248; email: publications@bankofcanada.ca
or visit our website: http://www.bankofcanada.ca

Communication: A Vital Tool in the Implementation of Monetary Policy

Remarks by Paul Jenkins
Senior Deputy Governor
Bank of Canada
to the FMAC/FMA-USA Joint Conference 2004
Toronto, Ontario
30 September 2004

I t is a pleasure to have the opportunity to address this joint conference of financial market professionals from Canada and the United States. At the outset, I want to thank the Financial Markets Association of Canada and the Financial Markets Association of the United States for inviting me to be your conference keynote speaker.

The members of these two organizations play an instrumental role in ensuring the efficient functioning of North America's financial markets and, from a central bank perspective, the efficient transmission of monetary policy. You are, therefore, among the Bank of Canada's key target audiences. We rely on the effective two-way flow of information between the Bank and financial markets in order to fulfill our mandate efficiently and serve the public interest responsibly. In aiming to do so, our overriding priority is to provide markets with the confidence that the value of money will be preserved through sound monetary policy. Put differently, financial markets embody the views of savers, investors, and borrowers, and the most basic consideration in the formulation of such views is confidence in the future value of money.

Many of you who have worked in financial markets for some years may well take for granted the evolution in the way monetary policy is conducted. But if Rip Van Winkle had been a monetary policy "wonk"

and had awakened from his 20-year sleep today, he would surely be bewildered by the extraordinary changes that have occurred in central banking, especially in the way central banks communicate.

While central banks used to say little and let actions speak for themselves, today it would be accurate to say that words can, and often do, speak louder than actions.

The fact is, few aspects of the conduct of monetary policy have changed quite so dramatically as the role of public communications. We have gone from a communication approach that not so long ago had central banks doing little to let people know what they were up to and why, to one that is now progressively transparent and deliberately forthcoming. Indeed, while central banks used to say little and let actions speak for themselves, today it would be accurate to say that words can, and often do, speak louder than actions.

Central bank practitioners of monetary policy have become far more preoccupied with communication because communication is so tightly bound to achieving good economic outcomes. As financial market players, you are one of the publics that are most sensitive to this new reality.

Bearing all this in mind, I want to focus my remarks today on communication and monetary policy. I will structure my remarks to address three key issues:

- first, why communication has become so important in conducting monetary policy;
- second, the need for central banks to be strategic in their communication approach;
- and third, some practical challenges central banks must manage in implementing their communication strategies.

Importance of Communication in Conducting Monetary Policy

Let me begin, then, with the importance of communication. For the Bank of Canada, communication is a strategic priority in supporting our goal of preserving low, stable, and predictable inflation. Indeed, I would submit that effective communication has become a vital tool in the implementation of monetary policy.

> *Communication is a strategic priority in supporting our goal of preserving low, stable, and predictable inflation. Indeed . . . effective communication has become a vital tool in the implementation of monetary policy.*

Why this emphasis on communication as an important monetary policy tool? There are at least two key reasons: first, experience has shown that communication improves the effectiveness of monetary policy or, put another way, monetary policy is most effective when it is effectively communicated; and second, communication helps central banks to be more accountable.

I want to touch on each of these points in turn.

Like all public policies, monetary policy benefits from increased public understanding and support. This translates into what I call "legitimacy of policy." Through clear explanation of why our policy objectives and actions are the right ones, we aim to gain public support for what we are doing. With success on this front, we begin to shape expectations and influence behaviour in ways that support policy outcomes.

Central to our effort is clarity of purpose. We at the Bank of Canada have found that a clear statement of our objective—an explicit inflation target—is crucial. With the clear recognition and appreciation of this

objective, agents in the economy—consumers, investors, businesses, financial market participants—begin to adjust their behaviour in ways consistent with an expectation that future inflation will be firmly in line with the inflation target. Price, wage, and financial decisions will tend to be consistent with the target. And the net effect will be a more stable macroeconomic environment and greater success in keeping inflation low and stable.

The second reason why communications is important is accountability. A clear basis for judging a central bank's performance is extremely important to its credibility and independence. For the Bank of Canada, the explicit inflation target is that basis for accountability. Put simply, the public can measure our performance by how successful we are in achieving the 2 per cent inflation target. The fact that we have had a pretty good record in this regard has reinforced our credibility and the public's confidence that we will keep inflation at, or near, the target.

But for the Bank to be fully accountable, we must not only communicate the information that the public needs to understand our policy objective and our progress in meeting that objective, but also the challenges that arise in the economic environment and the factors that we take into account in making decisions. Communicating all this information has become one of the Bank's chief activities.

The Need to be Strategic in Our Communications

To communicate successfully, we need to be strategic. That requires an effective, proactive approach to communications. So we have to identify who our audiences are and what communication vehicles are most effective in reaching them.

> *To communicate successfully, we need to be strategic.*

We aim for effective dialogue with the public, the media, the markets, and other interested and influential constituencies. We want to further *their* understanding of monetary policy and foster public support for our goals and actions. At the same time, and equally important, we want to increase *our* understanding of the public's views.

This is clearly a continuous and iterative process. And the old communications principle, "Repeat, Repeat, Repeat," is entirely appropriate. By repeating our fundamental messages about the framework we use to conduct policy and about our policy goals and why they are important, we are increasing the odds that these messages will take hold in the public consciousness and resonate in shaping behaviour.

Through all our communications, we are providing the opportunity for public critique of our economic analysis, by economists, financial market players, journalists and reporters, politicians, and the public more broadly. This is constructive. Engaging the public in the issues is important in broadening awareness and understanding of monetary policy.

Let me be a little more specific about this. As I have already noted, expectations play a critical role in the conduct of monetary policy. First and foremost, we want to anchor expectations about future inflation to our 2 per cent target. Financial market expectations about future policy actions are also important to us. Market expectations get reflected in medium- and longer-term interest rates, as well as prices of other financial assets, and these financial prices make up part of the overall financial conditions in the economy. We therefore pay close attention to market expectations, and indeed look to financial markets to get an independent view of the expected future path of interest rates.

Bank staff, in our trading room and in our regional offices, are in regular contact with market dealers and investors in key financial centres, including Toronto, Montréal, New York, and elsewhere around the world. We also apply analytic techniques to extract from asset prices the views of market participants about the future path of interest rates. We look at interest rate futures, expectations implicit in the term structure of interest rates, and markets for instruments such as bankers' acceptances, term repos, and treasury bills. This involves assessment about relevant term, risk, and liquidity premiums. In this way, we keep our finger on the pulse of the market, on its interpretation of our decisions and statements, and on its views as to where policy interest rates are headed. We also stay on top of published economic analyses and commentaries from financial institutions. And we review the surveys of economists' and market participants' expectations for interest rates that are published by the major wire services.

All of this information, together with other economic and financial analysis, feeds into the Bank's delibera-

tions leading to our interest rate decisions and then into the messages we communicate about the decision to the public. If the iterative process and the two-way communication that I have just described work as they should, the views of the Bank and the markets should be broadly consistent. And this should help create an environment in which positive economic outcomes are achieved in an efficient manner.

The Bank of Canada's communications strategy is based on reaching our target audiences through a schedule of key publications and communications events throughout the year. This gives us a regular, continuous, and integrated program of communication with the public. It permits us to communicate our evolving views on the economy and the trend of inflation on a regular basis through the course of the year.

These communications events include eight scheduled policy interest rate announcements, when we issue a press release, publication of our semi-annual *Monetary Policy Report* in April and October, *Updates* to the *Report* in January and July, frequent speeches by the Governor and other Governing Council members, public appearances before parliamentary committees, press conferences, and other media events and interviews. And a recent initiative has been to publish our regional office *Business Outlook Survey,* which summarizes business and industry views on their outlook for the economy and inflation.

From the Bank's perspective, we are encouraged by the progress we are making in engaging public interest in economic and monetary policy issues. The quantity and quality of media coverage of the Bank—both electronic and print—has increased markedly in recent years, especially since the adoption of a fixed schedule of regular dates for announcing policy interest rates. The C.D. Howe Institute's creation of a shadow Monetary Policy Council last year to provide an independent analysis and view on interest rate decisions is making a constructive contribution to public awareness and debate. And the public traffic to the Bank's Web site has grown enormously, indicating a growing public appetite for our published statements and information. These are encouraging indications that the public is reacting to our communications and, in many cases, providing us with tangible feedback.

Some Practical Challenges to a Successful Communications Strategy

Implementing an effective communications strategy for monetary policy in 2004 has some very real challenges. Today, I want to touch on a couple of these: first, how to communicate uncertainty; and second, how to capitalize on new technologies, specifically an effective Web site.

How to communicate about an uncertain future

After many years of being involved in developing and communicating monetary policy, I have found that dealing with the simple fact that the future is uncertain is one of the most difficult communications challenges a central bank faces. Clearly, financial markets are hypersensitive to anything a central bank says about the future because the markets are looking for indications about where interest rates may be going. This makes talking about the future all the more challenging.

Let's remember, central banks do not have a crystal ball. Economies are always subject to events and shocks that are unforeseen. And the fact that monetary policy operates over a medium-term time frame compounds the communications challenge.

How can a central bank best address this communications challenge?

I believe that we must be able to tell a coherent narrative—in other words, a story. The story has to explain the logic of central bank decisions, but allow the public and the markets to make their own assessment of future Bank decisions. The story must be set in the context of a clear statement of the objective of policy, a view of the key macroeconomic relationships, especially the inflation process, and an understanding of the tools and the actions used to achieve our policy objective.

But the story also has to recognize the forward-looking nature of monetary policy; that is, the considerable time lags between monetary policy actions and their effects. And it has to recognize that the outlook is uncertain and that the future path of interest rates will be linked to developments in the economy. In other words, the outlook is conditional—conditional on assumptions, such as an assumption about the world price of oil, and on views and analysis based on circumstances at a given point in time.

This may not be an easy story to tell. But for it to be as clear as possible, the elements have to add up in a way that reflects the monetary policy framework we have adopted to conduct policy. This includes how the exchange rate fits into the framework. Fundamen-

tally, we have to assess the implications of movementsin the currency for aggregate demand since, in setting policy, we aim to keep aggregate demand and supply in balance in order to help keep inflation close to our target. Another important aspect of the story is to communicate a sense of the risks and uncertainties facing the economy. If our story does all this, then it will properly convey the key relationships, nuances, and conditional nature of policy.

More specifically, what we do, primarily through our *Monetary Policy Reports* and *Updates*, is to provide a projection of those key macroeconomic variables—real GDP growth, the output gap, and inflation—that drive monetary policy decisions and give indication to the general direction of policy. We do not provide an interest rate path as part of these projections. Under an inflation-targeting framework, the policy consequences of changing circumstances or unanticipated events fall primarily on interest rates, and thus any projected interest rate path would be an unreliable guide to future policy actions.

Our commitment is to the policy objective, not to a particular interest rate path.

In other words, our commitment is to the policy objective, not to a particular interest rate path. Our communication focus is therefore on presenting and updating our macroeconomic "base-case" projection consistent with eliminating any output gap—positive or negative—and achieving the 2 per cent inflation target over the policy horizon of roughly 1 1/2 to 2 years. But in order to underscore the conditional nature of the base-case projection, we also discuss the main risks and uncertainties that we see, and we identify those issues that we will be watching closely.

Let me offer a specific example from the Bank of Canada's fairly recent experience. In the spring of 2002, there was evidence that demand pressures in the economy were growing more rapidly than had been anticipated, even though they were not yet showing up in price increases. Based on the evidence at the time, we raised our policy interest rate three times. By the first quarter of 2003, there was further evidence that inflation was above target, suggesting that strong domestic demand was putting pressure on the economy's production capacity. So we raised our target overnight rate further in March and again in April. At that time, we concluded that the risks to the global economic outlook were more evenly balanced than they were the previous autumn, and we said so.

Then the Canadian economy was sideswiped by a number of unanticipated developments, most notably SARS, BSE, and a rapid rise in the value of the Canadian dollar as part of a broad-based weakness in the U.S. dollar. The impact of these developments caused us to alter our outlook for economic activity and inflation in Canada. With inflation pressures easing, we lowered the policy interest rate in July and September to help support domestic demand.

Through this period, there was some criticism of the Bank, that we had acted prematurely in raising rates and that, as a result, we had to reverse our decision. The fact of the matter is that conditions did change significantly. So our analysis and outlook changed accordingly, and we communicated the evolving story consistent with our monetary policy framework and its forward-looking nature. Like the baseball umpire says, "There's strikes and there's balls, and I calls 'em as I sees 'em."

Communication technologies: capitalizing on a good Web site

A second communications challenge that I want to highlight is capitalizing on new technology. By shrinking time and space, new communication technologies have created enormous pressure to provide markets and the public with access to real-time information about monetary policy.

Fortunately, these technologies offer the means to help address these pressures. So the Bank of Canada has put a lot of emphasis on developing and maintaining a high-calibre Web site. The Web has become particularly important for monetary policy communication because it helps facilitate equal treatment of target audiences and it enables us to respond more quickly to information needs. Our site gives the general public and more specialized audiences direct and immediate access not only to our releases, publications, speeches, and technical information, but also to more easily understandable information about the Bank and monetary policy. Thus, the Web supports our objective of being proactive in reaching the public, the markets, and specialized audiences with news and information.

Last year, we were honoured to be presented with the "Central Bank Website of the Year" award by Central Banking Publications and Lombard Street Research. Nonetheless, we continue to work at improving and expanding the site. (If I might add a plug, our Web site address is bankofcanada.ca; banqueducanada.ca.)

Our audio "Webcasts" of speeches and press conferences by the Governor have been highly successful. They provide the instant access that markets and media want, to what the Bank is saying on monetary policy issues, as we say it. They also enable journalists and market participants from anywhere in the world to tune in "in real time."

Our Web site plays an important role in supporting our financial market activities. Dealers and distributors can find up-to-the-minute information on securities auctions and tenders, plus historical yield data and a variety of technical documents. And the site permits much wider distribution of the Bank's research than was possible in the past.

The Web is maturing as a medium, and the Bank will continue to exploit it to communicate more directly and effectively with its target audiences.

Conclusion

Let me conclude by summarizing my main points. First, communication has become another vital tool in the implementation of monetary policy. Thanks in part to effective communication, Canadians are now more confident that inflation will be kept near the 2 per cent target, and this expectation is feeding into their day-to-day decision-making.

> *By communicating in a timely and effective way, we can engage the markets and the public in the issues we face. At the same time, public input helps make monetary policy more effective.*

Second, central banks need to be strategic in their approach to communications. By communicating in a timely and effective way, we can engage the markets and the public in the issues we face. At the same time, public input helps make monetary policy more effective.

And finally, there will continue to be numerous day-to-day challenges in communicating monetary policy. But in addressing these challenges, be they complex ones like the conditionality and forward-looking nature of monetary policy or technical ones like capi-talizingonnew technology, we are always striving to achieve better,more effective policy.

Communications is indeed a vital tool in helping the Bank achieve the goal of low, stable, and predictable inflation. But it is important to remember that low inflation is not an end in itself. Ultimately, it is the means by which monetary policy contributes to Canada's solid economic performance and to the rising living standards of Canadians.

Endnotes

Chapter One

1   Bank economists sometimes employ the term 'monetary-policy framework' as an alternative to 'monetary-policy process.' For the sake of consistency, however, I will use the latter term throughout the book. I have also followed this practice in editing quotations from Bank economists.

2   I take the term 'written knowledge' from Charles Bazerman (1988) to refer to knowledge that is constituted through, instantiated in, and communicated by written discourse. I need to make the point, however, that referring to knowledge as 'written' does not preclude the possibility of other analytic practices being involved in its production or of non-linguistic symbols appearing in its textual form.

3   The 1985 revision of the 1934 Bank of Canada Act describes the mandate of the central bank as follows: 'to regulate credit and currency in the best interests of the economic life of the nation, to control and protect the external value of the national monetary unit and to mitigate by its influence fluctuations in the general level of production, trade, prices and employment, so far as may be possible within the scope of monetary action, and generally to promote the economic and financial welfare of Canada.'

4   Lave and Wenger define a community-of-practice as a 'set of relations among persons, activity, and world, over time and in relation to other tangential and overlapping communities of practice.' They go on to assert that a 'community-of-practice is an intrinsic condition for the existence of knowledge, not least because it provides the interpretive support necessary for making sense of its heritage. Thus, participation in the cultural practice in which knowledge exists is an epistemological principal of learning' (1991, p. 99).

Chapter Two

1   In *Ideology: An Introduction*, Terry Eagleton begins his discussion by acknowledging the wide range of conventional meanings associated with the term 'ideology,' noting 16 different definitions 'currently in circulation' (pp. 1–2). In the present study the term is used not, as it is sometimes employed, to refer to the Marxist notion of false consciousness or the wilful distortion of reality in the service of political or economic advantage; rather, in

speaking of a social group's 'ideology' I mean a shared world-view, in the sense suggested by Robert Heilbroner and by Mikhail Bakhtin in Speech Genres. As Heilbroner (1990) points out, 'Ideologies in this sense are 'social constructions of reality' in Berger and Luckman's (1966) terminology. They are conceptual frameworks by which order is imposed on, and moral legitimacy accorded to, the raw stuff out of which social understandings must be forged' (p. 102).

2   My thinking about conceptual economies was initially prompted by conversations with Peter Medway concerning his notion of the 'virtual building' – a discursive construct created by architects, builders, municipal authorities, and site workers to guide the planning and construction of a material building. See, for example, Medway, 1996.

3   I am grateful to Janet Giltrow for suggesting this metaphor in a personal communication.

4   The Bank is committed to 'a gradual approach to price stability as the central objective of monetary policy' (Duguay & Poloz, 1994, p. 190). According to the Governor, 'The focus of Canadian monetary policy is on price stability. However, the Bank of Canada does not pursue price stability for its own sake but rather as a means of contributing to a well-functioning, productive economy, capable of providing Canadians with a rising standard of living' (from a speech given at *The World in* 1996 *Conference*, Toronto, January 19,1996). In 1991, in collaboration with the Department of Finance, the Bank announced a series of 'inflation-control targets' running out to 1995, a commitment that in 1993 was extended to 1998, and then in 2000 extended again to 2006. (The Bank's argument for focusing on price stability as the primary goal of monetary policy can be found in John Crow's 1988 'Hansen Lecture' and in the 1990 *Bank* of *Canada Annual Report*.)

As with other central banks, and perhaps all influential public-sector institutions, the Bank of Canada is not without its critics. Indeed, the Bank's focus on controlling inflation as the primary goal of monetary policy has been questioned both by academics such as Lars Osberg and Pierre Fortin (1996) and by financial journalists such as Linda McQuaig. In her polemic on the Canadian government's preoccupation with the deficit and national debt, *Shooting the Hippo*, McQuaig takes dead aim, so to speak, at the Bank's approach to monetary policy.

5   The interviews with the informants quoted in the study were tape-recorded. I have edited the quotes to remove false starts, hesitations, fillers, and redundancy.

6 As explained earlier in the book, the Bank's aim is to guide the Canadian economy towards price stability, or low inflation, with specific inflation-control targets set for given points in the future.

7 Here we begin to see the tension, alluded to in Chapter One, between, on the one hand, the notion that organizations exert a deterministic, 'normalizing' influence on human perception and reasoning, as reflected, for example, in the economists' shared paradigm of the Canadian economy, and on the other hand, the diversity of views and the lively debates that characterize Bank discourse. As we will see, the study presented here includes evidence of both tendencies.

Chapter Three

1 I would certainly not claim to have identified all the genres in play within the activity of the Bank's knowledge-building and policy-making; rather, the list is simply the most accurate representation I have been able to infer from a particular body of data. And of course, given the plasticity of genres and the ever-changing character of a genre set, any list of this kind must be viewed as an abstraction of reality.

2 Economists are far from alone in using computer-run mathematical models. In my experience as a freelance writing consultant in a range of organizations, I have also seen such models used to support analysis in engineering and epidemiology. As well, in reading or in talking with other people, I have heard of the use of computer-run mathematical models in physics, geology, climatology, oceanography, medicine, demography, and environmental science.

3 In 1965 the Bank of Canada hired a group of university economists to build a computer-run macroeconomic model for policy simulations. In 1968 the model RDX1 was completed and then in 1972 a second version, RDX2, was released. In the mid-1970s, the Bank realized it needed to develop a model that was also capable of economic forecasting and in 1977 RDXF was implemented. By the early 1980s, however, it was clear that RDXF no longer reflected the Bank's view of the Canadian economy and another model, SAM (Small Annual Model), was developed. While SAM was theoretically more sophisticated than RDXF, it did not have the capacity to function as the Bank's major analytic model of the economy and a much-elaborated version of RDXF continued to be used.

4 Reflecting current theory and methodology in economics, QPM is a smaller, more highly aggregated model than RDXF, which was composed of approximately 400 mathematical equations. However, QPM, with its set

of 30 equations, is supplemented by a number of adjunct 'satellite models,' used by staff economists to analyze developments in particular sectors of the economy.

5   QPM's 'general equilibrium' structure and its 'steady state,' 'forward-looking,' and 'stock-flow' properties reflect several theoretical assumptions: that an economy is constituted of numerous interconnected processes that act upon one another, simultaneously, in extremely complex ways; that an economy using its resources efficiently has an 'ideal' level of output that can be achieved without creating inflationary pressures; that people's decisions are based on expectations about future economic trends; and that accumulated 'stocks,' such as government debt, influence the performance of an economy.

6   As described by one staff economist, an economic projection answers the question, 'Given where we are today and where we think the economy's going and given where we want to be in terms of the Bank's inflation-control objectives in, say, two to three years from now, what do we have to do with monetary policy to get there?' This is different from an economic forecast, where the question is, 'OK, given where we are today, where are we going to be, say, two years from now?' (Staff Economist 10). According to this distinction, a forecast is one component of a projection.

7   For Bank economists, the term 'formalize' appears to refer to the use of mathematics to represent some facet of the economy.

8   The Bank actually does two 'major' projections a year, in September and March, and two 'update' projections, in December and June. While there are significant differences between major and update projections (for example, the former look ahead over a six- or seven-year horizon, and the latter over a two-year horizon), the underlying activity is similar for both, and so for my purposes here these differences will be ignored.

9   Prior to the beginning of the Projection Exercise, developments in the U.S economy are analyzed, along with those in the 'overseas' economies (of France, Germany, Great Britain, Italy, and Japan) and in Mexico. These analyses are then treated as 'exogenous' or external factors in the Projection Exercise, which focuses on the Canadian economy.

10 Areas of the economy monitored by sector specialists include consumption, investment, employment, prices, wage settlements, exchange rates, exports and imports, and trade in services.

11 The 'monetary aggregates' are several different measures of the overall supply of money in the economy. For a period of time in the late 1970s and early 1980s, these measures played a central part in the central bank's direction of monetary policy.

12　The National Accounts is a compendium of statistics on various aspects of the Canadian economy that is produced four times a year by Statistics Canada.

13　The 'terms-of-trade' is defined as the ratio of the index (or weighted average) of export prices to the index of import prices.

14　While I discuss the function and discourse structure of the *White Book* in this section, I am not able to quote from the document, given its 'protected' status as policy advice.

15　Other sources of information for the Executives are 'independent private-sector forecasts, views obtained directly from outside contacts, and [reports on] conditions in financial and foreign exchange markets' (Duguay & Poloz, 1994, p. 196). 'Outside contacts' include, for example, the executives' counterparts in other central banks and financial institutions, as well as academics and people in industry.

16　While in one sense the construction of the 'monetary-policy story' can indeed be viewed as a linear process, temporally, in another sense this distorts reality somewhat. For example, the creation of the executives' version of the story is actually more of an ongoing process than a discursive episode that occurs at one particular point each quarter.

17　This is in addition to the alternative scenarios already included by the Secretariat in the version of the *White Book* presented to the Governing Council.

18　The Bank also publishes two *Updates* to the *Monetary Policy Report* each year.

19　The interviews generally lasted between forty-five minutes and an hour and fifteen minutes. Almost invariably, I interviewed people in their own offices – 'on their own territory,' as Hammersley and Atkinson (1983, p. 150) recommend.

Chapter Four

1　This image and others like it quoted in this chapter recall Deidre McCloskey's (1985) observation about the widespread use of metaphor in economists' discourse.

2　The 'transmission mechanism' refers to the chain of events through which the Bank's monetary policy achieves its effect on the economy. An Executive explains: 'We have a view of how the Bank's actions serve to accomplish our policy objectives, going from the day-to-day interest rate, to monetary conditions; and how that influences spending, which then affects inflation.' (Executive 3).

3   Thomas Bayes was an English mathematician who lived from 1702–1761. Bayesian analysis refers to the research practice of combining new information with conventional wisdom derived from prior research.

4   The reference here is apparently to Paul Samuelson's *Foundations of Economic Analysis*. Cambridge: Harvard University Press, 1947.

5   The department chief's description of the evolution in economic modelling parallels Donald Schon's (1983) account of the disillusionment in the professions with the use of large computer-driven mathematical models as comprehensive analogues of reality. According to Schon, this has led to a more realistic attitude on the part of practitioners, who 'have decided to treat formal models as 'probes' or 'metaphors' useful only as sources of new perspectives on complex situations' (p. 44). This characterization fits the Bank's economists quite well. Earlier I described how, in analyzing developments in the economy, they combine the mathematical logic of the Quarterly Projection Model with a large measure of professional judgment. In this sense, they would indeed appear to employ the model as a 'probe' or 'metaphor' offering a useful, but recognizably constrained, way of looking at the complex reality of economic events.

6   This expertise with the modal involved both familiarity with the four hundred interconnected equations that comprised RDXF and skill in the econometric technique of using historical data to 'estimate' the numerical values ascribed to the different equations.

7   Poloz, S., Rose, D., and Tetlow, R. 1994. The Bank of Canada's new Quarterly Projection Model. *Bank of Canada Review*, Autumn, pp. 23–39.

8   As mentioned earlier, Pierre Duguay is a deputy governor at the Bank; David Longworth is also a deputy governor.

9   Presumably, each reader familiar with the formal mathematical structure of QPM carries a mental image of it that is in certain ways identical, or at least very similar, to the mental image carried by colleagues, while also having a perception of the model that, in other ways, is unique to that individual.

Chapter Five

1   See the July 2004 special issue of *Journal of Business and Technical Communication* for further research and theorizing on ITexts.

2   Again, as I pointed out with the genres of knowledge-building and policy-making, I would certainly not claim to have identified all the genres in play

within the activity of the Communications Strategy. With the plasticity of genres and the constantly changing character of a genre set, any list of this kind is an abstraction of reality.

3   A former Bank economist provides an historical perspective on this shift towards 'transparency' in the Bank of Canada:

'After the James Coyne episode of the early 1960's [in which the Governor of the Bank was forced from office by the Canadian Prime Minister of the day, John Dieffenbaker], Lou Razminsky was recruited [as Governor] to re-establish the authority of the Bank and he did so, in my view, by taking the Bank from the public eye and speaking 'ex cathedra' on the fewest possible occasions. ... Transparency was certainly not the word of the day! Indeed virtually the Bank's sole (soul!) publication was the Annual Report upon which work began in the fall headed for an end of February tabling. The purpose of this long gestation, far from transparency, was to minimize any risk to the Bank of careless prose escaping its vaults. ... Gordon Thiessen, on the other hand and as you point out, confronted the threats to the Bank in the early 1990's by moving in precisely the opposite way – towards greater transparency and communication.'

References

Ackerman, John & Oates, Scott. 1996. Image, text, and power in architectural design and workplace writing. In Anne Hill Duin and Craig Hansen (eds) *Non-academic writing*: *Social theory and technology* (pp. 81–122). Mahwah, NJ: Lawrence Erlbaum.

Adler, Peter & Adler, Patricia. 1987. *Membership roles in field research*. Newbury Park, CA: Sage.

Agar, Michael. 1980. *The professional stranger*: *An informal introduction to ethnography*. New York: Academic Press.

Agar, Michael. 1986. *Speaking of ethnography*. Beverly Hills, CA: Sage.

Anderson, Gary. 1990. *Fundamentals of educational research*. London: Falmer Press.

Athanases, Steven & Heath, Shirley Brice. 1995. Ethnography in the study of the teaching and learning of English. *Research in the Teaching of English 29*, 263–287.

Atkinson, Paul. 1992. *Understanding ethnographic texts*. Beverly Hills, CA: Sage.

Bakhtin, Mikhail. 1981. *The dialogic imagination*: *Four essays*. Michael Holquist (ed.) Carlyn Emerson & Michael Holquist (trans.). Austin: University of Texas Press.

Bakhtin, Mikhail. 1986. *Speech genres and other late essays*. Carlyn Emerson & Michael Holquist (eds) & Vern W. McGee (trans.). Austin: University of Texas Press.

Bargiela-Chiappini, Francesca & Nickerson, Catherine. 1999. *Writing business*: *Genres, media and discourses*. London: Longman.

Barron, Colin, Bruce, Nigel & Nunan, David. 2002. *Knowledge and discourse*: *Towards an ecology of language*. Harrow, UK: Pearson Education Limited.

Basso, Keith & Selby, Henry. 1976. Introduction to Keith Basso & Henry Selby (eds) *Meaning in anthropology* (pp. 1–9). Albuquerque, NM: University of New Mexico Press.

Bauman, Richard. 2004. *A world of other's words: cross-culturalperspectives on intertextuality*. Oxford: Blackwell.

Bazerman, Charles. 1991. How natural philosophers can cooperate. In C. Bazerman and J. Paradis (eds) *Textual dynamics of the professions* (pp. 13–44). Madison: University of Wisconsin Press.

Bazerman, Charles. 1988. *Shaping written knowledge*: *The genre and activity of the experimental article in science*. Madison: University of Wisconsin Press.

Bazerman, Charles. 1994a. *Constructing experience*. Carbondale: Southern Illinois University Press.

Bazerman, Charles. 1994b. Systems of genres and the enactment of social intentions. In Aviva Freedman & Peter Medway (eds) *Genre and the new rhetoric* (pp. 79–101). London: Taylor & Francis.

Bazerman, Charles. 1999. *The languages of Edison's light*. Cambridge, MA: The MIT Press.

Bazerman, Charles. 2000. Letters and the social grounding of differentiated genres. In D. Barton & N. Hall (eds) *Letter writing as a social practice*. (pp. 15-30). Amsterdam: John Benjamins.

Bazerman, Charles. 2001. Nuclear information: One rhetorical moment in the construction of the information age. *Written Communication 18*, 259–295.

Bazerman, Charles, Little, Joseph & Chavkin, Teri. 2003. The production of information for genred activity spaces. *Written Communication 20*, 455–477.

Bazerman, Charles & Russell, David. (eds) 2003. *Writing selves/writing societies: Research from activity perspectives*. Fort Collins, Colorado: The WAC Clearinghouse and *Mind, Culture, and Activity*.

Beaufort, Anne. 1999. *Writing in the real world: Making the transition from school to work*. New York: Teachers College Press.

Becker, H. 1970. *Sociological work: Method and substance*. Chicago: Aldine.

Berkenkotter, Carol & Huckin, Thomas. 1995. *Genre knowledge in disciplinary communication: Cognition/culture/power*. Hillsdale, NJ: Lawrence Erlbaum.

Bhagwati, Jagdish. 2004. *In defense of globalization*. New York: Oxford University Press.

Bhatia, Vijay. 1993. *Worlds of written discourse: A genre-based view*. London & New York: Continuum.

Bhatia, Vijay. 2004. *Analyzing genre: Language use in professional settings*. London: Longman.

Blyler, Nancy. 1995. Research as ideology in professional communication. *Technical Communication Quarterly 4*, 285–313.

Bourdieu, Pierre. 1991. *Language and symbolic power*. Cambridge, MA: Harvard University Press.

Bowker, Jeoffrey & Star, Susan Leigh. 1999. *Sorting things out: Classification and its consequences*. Cambridge, MA: The MIT Press.

Brodkey, Linda. 1987. Writing ethnographic narratives. *Written Communication 4*, 25–50.

Brown, Vivienne. 1993. Decanonizing discourses: Textual analysis and the history of economic thought. In Willie Henderson, Tony Dudley-Evans & Roger Backhouse (eds) *Economics and language* (pp. 64–84). London: Routledge.

Brown, John Seely & Duguid, Paul. 2000. *The social life of information*. Boston: Harvard Business School Press.

Candlin, Chris & Maley, Yon. 1999. In Britt-Louise Gunnarsson, Per Linell & Bengt Nordberg (eds) *The construction of professional discourse* (pp. 201–222). London: Longman

Carlson, Patricia. 2001. Information technology and organizational change. *Journal of Technical Writing and Communication 31*, 77–96.

Chouliaraki, Lilie & Fairclough, Norman. 1999. *Discourse in late modernity*: *Rethinking critical discourse analysis*. Edinburgh: Edinburgh University Press.

Cintron, Ralph. 1993. Wearing a pith helmet at a sly angle: Or, can writing researchers do ethnography in a postmodern era? *Written Communication 10*, 371–412.

Colander, David. 1991. *Why aren't economists as important as garbagemen? Essays on the state of economics*. New York: M.E. Sharpe.

Cole, Michael & Engeström, Yrjö. 1993. A cultural-historical approach to distributed cognition. In Gavriel Salomon (ed.) *Distributed cognitions*: *Psychological and educational considerations* (pp. 1–46). Cambridge, UK: Cambridge University Press.

Collins, Lyndhurst. (ed.) 1976. *The use of models in the social sciences*. Boulder, CO: Westview Press.

Cross, Geoffrey. 2001. *Forming the collective mind*: *A contextual exploration of large-scale collaborative writing in industry*. Cresskill, NJ: Hampton Press.

Crow, John. 1988. *The work of Canadian monetary policy*. Eric J. Hanson Memorial Lecture, University of Alberta, Edmonton.

Davis, Philip & Hersh, Reuben. 1987. Rhetoric and mathematics. In John Nelson, Allan Megill & Deidre McCloskey (eds) *The rhetoric of the human sciences*: *Language and argument in scholarship and public affairs* (pp. 53–68). Madison: University of Wisconsin Press.

Denzin, Norman. 1997. *Interpretive ethnography*: *Ethnographic practices for the 21st century*. Thousand Oaks, CA: Sage

Denzin, Norman. 1999. Interpretive ethnography for the next century. *Journal of Contemporary Ethnography 28*. 510–519.

Devitt, Amy. 1991. Intertextuality in tax accounting: Generic, referential, and functional. In Charles Bazerman & James Paradis (eds) *Textual dynamics of the professions*: *Historical and contemporary studies of writing in profes-sional communities* (pp. 336–357). Madison: University of Wisconsin Press.

Devitt, Amy. 2004. *Writing genres*. Carbondale: Southern Illinois University Press.

Dias, Patrick. 1987. *Making sense of poetry*. Portsmouth, NH: Heinemann/ Boynton Cook.

Dias, Patrick, Freedman, Aviva, Medway, Peter & Paré, Anthony. 1999. *Worlds apart*: *Acting and writing in academic and workplace settings*. Mahwah, NJ: Lawrence Erlbaum.

Dias, Patrick, Freedman, Aviva, Medway, Peter & Paré, Anthony. 1992. *Rhetoric, innovation, technology*: *Case studies of technical communication in technology transfers*. Cambridge: The MIT Press.

Douglas, Mary. 1986. *How institutions think*. Syracuse: Syracuse University Press.

Duguay, Pierre & Poloz, Stephen. 1994. The role of economic projections in Canadian monetary policy formulation. *Canadian Public Policy 2*, 189–199.

Duguay, Pierre & Longworth, David. 1997. Macroeconomic models and policymaking at the Bank of Canada. Paper presented at the 10th Anniversary Congress of the Tinbergen Institute, Amsterdam.

Ede, Lisa & Lunsford, Andrea. 1990. *Singular texts/plural authors*: *Perspectives on collaborative writing*. Carbondale and Edwardsville: Southern Illinois University Press.

Eisner, Elliot. 2001. Concerns and aspirations for qualitative research in the new millennium. *Qualitative Research 1*, 135–145.

Engeström, Yrjö. 1987. *Learning by expanding*: *An activity-theoretical approach to developmental research*. Orienta-Konsultit Oy.

Engeström, Yrjö. 1992. *Interactive expertise*: *Studies in distributed working intelligence*. Research Bulletin 83. Department of Education, Helsinki University.

Engeström, Yrjö & Middleton, David. 1998. *Cognition and communication at work*. Cambridge, UK: Cambridge University Press.

Fairclough, Norman. 1992. *Language and social change*. Cambridge, UK: Polity Press.

Fairclough, Norman. 1995. *Critical discourse analysis*: *The critical study of language*. London: Longman.

Fairclough, Norman. 2000. Discourse, social theory, and social research: The discourse of welfare reform. *Journal of Sociolinguistics 4*, 163–95.

Fairclough, Norman. 2003. *Analyzing discourse*: *Textual analysis for social research*. London: Routledge.

Ferber, Marianne & Nelson, Julie. (eds) 1993. *Beyond economic man*: *Feminist theory and economics*. Chicago: University of Chicago Press.

Fishman, Stephen & McCarthy, Lucille. 2001. An ESL writer and her discipline-based professor: Making progress even when goals don't match. *Written Communication 18*, 180–228.

Flowerdew, John. 2004. The discursive construction of a world-class city. *Discourse and Society 5*, 579 – 605.

Foucault, Michel. 1972. *The archeology of knowledge*. A. Sheridan-Smith (Trans.). New York: Harper and Row.

Freadman, Anne. 1994. Anyone for tennis? In Aviva Freedman & Peter Medway (eds) *Genre and the new rhetoric* (pp. 43–66). London: Taylor & Francis.

Freedman, Aviva & Medway, Peter. (eds) 1994. *Genre and the new rhetoric*. London: Taylor & Francis.

Freedman, Aviva & Adam, Christine. 2000. Write where you are: Situating learning to write in university and workplace settings. In Patrick Dias & Anthony Paré (eds) *Transitions*: *Writing in academic and workplace settings* (pp. 31–60). Cresskill, NJ: Hampton.

Freedman, Aviva & Smart, Graham. 1997. Navigating the current of economic policy: Written genres and the distribution of cognitive work at a financial institution. *Mind, Culture, and Society 4*, 238–255.

Freedman, Aviva, Adam, Christine & Smart, Graham. 1994. Wearing suits to class: Simulating genres and simulations as genre. *Written Communication 11*, 193–226.

Gee, James. 1992. Socio-cultural approaches to literacy (literacies). *Annual Review of Applied Linguistics 12*, 31–48.

Gee, James. 1999. *An introduction to discourse analysis*: *Theory and method*. London: Routledge.

Geertz, Clifford. 1973. *The Interpretation of Cultures*. New York: Basic Books.

Geertz, Clifford. 1983. *Local Knowledge*. New York: Basic Books.

Geisler, Cheryl. 2001. Textual objects: Accounting for the role of texts in the everyday life of complex organizations. *Written Communication 18*, 296–325.

Geisler, Cheryl. 2004. Introduction to the special issue: The IText revolution. *Journal of Business and Technical Communication 18*: 267–269.

Geisler, Cheryl et al. 2001. Future directions for research on the relationship between information technology and writing. *Journal of Business and Technical Communication 15*, 269–308.

Giddens, Anthony. 1979. *Central problems in social theory*. London: Macmillan.

Giddens, Anthony. 1984. *The constitution of society*: *Outline of the theory of structuration*. Berkeley: University of California Press.

Gilbert, Nigel. 1976. The transformation of research findings into scientific knowledge. *Social Studies of Science 6*, 281–306.

Giltrow, Janet. 2002. Meta-genre. In Richard Coe, Loreli Lingard & Tatiana Teslenko (eds) *The rhetoric and ideology of genre* (pp. 187–205). Cresskill, NJ: Hampton Press.

Giltrow, Janet & Valiquette, Michele. 1994. Genres and knowledge: Students writing in the disciplines. In Aviva Freedman and Peter Medway (eds) *Learning and teaching genre* (pp. 47–62). Portsmouth, NH: Heinemann/ Boynton Cook.

Glaser, Barney & Strauss, Anselm. 1967. *The discovery of grounded theory*: *Strategies for qualitative research*. New York: Aldine.

Goetz, Judith & LeCompte, Margaret. 1981. Ethnographic research and the problem of data reduction. *Anthropology and Education Quarterly 12*, 51–70.

Goetz, Judith & LeCompte, Margaret. 1984. *Ethnography and qualitative design in educational research*. Orlando: Academic Press.

Goodson, Ivor. 1985. History, context and qualitative methods in the study of curriculum. In Robert Burgess (ed.) *Strategies of educational research: Qualitative methods* (pp. 121–152). London: Falmer Press.

Goodson, Ivor. 1993. The story so far: Narrative and the political in media and research. Centre for Research on Language in Education and Work, Carleton University, Ottawa, Canada (Working Paper 2).

Goodwin, Charles. 1997. The blackness of black: Color categories as situated practice. In Lauren Resnick, Roger Säljö, Clotilde Pontecorvo & Barbara Burge (eds) *Discourse, tools, and reasoning: Essays on situated cognition* (pp. 111–140). Berlin: Springer.

Gunnnerson, Britt-Louise. 1997. On the sociohistorical construction of scientific discourse. In Britt-Louise Gunnarsson, Per Linell & Bengt Nordberg (eds) *The construction of professional discourse* (pp. 99–126). London: Longman.

Gunnarsson, Britt-Louise. 1998. Promoting images. The discursive construction of a bank. In Lita Lundquist, Heribert Picht & Jacques Qvistgaard (eds) *LSP identity and interface research, knowledge and society* (pp. 623–636). Proceedings of the 11th European Symposium on LSP. Copenhagen, August 1997. Volume II. Copenhagen Business School.

Gunnarsson, Britt-Louise. 2000. Discourse, organizations and national cultures. *Discourse Studies 2*, 5–34.

Haas, Christina. 1996. Writing technology: Studies on the materiality of writing. Mahwah, NJ: Lawrence Erlbaum.

Haas, Christina & Flower, Linda. 1988. Rhetorical reading strategies and the construction of meaning. *College Composition and Communication 39*, 167–83.

Halmari, Helena & Virtanen, Tuija. (eds) 2005. *Persuasion across genres: A linguistic approach*. Amsterdam: John Benjamins.

Hammersley, Martyn. 1992. *What's wrong with ethnography?* London: Routledge.

Hammersley, Martyn & Atkinson, Paul. 1995. *Ethnography: Principles in practice*. London: Routledge.

Harper, Richard. 1998. *Inside the IMF: An ethnography of documents, technology and organizational action*. London: Academic Press.

Harre, R. 1970. *The principles of scientific thinking*. Chicago: University of Chicago Press.

Heath, Christian & Luff, Paul. 2000. *Workplace studies: Recovering work practice and informing system design*. Cambridge, UK: Cambridge University Press.

Henderson, Kathryn. 1999. *On line and on paper: Visual representations, visual culture, and computer graphics in design engineering*. Cambridge, MA: The MIT Press.

Heilbroner, Robert. 1990. Economics as ideology. In Warren Samuels (ed.) *Economics as discourse: An analysis of the language of economists* (pp. 101–116). Boston: Kluwer Academic Publishers.

Hofstede, Geert. 2003. *Culture's consequences: Comparing values, behaviors, institutions and organizations across nations.* Thousand Oaks, CA: Sage.

Huckin, Thomas. 1987. Surprise value in scientific discourse. A paper presented at the Conference on College Composition and Communication, Atlanta.

Hutchins, Edwin. 1991. The social organization of distributed cognition. In Lauren Resnick, John Levine & Stephanie Teasley (eds) *Perspectives on socially shared cognition* (pp. 283–307). Washington, DC: American Psychological Association.

Hutchins, Edwin. 1993. Learning to navigate. In Seth Chaiklin & Jean Lave (eds) *Understanding practice: Perspectives on activity and context* (pp. 35–63). Cambridge: Cambridge University Press.

Hutchins, Edwin. 1995. *Cognition in the wild.* Cambridge, MA: The MIT Press.

Iedema, Rick. 2003. *Discourses of post-bureaucratic organization.* Amsterdam & Philadelphia: John Benjamins.

Jarratt, Susan. 1987. Towards a sophistic historiography. *PRE/TEXT 8*, 9–26.

Journet, Debra. 1990. Writing, rhetoric, and the social construction of scientific knowledge. *IEEE Transactions on Professional Communication 33*, 162–167.

Journet, Debra. 1995. Ecological theories as cultural narratives. *Written Communication 8*, 446–472.

Keynes, John Maynard. 1936. *The general theory of employment, interest and money.* New York: Harcourt.

Klamer, Arjo. 1984. *The new classical macroeconomics: Conversations with the new classical economists and their opponents.* Brighton, Sussex: Harvester Press.

Klamer, Arjo. 1990. The textbook presentation of economic discourse. In W. Samuels (ed.) *Economics as discourse: An analysis of the language of economists* (pp. 129–154). Boston: Kluwer Academic Publishers.

Kress. Gunther. 2003. *Literacy in the new media age.* London: Routledge.

Kress, Gunther & van Leeuwen, Theo. 2000. *Multimodal discourse: The modes and media of contemporary communication.* London: Arnold.

Krugman, Paul. 2000. *The return of depression economics.* New York: Norton.

Latour, Bruno. 1987. *Science in action: How to follow scientists and engineers through society.* Cambridge, MA: Harvard University Press.

Latour, Bruno. 1990. Drawing things together. In Michael Lynch & Steve Woolgar (eds) *Representation in scientific practice* (pp. 19–68). Cambridge, MA: The MIT Press.

Latour, Bruno & Woolgar, Steve. 1986. *Laboratory life: The social construction of scientific facts* (second edition). Beverly Hills: Sage.

Lave, Jean. 1988. *Cognition in practice: Mind, mathematics and culture in everyday life.* Cambridge, UK: Cambridge University Press.

Lave, Jean. 1996. The practice of learning. In Seth Chaiklin & Jean Lave (eds) *Understanding practice: Perspectives on activity and context.* New York: Cambridge University press.

Lave, Jean & Wenger, Etienne. 1991. *Situated learning: Legitimate peripheral participation*. Cambridge, UK: Cambridge University Press.

Lay, Mary & Karis, Bill. (eds) 1991. *Collaborative writing in industry: Investigations in theory and practice*. Farmington, NY: Baywood.

LeCompte, Margaret & Goetz, Judith. 1982. Problems of reliability and validity in ethnographic research. *Review of Educational Research 52*, 31–60.

LeCompte, Margaret & Preissle, Judith. 1993. *Ethnography and qualitative design in educational research* (2nd ed.). San Diego, CA: Academic Press.

Ledwell-Brown, Jane & Dias, Patrick. 1994. The way we do things here: The significance of narratives in research interviews. *Journal of Business & Technical Communication 8*, 165–177.

Leont'ev, Aleksei. 1978. *Activity, consciousness, and personality*. Englewood Cliffs, NJ: Prentice Hall.

Lincoln, Yvonne. & Guba, Egon. 1985. *Naturalistic inquiry*. Beverly Hills, CA: Sage.

Loos, Eugène. 1999. Intertextual networks in organizations: The use of written and oral business discourse in relation to context. In Francesca Bargiela-Chiappini & Catherine Nickerson (eds) *Writing business: Genres, media and discourses* (pp. 315–332). London: Longman.

Luff, Paul, Hindmarsh, Jon & Heath, Christian. (eds) 2000. *Workplace studies: Recovering work practice and informing system design*. Cambridge, UK: Cambridge University Press.

Luria, Aleksandr. 1976. *Cognitive development: Its cultural and social foundations*. Cambridge, MA: Harvard University Press.

Lynch, Michael. 1990. The externalized retina: Selection and mathematization in the visual documentation of objects in the life sciences. In Michael Lynch & Steve Woolgar (eds) *Representation in scientific practice* (pp. 153–186). Cambridge, MA: The MIT Press.

Maines, D. 1993. Narrative's moment and sociology's phenomena: Toward a narrative sociology. *Sociological Quarterly 34*, 17–38.

McCarthy, Lucille. 1991. A psychiatrist using *DSM-III*: The influence of a charter document in psychiatry. In Charles Bazerman & James Paradis (eds) *Textual dynamics of the professions: Historical and contemporary studies of writing in professional communities* (pp. 358–378). Madison: University of Wisconsin Press.

McCloskey, Deidre. 1985. *The rhetoric of economics*. Madison: University of Wisconsin Press.

McCloskey, Deidre. 1990. *If you're so smart: The narrative of economic expertise*. Chicago: University of Chicago Press.

McCloskey, Deidre. 1994. *Knowledge and persuasion in Economics*. Cambridge, UK: Cambridge University Press.

McQuaig, Linda. 1995. *Shooting the hippo: Death by deficit and other Canadian myths*. Toronto: Penguin.

Medway, Peter. 1996. Virtual and material buildings: Construction and constructivism in architecture and writing. *Written Communication 13*, 473–514.

Merriam, Sharan. 1988. *Case study research in education: A qualitative approach*. San Francisco: Jossey-Bass.

Merriam, Sharan. 1998. *Qualitative research and case study applications in education*. San Francisco: Jossey-Bass.

Miller, Carolyn. 1984. Genre as social action. *Quarterly Journal of Speech 70*, 151–67.

Miller, Carolyn. 1994. Rhetorical community: The cultural basis of genre. In Aviva Freedman & Peter Medway (eds) *Genre and the new rhetoric* (pp. 23–42). London: Taylor & Francis.

Mishler, Elliot. 1986. *Research interviewing*. Cambridge, MA: Harvard University Press.

Moll, Luis, Tapia, Javier & Whitmore, Kathryn. 1993. Living knowledge: The social distribution of cultural resources for thinking. In Gavriel Salomon (ed.) *Distributed cognitions: Psychological and educational considerations* (pp. 139–163). Cambridge: Cambridge University Press.

Monetary policy report, April 2004.

Monetary policy report, April 2005.

Myers, Greg. 1990. *Writing biology: Texts in the social construction of knowledge*. Madison: University of Wisconsin Press.

New London Group. 1996. A pedagogy of multiliteracies: designing social futures. *Harvard Educational Review 66*, 60–92.

Orlikowski, Wanda. 2001. Improvising organizational transformation over time: A situated change perspective. In JoAnne Yates and John Van Maanen (eds) *Information technology and organizational transformation: History, rhetoric, and practice* (pp. 223–274). Thousand Oaks, CA: Sage Publications.

Orlikowsky, Wanda & Yates, JoAnne. 1994. Genre repertoire: Examining the structuring of communicative practices in organizations. *Administrative Science Quarterly 39*, 541–574.

Ormerod, Paul. 1994. *The death of economics*. London: Faber and Faber.

Ormerod, Paul. 1999. *Butterfly economics: A new general theory of social and economic behavior*. New York: Basic Books.

Osberg, Lars & Fortin, Pierre. (eds) 1996. *Unnecessary debts*. Toronto: James Lorimer.

Paradis, James, Dobrin, David & Miller, Richard. 1985. Writing at Exxon ITD: Notes on the writing environment of an R & D organization. In Lee Odell and Dixi Goswami (eds) *Writing in non-academic settings* (pp. 281–307). New York: Guilford Press.

Paradis, James, Dobrin, David & Miller, Richard. 2000. Writing as a way into social work: Genre sets, genre systems, and distributed cognition. In Patrick Dias & Anthony Paré (eds) *Transitions: Writing in academic and workplace settings* (pp. 145–166). Cresskill, NJ: Hampton Press.

Paré, Anthony & Smart, Graham. 1994. Observing genres in action: Towards a research methodology. In Aviva Freedman and Peter Medway (eds) *Genre and the new rhetoric* (pp. 146–154). London: Taylor & Francis.

Pea, Roy. 1993. Practices of distributed intelligence and designs for education. In Gavriel Salomon (ed.) *Distributed cognitions: Psychological and educational considerations* (pp. 47–87). Cambridge: Cambridge University Press.

Piazza, Carolyn. 1987. Identifying context variables in research on writing: A review and suggested directions. *Written Communication 4*, 107–137.

Polanyi, Michael. 1966. *The tacit dimension*. Garden City, NY: Doubleday.

Poloz, Stephen, Rose, David & Tetlow, Robert. 1994. The Bank of Canada's new Quarterly Projection Model. *Bank of Canada Review*, Autumn, 23–39.

Resnick, Lauren. 1991. Shared cognition: Thinking as social practice. In Lauren Resnick, John Levine & Stephanie Teasley (eds) *Perspectives on socially shared cognition* (pp. 1–22). Washington, DC: American Psychological Association.

Ricoeur, Paul. 1981. Narrative time. In W. J. T Mitchell (ed.) *On narrative* (pp. 1–23). Chicago: University of Chicago Press.

Russell, David. 1997. Rethinking genre in school and society: An activity theory analysis. *Written Communication 14*, 504–554.

Sachs, Jeffrey. 2005. *The end of poverty: Economic possibilities for our time*. New York: The Penguin Press.

Salomon, Gavriel. 1993. Editor's introduction. In Gavriel Salomon (ed.) *Distributed cognitions: Psychological and educational considerations* (pp. xi-xxi). Cambridge, UK: Cambridge University Press.

Samuelson, Paul. 1947. *Foundations of economic analysis*. Cambridge, MA: Harvard University Press.

Sanjek, Roger. 1990. On ethnographic validity. In Roger Sanjek (ed.) *Fieldnotes: The making of anthropology*. Ithaca, NY: Cornell University Press.

Sarangi, Srikant. 2000. Activity types, discourse types and interactional hybridity: The case of genetic counselling. In Srikant Sarangi & Malcolm Coulthard (eds) *Discourse and social life*. London: Longman.

Sauer, Beverly. 2003. *The rhetoric of risk: Technical documentation in hazardous environments*. Mahwah, NJ: Lawrence Erlbaum.

Schön, Donald. 1983. *The reflective practitioner: How professionals think in action*. New York: Basic Books.

Schryer, Catherine. 1993. Records as genre. *Written Communication 10*, 200–234.

Schryer, Catherine. 2002. Genre and power: A chronotopic analysis. In Richard Coe, Loreli Lingard & Tatiana Teslenko (eds) *The rhetoric and ideology of genre* (pp. 73–102). Cresskill, NJ: Hampton Press.

Sellen, Abigail & Harper, Richard. 2002. *The myth of the paperless office*. Cambridge, MA: The MIT Press.

Shore, Chris & Wright, Susan. (eds) 1997. *The anthropology of policy: Critical perspectives on governance and power*. London: Routledge.

Smart, Graham. 1993. Genre as community invention: A central bank's response to its executives' expectations as readers. In Rachel Spilka (ed.) *Writing in the workplace: New research perspectives* (pp. 124–140). Carbondale: Southern Illinois University Press.

Smart, Graham. 1998. Mapping conceptual worlds: Using interpretive ethnography to explore knowledge-making in a professional community. *The Journal of Business Communication 35*, 111–127.

Smart, Graham. 1999. Storytelling in a central bank: The role of narrative in the creation and use of specialized economic knowledge. *Journal of Business and Technical Communication 13*, 249–273.

Smart, Graham. 2000. Reinventing expertise: Experienced writers in the workplace encounter a new genre. In Patrick Dias & Anthony Paré (eds) *Transitions: Writing in academic and workplace settings* (pp. 223–252). Cresskill, NJ: Hampton Press.

Smith, Adam. 1978. *Lectures on Jurisprudence*. R. L. Meek, D. D. Raphael, and F. G. Stein (eds). Oxford: Clarendon Press.

Smith, Dorothy. 1974. The social construction of documentary reality. *Sociological Inquiry 44*, 257–268.

Smith, Dorothy. 1990. *Texts, facts, and femininity: Exploring the relations of ruling*. London: Routledge.

Smith, Dorothy. 1999. *Writing the social: Critique, theory, and investigations*. Toronto: University of Toronto Press.

Smith, Dorothy. 2005. *Institutional ethnography: A sociology for people*. Oxford, UK: AltaMira Press.

Spilka, Rachel. 1993. Moving between oral and written discourse to fulfil rhetorical and social goals. In R. Spilka (ed.) *Writing in the workplace: New research perspectives* (pp. 71–83). Carbondale: Southern Illinois University Press.

Spinuzzi, Clay. 2003. Tracing genres through organizations: A sociocultural approach to information design. Cambridge, MA: The MIT Press.

Spinuzzi, Clay & Zachry, Mark. 2000. Genre ecologies: An open-system approach to understanding and constructing documentation. *ACM Journal of Computer Documentation 24*, 169–181.

Stiglitz, Joseph. 2002. *Globalization and its discontents*. New York: Norton.

Strauss, Anselm. 1987. *Qualitative analysis for social scientists*. New York: Cambridge University Press.

Strauss, Anselm & Corbin, Juliet. 1998. *Basics of qualitative research: Techniques and procedures for developing grounded theory*. Thousand Oaks, CA: Sage Publications.

Suchman, Lucy. 1998. Constituting shared workplaces. In Yrjö Engeström & David Middleton (eds) *Cognition and communication at work*. Cambridge, UK: Cambridge University Press.

Suchman, Lucy. 2000. Making a case: 'Knowledge' and 'routine' work in document production. In Paul Luff, Jon Hindmarsh & Christian Heath (eds)

Work, interaction and technology: *Recovering work practice and informing system design* (pp. 29–45). Cambridge, UK: Cambridge University Press.

Swales, John. 1990. *Genre analysis*: *English in academic and research settings*. New York: Cambridge University Press.

Swales, John. 1998. *Other floors, other voices*: *A textography of a small university building*. Mahwah, NJ: Lawrence Erlbaum.

Swales, John. 2004. *Research genres*: *Exploration and applications*. New York: Cambridge University Press.

Tardy, Christine. 2003. A genre system view of the funding of academic research. *Written Communication 20*, 7–36.

Thurlow, Lester. 1997. *The future of capitalism*: *How today's economic forces shape tomorrow's world*. New York: Penguin.

Toulmin, Stephen. 1985. *The inner life of the outer mind*. Worcester, MA: Clark University Press.

Van Dijk, Tuen. 2003. The discourse-knowledge interface. In Gilbert Weiss & Ruth Wodak (eds) *Critical discourse analysis*: *Theory and disciplinarity*. New York. Palgrave Macmillan.

Van Maanen, John. 1979. The fact of fiction in organizational ethnography. *Administrative Science Quarterly 24*, 539–550.

Van Maanen, John. 1988. *Tales of the field*: *On writing ethnography*. Chicago: University of Chicago Press.

Van Maanen, John. (ed.) 1995. *Representation in ethnography*. Beverly Hills, CA: Sage.

Van Nostrand, A.D. 1997. *Fundable knowledge*: *The marketing of defense technology*. Mahwah, NJ: Lawrence Erlbaum.

Vygotsky, Lev. 1978. *Mind in society*: *The development of higher psychological processes*. Cambridge, MA: Harvard University Press.

Waern, Yvonne. 1979. *Thinking aloud during reading*: *A descriptive model and its application*. University of Stockholm, Department of Psychology Report No. 546.

Waring, Marilyn. 1999. *Counting for nothing*: *What men value and what women are worth* (second edition). Toronto: University of Toronto Press.

Wenger, Etienne. 1998. *Communities of practice*: *Learning, meaning, and identity*. Cambridge, MA: Cambridge University Press.

Wenger, Etienne, McDermott, Richard & Snyder, William. 2002. *Cultivating communities of practice*. Boston: Harvard Business School Press.

Wertsch, James. 1991. *Voices of the mind*: *A sociocultural approach to mediated action*. Cambridge, MA: Harvard University Press.

Wertsch, James. 1997. *Mind as action*. New York: Oxford UP.

Winsor, Dorothy. 1992. What counts as writing? An argument from engineers' practice. *Journal of Advanced Composition 12*, 337–347.

Winsor, Dorothy. 1996. *Writing like an engineer*: *A rhetorical education*. Mahwah, NJ: Erlbaum.

Winsor, Dorothy. 1999. Genre and activity systems: The role of documentation in maintaining and changing engineering activity systems. *Written Communication 16*, 200–224.

Winsor, Dorothy. 2003. *Writing power: Communication in an engineering center*. Albany: State University of New York Press.

Witte, Stephen. 1992. Context, text, intertext: Toward a constructivist semiotic of writing. *Written Communication 9*, 237–308.

Woolgar, Steve. 1990. Time and documents in researcher interaction: Some ways of making out what is happening in experimental science. In Michael Lynch & Steve Woolgar (eds) *Representation in scientific practice* (pp. 123–152). Cambridge, MA: The MIT Press.

Yates, JoAnne. 1989. *Control through communication: The rise of system in American management*. Baltimore: Johns Hopkins University Press.

Yates, JoAnne & Orlikowski, Wanda. 1992. Genres of organizational communication: A structurational approach to studying communication and media. *Academy of Management Review 17*, 299–326.

Yates, JoAnne & Orlikowski, Wanda. 2002. Genre systems: Chronos and kairos in communicative interaction. In Richard Coe, Loreli Lingard & Tatiana Teslenko (eds) *The rhetoric and ideology of genre* (pp. 103–121). Cresskill, NJ: Hampton Press.

Index

Printed in the United States
73407LV00003B/1-48